Praise for *The Rise of the Female Executive*

"We need to encourage and enable more women to achieve positions of leadership and to use those positions to change the culture within their organisations. We need to generate cultures in our companies that appeal to both men and women at all stages of their careers and in which women are able to succeed in great numbers. This book, and the continued work of the Foundation, in supporting able women at different stages of their careers, make important contributions to bringing about that change."

– Sir Philip Hampton, Chairman, GlaxoSmithKline plc

"It is increasingly acknowledged that mentoring plays an important role in accessing and developing diverse talent to the most senior management and boards of companies. What may not always be quite so apparent is the secondary benefit to the mentee's organisation in terms of morale and inclusion and - dare I say it - to the sense of achievement of the mentor! Peninah Thomson has done a great service not only in championing the concept of mentoring but also in writing about it so lucidly and passionately."

– Sir Win Bischoff, Chairman, Financial Reporting Council

"In my nearly 25 years of training and development in the civil service, the last 18 months working with my mentor on the FTSE Programme have been the most precious, the most interesting and the most challenging. He shifted my way of thinking; we had different sorts of conversations."

– Sharon White, Chief Executive Officer, Ofcom

"This book, by Peninah Thomson and colleagues at The Mentoring Foundation, is very timely as a breakthrough is now occurring in terms of female representation on boards, and it needs to be sustained by mentoring a growing pipeline. I am delighted to see that, having set up a process with Lord Davies and his team, a voluntary approach based on the self-interest of companies in tapping into the female talent pool is now bearing fruit."

– Sir Vince Cable, Former MP and Secretary of State
for Business, Innovation and Skills

"FTSE 250 companies need to ensure they equip themselves to be competitive in an international marketplace as business culture evolves in the 21st century. As a Chairman Mentor on the FTSE 100® Cross-Company Mentoring Programme, I believe that encouraging women to join boards is crucial to modernising organisational culture, improving how both companies and boards function, and this book outlines how companies (and individuals) can go about it."

– Nigel Rich CBE, Chairman, Segro plc

"Discussions of Venus and Mars are now generational. The new generation Y/Z is omni-channel. CEOs of today's businesses need to get it, or they won't be around in 20 years. For women, the next challenge is the pipeline, and women's representation on Executive Committees. The biggest question is work-life balance. Culture's critical. We need to start by knowing ourselves – compensate for your own weaknesses through your choice of team. We can learn a lot from the sporting world. Sports coaches apply science and psychology. Business needs to do the same."

– Lord Davies of Abersoch, CBE
at The Mentoring Foundation Colloquium, 2014, Inner Temple

"Our collaboration with The Mentoring Foundation has helped to stimulate great discussion and debate across our business, the FTSE 100® and beyond. As well as preparing senior women for board appointments, it has been very positive to focus on the development of women at an earlier stage in their career. The Next Generation Women Leaders Programme, described in this book, ensures that these talented women are gaining from the valuable experience of others to help them to achieve success and take ownership of a fulfilling career. I strongly believe that they will encourage diversity of thought which will have an impact on the culture of organisations as they progress."

– Nigel Wilson, Group Chief Executive Officer, Legal & General Group plc

"Historically, the diversity debate has been long on aspiration and short on delivery. This is where the FTSE 100® Cross-Company Mentoring Programmes really make a difference, as this book demonstrates. By pairing talented women on the fast-track with senior business people with a record of success, wisdom and experience can be shared and self-confidence and poise created. And by organising the mentoring programme on a dynamic basis, the process can be tailored to the individual, the better to help them develop."

– Marcus Agius, Chairman, PA Consulting Group

"Talent is the rarest commodity. Yet we have sought to succeed as companies, institutions and nations while merely skimming the surface of that half of the talent pool which is female. How stupid can that be? We should be desperate for any help in addressing this imbalance – and here it is. The case is powerfully made, remarkably valuable experience is shared, we are provided with the tool kit. Read *The Rise of the Female Executive*. The survival of your organisation depends upon it."

– Niall FitzGerald KBE, Chairman, The Leverhulme Trust

"The great value of mentoring, and cross-company mentoring in particular, is the opportunity to help women to better assess how to progress in their career, and to discuss issues more independently and objectively. I believe mentoring has an important role to play in helping us ensure that we fully harness the capabilities and potential of the UK's enviably large population of talented women. This wise book makes a compelling case for redoubling our efforts. Our businesses and the wider economy will be the beneficiaries."

– António Horta-Osório, Chief Executive Officer, Lloyds Banking Group plc

Also by Peninah Thomson

'Public sector human resource management: An agenda for change', in Michael Armstrong (ed.) *Strategies for Human Resource Management*, Kogan Page, 1992.

'Public sector management in a period of radical change 1979–1992', in Norman Flynn (ed.) *Change in the Civil Service: A Public Finance Foundation Reader*, Chartered Institute of Public Finance and Accountancy, 1994.

'Aftermath: Making public sector change work: Part 1', *Public Policy Review*, 3(1), pp. 54–6, 1995.

'A paradigm shift: Making public sector change work: Part II', *Public Policy Review*, 3(2), pp. 60–4, 1995.

The Changing Culture of Leadership: Women Leaders' Voices, with Elizabeth Coffey and Clare Huffington, The Change Partnership, 1999.

'Making the case for business: The change agenda', *Work-Life Strategies for the 21st Century*, Report by the National Work-Life Forum, 2000.

'Introduction' to *10 Things That Keep CEOs Awake and How to Put Them to Bed*, Elizabeth Coffey and colleagues from The Change Partnership, McGraw-Hill Business Books, 2002.

'Corporate governance, leadership and culture change in business', Royal Society of Arts, Manufactures and Commerce, 2003.

A Woman's Place is in the Boardroom, with Jacey Graham and Tom Lloyd, Palgrave Macmillan, 2005.

'Why a woman's place is in the boardroom', *Finance and Management*, pp. 13–14, November 2005.

'Women on the board: Choice or necessity?' *Business Voice*, pp. 26–7, March 2006.

'The FTSE 100® Cross-Company Mentoring Programme', *Mentoring- A Powerful Tool for Women*, Women@Work No. 7, ed. Thérèse Torris, Publications@EuropeanPWN.net,2007.

'Being on a board', *Women on Boards: Moving Mountains*, Women@Work No. 8, ed. Mirella Visser and Annalisa Gigante, Publications@EuropeanPWN.net, 2007.

'It's still a man's world: Businesses need to find new ways of keeping talented women in the workplace', p. 61, *World Business*, June 2007.

'The FTSE 100® Cross-Company Mentoring Programme', *The Brown Book*, Lady Margaret Hall, Oxford, 2008.

A Woman's Place is in the Boardroom: The Roadmap, with Jacey Graham and Tom Lloyd, Palgrave Macmillan, 2008.

'Step this way', *Coaching at Work*, pp. 33–5 December 2008.

'Balancing the board, *Edge* (Journal of the Institute of Leadership and Management), pp. 36–41, August 2009.

'Countries where women executives fare best', *FT.com magazine*, September 2009.

'Should women be fast-tracked to top jobs?', *Stylist Magazine*, pp. 33–4, October 2009.

'The FTSE 100® Cross-Company Mentoring Programme: Steady progress; more to do', *Women in Banking and Finance*, pp. 9–10, January 2010.

'Women at the top: ask our experts', *FT.com magazine*, October 2010.

Women & the New Business Leadership, with Tom Lloyd, Palgrave Macmillan, 2011.

'Who Cares?', *Economia*, pp. 59–61, November 2014.

'The kindness of strangers', *Financial Times*, 9 January 2014.

Also by Tom Lloyd

Dinosaur & Co: Studies in Corporate Evolution, RKP, 1984; Penguin, 1985.

Managing Knowhow, with Karl-Erik Sveiby, Bloomsbury, 1987; Campus Verlag, Germany, 1990; FrancoAngeli, Italy, 1990; InterEditions, France, 1990; Centrum, Poland, 1994.

The "Nice" Company, Bloomsbury, 1990; Calmann-Levy, France, 1992; FrancoAngeli, Italy, 1993.

Entrepreneur!, Bloomsbury, 1992.

The Charity Business, John Murray, 1993.

A Woman's Place is in the Boardroom, with Peninah Thomson and Jacey Graham, Palgrave Macmillan, 2005.

A Woman's Place is in the Boardroom: The Roadmap, with Peninah Thomson and Jacey Graham, Palgrave Macmillan, 2008.

Business at a Crossroads: The Crisis of Corporate Leadership, Palgrave Macmillan, 2009.

Women & the New Business Leadership, with Peninah Thomson, Palgrave Macmillan, 2011.

The Rise of the Female Executive

How Women's Leadership is Accelerating Cultural Change

Peninah Thomson, OBE

and Clare Laurent

with Tom Lloyd

palgrave
macmillan

First published 2015 by
PALGRAVE MACMILLAN

Palgrave Macmillan in the UK is an imprint of Macmillan Publishers Limited, registered in England, company number 785998, of Houndmills, Basingstoke, Hampshire RG21 6XS.

Palgrave Macmillan in the US is a division of St Martin's Press LLC, 175 Fifth Avenue, New York, NY 10010.

Palgrave is the global academic imprint of the above companies and has companies and representatives throughout the world.

Palgrave® and Macmillan® are registered trademarks in the United States, the United Kingdom, Europe and other countries.

ISBN 978–1–137–45142–2 hardback

This book is printed on paper suitable for recycling and made from fully managed and sustained forest sources. Logging, pulping and manufacturing processes are expected to conform to the environmental regulations of the country of origin.

A catalogue record for this book is available from the British Library.

Thomson, Peninah.
The rise of the female executive: how women's leadership is accelerating cultural change / Peninah Thomson, CEO The Mentoring Foundation, Clare Laurent, Associate, The Mentoring Foundation, Tom Lloyd, Management Writer.
    pages cm
Includes index.
ISBN 978–1–137–45142–2
1. Women executives. 2. Leadership in women.   I. Laurent, Clare. II. Lloyd, Tom.   III. Title.
HD6054.3.T457 2015
306.3--dc23   2015018397

Typeset by MPS Limited, Chennai, India.

For Alastair and Diana
and the young people who know me as Aunt, Godmother or friend
James, Kate, Tristan, Ben, Tom and Eleanor
– all making their contribution in the world –
and for Edward, who has just entered it.
Peninah Thomson, OBE

With love and thanks
to Stan, Elias and Alma who support my 'juggling' to an
almost saintly degree,
as well as to my much-missed mother, Mary, and Melanie, my sister,
two formidable role models for me of how to combine
motherhood with career.
Clare Laurent

Contents

List of Tables

Preface

When historians look back on the first 15 years of the 21st century, they may well conclude that the period witnessed the first stage of a fundamental rearrangement of civil society, exemplified by a substantial influx of women into leadership positions.

In big business, the numbers speak for themselves – the proportion of women on the boards of FTSE 100 companies increased from barely 6% in 1999 to 25% by the end of 2015 (assuming, as seemed likely in February 2015, the target set by Lord Davies in his 2011 Review is met).

Why has the number and proportion of women in leadership positions increased so much and so quickly not only in business but also in government, the professions, the not-for-profits, science and many other walks of life? Why did the UK government sponsor the Davies Review and then stand behind the Davies target with resources and rhetoric, in preference to enacting statutory quotas for women on company boards? Why have several European countries enacted such quota laws? And why is all this happening now, at this particular point in history?

As the reader will see in the following pages, there are many long and complicated answers to these questions. There's a short answer too.

There has been a sharp increase, in recent years, in the number of women in leadership positions because civil society *needs* them.

It needs more women, because it needs all the leadership talent at its disposal if it is to tackle the grave and growing problems that beset it.

And it needs more women, because in a world that is Volatile, Uncertain, Complex and Ambiguous (as the US military has characterised modern battlefields), diversity itself is a cardinal virtue. A wide variety of ideas, outlooks, abilities, perspectives and sensitivities in the boardroom and on the Executive Committee protects organisations from the perils of 'groupthink' and helps them manage the volatility, uncertainty, complexity and ambiguity of their environments.

But historians are likely to see the period 2000–15 as the first stage of a reconfiguration of civil society that we call the 'big project'. In previous books we have chronicled the origins and the progress of this first stage (*A Woman's Place is in the Boardroom*, 2005; and *A Woman's Place is in the Boardroom: The Roadmap*, 2008), and how and why it was given additional momentum in the aftermath of the 2007–8 banking crisis (*Women & the New Business Leadership*, 2011). In this book we focus on the second stage: the extension of the increase in gender diversity in governance to management and the adaptation of organisations, not only to the needs of women, but also to the needs of the new, 'connected' generations who will be running our organisations in the future.

We should celebrate the considerable gender-diversity achievements of the past 15 years, but we should also recognise that there is a great deal more to do.

Peninah Thomson, OBE
Clare Laurent

The authors can be contacted at:
Peninah.Thomson@mentoringfoundation.co.uk
Clare.Laurent@mentoringfoundation.co.uk

Observations and Thanks

As we discussed the ideas for this book, it felt timely to be taking a fresh look at how things are evolving in the quest to advance women's careers further and also to be considering our work in its broader context. This year, 2015, is a prominent milestone. By the time it ends, FTSE 100 companies are expected to have achieved the target set by Lord Davies in his 2011 Review, *Women on Boards*, for 25% female representation on FTSE 100 boards. It seems likely that the target will be met. The brevity of the previous sentence, and the ease it suggests, belie the efforts of the many individuals who have worked so hard to help UK businesses meet that target. As the end of the four-year review period approaches we've noticed that there is in some quarters the sense of a job done and of slight fatigue with the continued discussion on how to improve women's representation. But it is evident that this particular story is not at an end. The narrative is changing and a new conversation is beginning about how to effect deeper change in diversity at every level of organisations, not just at the very top.

There are also broader forces affecting our work. This is the fourth book we have written, and in each of them we placed our work in the context of national and international events. This book is no exception. At the time of writing, we stand on what seems uncharted territory. Many of the institutions that have been taken for granted in our lifetime face huge challenges of public confidence. This feeling was encapsulated by Philip Stephens, writing in the *Financial Times* on 25 February 2015 in an article entitled 'Disunited Kingdom. The Great Fragmentation'. Stephens described how

'The political system and constitution have been left stranded by modernity. Britain has outgrown its politics.' He believes that Britain has also outgrown other features of her Establishment: 'The City has fallen into disgrace ... The British Social Attitudes survey records that in 1983 some 90 per cent of workers thought banks were well-run institutions. By 2012 the level of trust had fallen to 19 per cent.' He warned that Britain needed a 'new way of governing itself and a new story – a binding narrative'.

At The Mentoring Foundation, our work is centred on people's stories and the stories of their organisations. We hear many individual narratives; and people tell us how mentoring relationships bringing together people of different genders, from different industries and different generations can affirm, nudge and even transform those narratives. Our raison d'être is also long-term change, through which companies and their boards will better reflect not only the broad spectrum of people that makes up Britain, but also the global customers they serve. This is our contribution to the 'new glue' that will bind us together in a different, more inclusive way for the future.

We might not express it in the same terms as Stephens, but we've become increasingly aware of the appetite for deeper change and the efforts being made to achieve it. In this book we consider the different strands that we see as pivotal to establishing this new world of work. We analyse progress in Britain, and internationally, in helping more women onto boards, as a case study for broader change. We include data from interviews with chairmen and top human resources executives about how companies are implementing detailed plans for cultural change, highlighting their experience of what really works and the benefits they have observed for their businesses of more diverse teams. We assess the contribution of bespoke mentoring relationships facilitated by our programmes in preparing current business leaders and aspiring women for the sharing of power among a broader 'elite'. Our mentees reflect on what the programmes have done for them as they prepare for larger executive or non-executive roles at the top of organisations. We include the voices of younger women from our new Next Generation Women Leaders Programme. Their narratives illuminate how they see their futures in the world of work and how their involvement in the programme is helping them stay engaged with their companies and their careers at a time when many women traditionally flow out of the pipeline leading to the top of their organisations. Finally, we keep our eye firmly on the future, outlining our ideas for a roadmap for broader cultural change.

We are privileged at the Foundation to enjoy unparalleled access to a committed group of chairmen, CEOs and business leaders who act as mentors on our programmes. The full list of mentors is shown in the Appendix. We are extremely grateful to them: without them nothing we do would be possible. The particular insights that a group of our Executive Programme Mentors have provided in our conversations with them for this book are invaluable. We are particularly grateful for their input to Sir Win Bischoff, Chairman Financial Reporting Council; Ian Coull, former Chairman, Galliford Try; David Cruickshank, Global Chairman, Deloitte LLP; Simon Davies, Firmwide Managing Partner, Linklaters LLP; Niall FitzGerald, KBE, Chairman, The Leverhulme Trust; Sir Philip Hampton, Chairman, GlaxoSmithKline; Nigel Rich, CBE, Chairman, Segro; John Stewart, Chairman, Legal & General Group; and Sir David Walker, Chairman, Barclays. We were not able to talk specifically to all of the almost 70 mentors on the Executive Programme about the topic of this book, but each of their contributions, both as mentors and in all the other activities they host and support for the Foundation, are fundamental to the success of the programmes.

A number of our mentees and alumnae have shared with us their experiences of the Executive and Next Generation Women Leaders Programmes and their broader ideas on how women's exercise of power can make a difference to wider society as well as business. Particular thanks go to Sarah Breeden, Bank of England; Helen Burton, Ashurst; Elizabeth Corley, Allianz Global Investors, Europe; Eva Eisenschimmel, formerly of Lloyds Banking Group; Dr. Emma FitzGerald, National Grid; Clare Francis, Lloyds Banking Group; Elizabeth Lee, Close Brothers Group; Joanna Mackle, the British Museum; Angela Pearson, Ashurst; Diane Varrin Eshleman, Barclays; Lynne Weedall, DixonsCarphone Group (all Executive Programme alumnae); and Hannah Reynolds, Bank of England

and Lizzie Rowlands, Tesco (both from our Next Generation Women Leaders Programme) who kindly provided their insights. Our network of mentees and alumnae continues to grow, today standing at 173 mentees and alumnae for the Executive Programme and 25 mentees and alumnae for the Next Generation Women Leaders Programme. By their generous sponsorship of the Executive Mentee Network and the Next Generation Women Leaders Mentee Network, Unilever and Old Mutual Group are closely connected with the Foundation. Through a mix of peer learning, mutual support and enthusiastic participation in Foundation events they make a significant contribution to the value of the programme and we are very grateful to Unilever and Old Mutual for their commitment to our work.

We would also like to thank the other business leaders and senior HR professionals from our sponsoring companies who talked to us about their thinking on various aspects of the book. In particular, thanks go to Lord Davies of Abersoch; Nigel Wilson, CEO, Legal & General Group; Elaine Arden, Group HR Director, Royal Bank of Scotland Group; Kirsty Bashforth, Group Head of Talent and Organisational Effectiveness, BP; and Fiona Cannon, OBE, Group Director, Diversity and Inclusion, Lloyds Banking Group. We would also like to thank our overseas collaborators Marie-Claude Peyrache, Co-Founder, BoardWomen Partners and Véronique Préaux-Cobti, Co-Founder and Director General, BoardWomen Partners, Diafora, for sharing their experience of the situation in France.

We benefit from a broad network of supporters and champions of our work. A powerful collaboration is building across organisations which, whilst each faces its own unique challenges in enhancing diversity, are learning from each other. A wonderful example of this is the unique flagship event for the Foundation hosted by the Royal Household at Buckingham Palace in May 2015. We were honoured that mentors, mentees and supporters of our programmes were invited to meet senior staff of the Royal Household to discuss some of the topics raised in this book. We are very grateful to Vice-Admiral Johnstone-Burt and his team for kindly offering to host and participate in that event and for their keen interest in the subject matter of this book.

We would also like to thank members of our Advisory Council, Sir Win Bischoff, Niall FitzGerald KBE, Sir Philip Hampton, Marcus Agius, and later Sir David Walker who have continued to provide us with unfailing support and wise counsel.

Particular thanks are also due to the members of The Mentoring Foundation's board, who have supported and encouraged us in our work on this book. They are Stephen Brenninkmeijer, Board member and former chairman, who was chairman at the time the board gave its approval to the writing of this book; Monica Burch, current chairman; Carolyn Bradley, NED; and Anita Chandraker, NED. Their wise oversight of the Foundation and its work is very much appreciated.

The small but efficient team of assistants at the Foundation, Becky Kean and Deirdre Stanley, have provided us with invaluable support and helped to ensure the continued smooth running of the Foundation's office while we worked to bring this book to fruition.

We are grateful also for the services of BoardEx, whose database and alerts help us keep track of all the individual moves, promotions and other achievements of women in corporate life.

Without the support and encouragement of our publishers, of course, there would be no book. We are delighted that Palgrave Macmillan approached us with the idea of another publication and particular thanks go to Stephen Partridge, Publisher, Professional Business, Global Head of Scholarly Business and Josephine Taylor, Editorial Assistant, Business Professional and Scholarly for their patient and enthusiastic support over the past year and a half.

Finally, we have been delighted to work once again with Tom Lloyd, our co-author. We continue to enjoy his intellectual input, rigour and good humour throughout. All three of us are proud of being able to play our part in contributing to the new thinking in relation to women at work.

Every effort has been made to trace all the copyright holders but if any have been inadvertently overlooked the publishers will be pleased to make the necessary arrangements at the first opportunity.

About the Authors

Peninah Thomson, OBE is CEO of The Mentoring Foundation, the company that owns and manages the FTSE 100® Cross-Company Mentoring Programme. Peninah's early career was in the UK Foreign Office. After doctoral studies at the University of Oxford, she joined PricewaterhouseCoopers, working for eight years in Government Services and Economics Division, and at Cabinet Office level in India, Africa, Singapore and Hong Kong. Seconded for two years to the UK Cabinet Office and to the European Investment Bank in Luxembourg, and promoted director, she then spent four years in PwC's Corporate Transformation Practice working at board level in FTSE 100 companies. After leaving PwC, Peninah worked for 14 years as a board-level executive coach with individual male and female senior executives, and with senior teams as groups on strategy, organisational change and leadership. Peninah is an international speaker and broadcaster, and has published four books and refereed articles on women's leadership and corporate governance. She directs the FTSE 100® Cross-Company Mentoring Programme, in which more than 70 FTSE 100 Chairmen, CEOs and other leaders mentor senior women from just below the board to become credible board candidates or otherwise to progress their careers. This highly successful programme has been running for twelve years in the UK and has been emulated in thirteen countries. She is co-author of *The Changing Culture of Leadership* (2000), and later of *A Woman's Place is in the Boardroom* (2005), *A Woman's Place is in the Boardroom: The Roadmap* (2008) and *Women & the New Business Leadership* (2011), all three published by Palgrave Macmillan. Peninah served on the Strategy Group of Lady Margaret Hall, University of Oxford. She was a member of the UK Commissioner for Public Appointments Advisory Board, and is a Companion of the Chartered Management Institute and a UK Director of the Center for Talent Innovation, New York. She was awarded an OBE for Services to Women and Equality in the Queen's Birthday Honours 2012.

Clare Laurent is an Associate with The Mentoring Foundation, where she helps Peninah in the running of the FTSE Programmes and related activities. Clare's career began in the City as a Solicitor specialising in internet law and regulation. She was General Counsel and SVP, Public Policy for AOL Europe from 1998 to 2002, with a diverse portfolio supporting multi-million pound commercial advertising deals, acting as company spokesperson for regulators, government and in the media and representing the industry as Chairman of the Internet Service Providers Association. She then joined Hutchison 3G as its Director of External and Regulatory Affairs for Europe where her work included renegotiating critical roaming deals and representing Hutchison before national and international regulators and the Competition Commission. It was her experience both of professional services firms and the dynamics of international matrixed organisations that gave rise to her interest in organisational behaviour and how coaching and mentoring might bring about change.

This interest led directly, after 15 years and a short career break in Hamburg, to her post-graduate Master's study of Career Management and Coaching at Birkbeck, University of London, from which she graduated with distinction. In her Master's thesis she examined women's career journeys and how mentoring helped them overcome obstacles to success. In parallel with her work at the Foundation, Clare is now undertaking doctoral studies into mentoring processes at Birkbeck, where she also assists with the teaching of postgraduate coaching modules.

Tom Lloyd is a former editor of *Financial Weekly* and *Management Today*. He was founding editor of Gemini Consulting's quarterly management journal *Transformation* and wrote the 'Working Brief' column in the *Sunday Telegraph* for several years. He has written six books including

Managing Knowhow (with Karl-Erik Sveiby, 1987), *The 'Nice' Company* (1990) and *Business at a Crossroads: The Crisis of Corporate Leadership* (Palgrave Macmillan, 2010). He was also a co-author of the successful *A Woman's Place is in the Boardroom* and *A Woman's Place is in the Boardroom: The Roadmap* (with Peninah Thomson and Jacey Graham, Palgrave Macmillan, 2005, 2008), and *Women & the New Business Leadership* (with Peninah Thomson, Palgrave Macmillan, 2011). He has also 'ghosted' several books for clients.

Introduction

At the time of writing in early 2015, there was a good chance that before the end of the year the proportion of women on the boards of the constituents of the Financial Times Stock Exchange (FTSE) 100 index would reach the 25% target set by Lord Davies in 2011 in his *Women on Boards Review*.

If the target is met, it will be an impressive achievement both by the women whose appointments have helped to raise the proportion of female representation on FTSE 100 boards from 12.5% in 2010 and by the male and female directors who believe more gender-balanced boards are better boards and have sought out the qualified women they need to give substance to that belief.

But three formidable challenges remain.

The first is to ensure there's no retreat from the higher level of gender balance on boards reached over the past few years. It's one thing to hit the target, and quite another to maintain the levels reached after the deadline date. Male and female directors retire or move to other jobs and must be replaced. If the rising trend in the percentage of women on FTSE 100 boards is to be maintained the annual average intake of women must be at least that percentage of FTSE 100 board appointments from now on.

The second challenge is to go even further and more than maintain the current percentage of women on FTSE 100 boards. Lord Davies's target was never a destination. It was a milestone within reach of where the UK's largest companies were in 2011 – but a good distance from the proportion of women in the general population.

The third challenge, the most formidable of all, but also the most important, is to increase the number of female executives on the boards and executive committees (ExCos) of large companies. Almost all the improvement in the gender balance of FTSE 100 boards in recent years is attributable to increases in the number of female non-executive directors (NEDs). The proportion of female executive directors (EDs) on FTSE 100 boards has increased from 5.5% in 2010 to 8.6% in March 2015, and by 2014 the proportion of women on FTSE 100 ExCos had fallen slightly from 14.2% in 2010 to 13.7%. (In this book, we use the figures compiled by the Cranfield University School of Management's International Centre for Women Leaders.)

Increasing the number of female NEDs is the easy part. It delivers valuable corporate governance benefits, but does relatively little to improve the quality of management and leadership.

We're under no illusions about how difficult it will be to get the proportions of female EDs, and female ExCo members, up to that of female NEDs. However, the sea changes in the way our organisations and institutions are run, which we call the 'big project', require women to play a bigger role in management as well as in governance.

The book begins, in Chapter 1, by describing the 'big project' and characterising it as a necessary adaptation to a new economic and social environment. Achieving better gender balance at the top of companies and other institutions is characterised as an important component of the 'big project'.

In Chapter 2, we summarise the state of play in the gender-balance environment by taking a close look at the numbers, surveying the relevant features of the environment, and describing some elements of the gender-balancing infrastructure that has begun to emerge.

Chapter 3 examines the political context of gender balance from an international perspective. It assesses the contributions statutory quotas for women on company boards have made in other countries in Europe, explains the absence of pressure for such quotas in the US and says the UK government's robust, but non-statutory approach to the 'women on boards' challenge has much to commend it.

The contribution of The Mentoring Foundation's pioneering FTSE 100® Cross-Company Mentoring Programme (FTSE Programme) to improvements since its creation in 2003 in gender balance at the top of large UK organisations is assessed in Chapter 4, from both a quantitative and qualitative perspective.

Chapter 5 looks at the use women make of networking in developing their careers, including internal and external networks. It casts doubt on the idea that women are not as good at networking as men, but acknowledges that, for historical reasons, women tend to have less 'network capital' than men and that it could take time to redress the imbalance.

With the help of FTSE Programme Mentors and Mentees we discuss in Chapter 6 the important issue of adaptation – the extent to which women need to adapt, or 'lean in' to what we call the 'settings' at the top of organisations the one hand, and the extent to which settings at the top of organisations can, or should, be modified to accommodate the needs of women, on the other hand.

Chapter 7 looks at the so-called 'pipeline' challenge. It explains why efforts to fill the pipeline of 'board-ready' women should be seen as concerned with executives, and suggests the focus of attention now should be on improving gender balance among EDs and members of executive committees. The chapter ends with a description of The Mentoring Foundation's Next Generation Women Leaders Programme (NGWL).

The pipeline metaphor is useful, but we argue in Chapter 8 that it obscures as much as it reveals. We address this weakness by asking NGWL mentees how they feel about their careers and prospects, what the key issues are for ambitious women and what insights they have gained from their NGWL mentors.

In Chapter 9 we look beneath the surface of things (below the policy statements of leaders) to the inner workings of organisations, and at how, and by whom, policy statements and goals are realised. The chapter includes a unique insight into how the trail-blazing goal of Lloyds Banking Group to get to the position where women account for 40% of its top 8,000 executive jobs, is being implemented.

A question begged by the approaching end-2015 deadline for meeting Lord Davies's 2011 target of 25% women on the boards of FTSE 100 Index constituents is 'what next?' In Chapter 10 we seek the views of several distinguished business people who are now, or have been, mentors on the FTSE Programme.

In the final chapter we summarise the arguments put forward in the earlier chapters and conclude that the gender-balance component of the 'big project' will have been completed when male and female (as opposed to male) organisational cultures are unremarkable.

The Big Project

The ascent of women up the hierarchies of organisations, to boards and their equivalents, has accelerated in recent years, thanks in part to the stimulus provided by targets set by Lord Davies in his 2011 *Women on Boards* Review.

At the time of writing, in early 2015, it seemed quite likely that the Davies target, a quarter of FTSE 100 board seats to be held by women by the end of the year, would be met. This will be a considerable achievement and a powerful endorsement of the UK's voluntary approach to increasing gender diversity at the top of our institutions. But, as with many goals, meeting the Davies target will beg questions about where we go from there.

We believe that when answering these questions we must look beyond gender and numbers.

Our preoccupation with gender leads us to focus exclusively on the problems women experience climbing organisational hierarchies. We forget that men also experience problems climbing hierarchies when 'cronyism' or political skill are perceived to be more important than ability in deciding who is promoted. And the dilemmas, pressures and difficult choices arising from the conflicting demands of work and home life are faced by both men and women.

Some mentors we know through the FTSE 100® Cross-Company Mentoring Programme (FTSE Programme) for female executives, who also mentor men, have told us that, if anything, their male mentees talk more than their female mentees about how hard it is to achieve a work–life balance, the tough choices they have had to make and the high price they have had to pay for advancement. Research published in 2014 by OnePoll.com found that 53% of UK fathers missed out on personal milestones, such as their children's first steps, first words and school prize givings; two-thirds had missed at least one parents' evening; 20% had not attended their child's most recent sports day, a third had missed most or all their children's Christmas plays and no less than 60% acknowledged that long working hours mean they only spent time with their children at weekends.[1]

That senior women who reach positions where top-level mentoring is made available talk less about work–life balance than their male peers may be partly to do with a belief that such concern is seen as a weakness in a woman, but a strength in a man. When giving the Mary Louise Smith lecture at the Catt Center for Women in Politics in 2007 Senator Hillary Clinton recalled a newspaper agony column she had read in the early 1980s. A reader had asked 'I'm about to get a big promotion, and I'm going to have my own office … What kind of decorations are appropriate for my office?' The columnist wanted to know if the writer was a man or a woman. If a man he was advised to display pictures of his family, because that gives the impression of 'a stable person with a good set of family values'. But if the reader was a woman she shouldn't put up pictures of her family, because that gives the impression she cannot keep her mind on the job.

We suspect, also, that women tend to confront these work–life balance issues earlier in their careers, and many have come to terms with the compromises and sacrifices they've had to make before they qualify for top-level mentoring.

When we discuss aims and objectives, we often talk about the numbers and percentages of women on company boards. But in our preoccupation with the numerical, we risk losing sight of the fundamental: we tend to forget that the numbers of women on boards are merely imperfect proxies for the influence of women on company management and governance.

The numbers or percentages of women on company boards are not ends in themselves, which they tend to become whenever targets are set or quotas are imposed. They are, rather, the means to the end of improving the performance and governance of our companies, and the well-being of those they employ.

The bigger picture

The energy and commitment that a growing number of individuals and organisations are investing in a collective effort to increase the influence of women in our institutions should be seen as part of a 'big project': finding assignments of power, roles and value-added in our society and institutions better adapted to the modern world than current assign-ments, and finding a balance between work and private life better adapted to the needs of the human spirit.

We will argue later in this book that, although the pressure on organisa-tions to improve the work–life balance for their top executives has been highlighted by efforts to improve gender balance on boards, it is as much a generational as a gender issue. The younger people, men and women, who will in due course replace the incumbent elites are looking for a new contract between individuals and organisations (see Chapter 8).

Evidence that a 'big project' of this kind is exercising the minds of our leading thinkers was an article in the *Financial Times* by the influential commentator Martin Wolf.[2] At the beginning of the year that marked the centenary of the outbreak of the First World War on 28 July 1914 Wolf attributed that great calamity, which cost nine million lives, to 'the failures of Europe's political, economic and intellectual elites'. He said the same elites were failing us again today. They did not understand 'the con-sequences of … financial liberalisation' (a huge expansion of debt) and failed to recognise 'the incentives at work and … the risks of a systemic breakdown'.

In what amounts to a disturbing warning issued in the pages of the elite's favourite newspaper, Wolf said: 'Complex societies rely on their elites to get things, if not right, at least not grotesquely wrong. When elites fail, the political order is likely to collapse...The elites need to do better. If they do not, rage may overwhelm us all.'

Wolf's argument seems to be that the calamitous discontinuities of the 1914–18 war and the 2008 banking crisis were both attributable to failures of governance, and that our governance systems need to be improved if further such failures are to be avoided.

Modern societies and economies are too complex to be governable in detail. All that can be done is to nudge the macro-features of our societies and institutions in what seems the right direction.

A conspicuous macro-feature of our societies and economies is that they consist of two genders. We believe that companies and other organisations are better governed by men *and* women, than by men *or* women, and that an integral part of the 'big project' is to assign power, roles and created value more equally between the genders. This will help to ensure more of our available talent, ability and experience moves to places where it can create the most economic and social value, and provide protection from the risks of another disastrous systemic failure.

It is one thing to imagine a better assignment of power, roles and value, a better allocation of human resources and a better way of living and working – but quite another to get to there, from where we are. By definition, elites have an enormous vested interest in the status quo and an almost instinctive compulsion to protect it from threats and challenges.

The quota debate

The inertia of the status quo has led in recent years to calls for statutory quotas for the proportion of women on boards. Advocates of quotas argue that the inefficiency and inequity represented by the low proportion of women on company boards has long been widely recognised, and that the glacial progress towards gender-balanced boards shows companies cannot be relied on to put their own houses in order. Government must, therefore, step in to oblige them to do so.

We understand the feelings of frustration that lead people to this view, but we do not believe statutory quotas contribute in a meaningful way to the 'big project'. Quotas are numbers and, as already noted, people tend to get hung up on numbers. We are interested in the numbers, but we see them as proxies for progress towards the ultimate objective, which is to increase the influence of women on the management and governance of our organisations.

Moreover, mandatory quotas, like all statutory interventions, have unintended and sometimes unwelcome consequences. It is not hard to imagine, for example, mandatory quotas leading to the emergence of a group of women who relinquish their executive roles in favour of several non-executive director (NED) roles. The number of board seats occupied by women is not necessarily the same as the number of women who are directors. Since the supply of suitable ('board-ready') women is inelastic in the short and medium terms, women who have board experience or are board-ready will be in demand for 'box-ticking' purposes after the enactment of quotas and may choose to serve as NEDs on more than one board. There are signs that something of the kind is happening in Norway where listed companies have been legally obliged to have boards comprising at least 40% women and men since 2006.

The proportion of women occupying four or more Norwegian boardroom seats at listed companies is twice that of men who occupy four or more boardroom seats. The multiple directorships held by Norwegian women have led them to be described as the 'golden skirts'.

It would, in our view, be a wasted opportunity if a consequence of statutory quotas was the emergence of a group of women whose main role was to help companies subject to a quota law comply with the quota. If, as seems probable, these professional compliance agents crowd out from boards other women who could make more substantial contributions to the 'big project', quota laws could be worse than a wasted opportunity; they could do real damage.

The Norwegian government's intervention has had another unintended consequence that suggests listed companies will go to considerable lengths to avoid quotas. A significant minority of Norway's listed companies have complied with the law, not by appointing more women to their boards but by de-listing (going private) and so escaping the reach of the quota.

Baroness Alison Wolf, Sir Roy Griffiths Professor of Public Sector Management at King's College London, is not a fan of quotas. In an article in *The Guardian* in early 2015 she said that Norway's quota 'has done nothing whatsoever for the female labour market generally. It has had no impact on female pay and promotion prospects in the companies concerned [and] … no positive impact on company profits either: replacing privileged men with privileged women doesn't seem to pay any "diversity" benefits. What Norway now has is a new group of "golden skirts": a small group of women who are very rich indeed.'[3]

This judgement seems overly harsh and premature, but Baroness Wolf is right to point out that there is more to this issue than quotas or numbers. As we have seen, the scope of the 'big project' extends beyond gender balance on boards.

Whether or not one supports quotas for the number or proportion of women on boards, it is important to recognise that quotas, threats of quotas and debates about the pros and cons of quotas represent the views of the ultimate authority in democracies, the people. As Martin Wolf observed, the people are dissatisfied with the performance of elites. They want to see some new faces, new approaches and new assignments of power, influence and roles.

Quotas or the threat of quotas is their message to companies. They are saying to companies through their representatives that they're impatient for reform within the business elite.

But quotas are not the only way. There is another, and we believe a better, way to comply with the demands of ordinary people. This uses diplomacy and negotiation, rather than *force majeure,* and has been made possible by a group of senior members of the business elite willing to engage in conversation across the genders and the management generations.

A better way

Among such distinguished diplomats are the FTSE 100® Cross-Company Mentoring Programme's roll of mentors. It's hard to exaggerate the importance of the willingness of these very distinguished business people to give a helping hand to able women as they climb up the last few rungs of organisational hierarchies. Many agreed to act as FTSE Programme mentors long before Lord Davies's 2011 review. They have voluntarily and often repeatedly committed themselves to helping women to join the male-dominated elite. They do not talk in these terms, but it's hard not to be impressed by the foresight and courage of a group consisting almost entirely of men who have devoted so much time to helping transfer power to a different and more diverse elite (see Appendix).

This engagement between the ruling establishment as it is now, and the ruling establishment it needs to become, will take many forms; conferences, debates in the media and parliament, opinion surveys, academic research and, above all, conversation. The FTSE Programme offers a forum for prolonged conversations across boundaries.

Although none of the conversations are specifically about the 'big project', they are lines of communication between groups of people on either side of the boundary separating the status quo from what may replace it. They improve mutual understanding between the groups, help to map out the common ground and contribute to the emergence of the trust necessary for bridging the divide.

We do not, of course, characterise the conversations that occur in the relationships we arrange in this way. Our focus is on narrower objectives: the careers of our mentees and how their mentors help them to realise their ambitions.

But when standing outside the mentoring process, knowing both participants in each mentoring pair, we can see a deep structure to these conversations. It is usually below the threshold of each mentoring pair's awareness, but it resembles a diplomatic engagement, preparatory to sharing power.

All mentoring relationships have a sub-text of this kind – the old guard playing tutors to the new. But in this case there is more to it. In addition to bringing on the next generation of leaders they are handing over to a new kind of elite; a more gender-balanced, less privileged elite, with the new faces, new approaches and new assignments of power and roles that society at large is seeking to achieve.

We believe that the FTSE Programme is making a small but important contribution to an implicit settlement between the elites running things today and the aspiring elites who will run things tomorrow. This is our contribution to the big project. We believe a good proportion of the new faces in the elites should be female faces.

We would not specify what proportion, because, as we have said, there's a tendency to get too hung up on numbers. Numbers are all we have to track the direction and speed of change, but we must be careful how we interpret them and attach significance to them.

Gender balance in Whitehall

When Gus O'Donnell (now Lord O'Donnell) was the head of Britain's civil service it was his proud boast that, on his watch, half the permanent secretaries were women. Jill Rutter of the Institute for Government pointed out in 2012 that this figure was never as robust as it seemed, because it excluded ambassadors of permanent secretary rank, and male permanent secretaries at departments with more than one permanent secretary. 'But ... some time in early 2011', Rutter acknowledged, O'Donnell could justifiably claim that half of those in charge of government departments were women, and, as Rutter put it, 'that marked a real change with what had gone before'.[4]

After O'Donnell retired, the proportion of female permanent secretaries fell to 26% by mid-2012. It rose a little subsequently.

What should we make of this? Should we conclude, as some say, that the 50% reached in early 2011 was an aberration, a consequence of O'Donnell's evangelism, and that the proportion of female permanent secretaries will never reach such heights again? Or should we point out that the 18 departments on which O'Donnell's 50% figure was based is a small sample and its gender split is very sensitive to the gender of the next joiner and the next leaver?

The latter seems to us to be the more reasonable reaction. Numbers describing the gender balance in a population or a group are just snapshots. People, including permanent secretaries, come and go. In a large group with constant immigration and emigration, such as FTSE 100 directors, it's extremely unlikely that the proportion of women at the end of one year will be the same as the proportion at the end of the previous year, or the next year. Targets should not be a specific measure for which we must reach and, once reached, to which we must cling. They should be moving averages or trends.

It's like the inflation target. This is set at a level that seems, in normal circumstances, to strike roughly the right balance between stimulating growth and containing inflation. But, because everyone knows circumstances are seldom normal, no one worries too much if actual inflation rises above the target a little or falls below it a little. The Governor of the Bank of England writes a letter to the Chancellor of the Exchequer, but no heads roll. Everyone knows there is normal variation around the trend.

Moving averages may not, of course, move in the right direction or at the required speed. On 5 September 2014, Sir Jeremy Heywood, Lord O'Donnell's successor as head of the civil service, said in a joint statement with cabinet office minister Francis Maude, that 'We are proud that women now account for almost 40% of our senior appointments and make up over half our entire workforce. But why do women only ... [hold] a third of the very top management posts in the Civil Service?' By practically every measure, the senior civil service is ahead of the UK company sector in gender diversity, but the proportion of female permanent secretaries had dropped to less than a third since O'Donnell's time. Heywood and Maude had, therefore, decided that henceforth all-male shortlists for permanent secretary positions would be banned in all but exceptional circumstances.[5]

Thanks partly to our mentors and to their mentees, the trend in the percentage of women on FTSE 100 boards has been steadier than in Whitehall. It has been rising slowly for several years. We expect the trend to begin to accelerate over the next few years, before slowing down, and finally levelling off in a classic 'S' curve. We expect considerable, year-to-year oscillations around the trend in the meantime.

Professional services firms

The professional services firms are beyond the scope of the Davies target and the public scrutiny that accompanies it, but they have, nonetheless, responded to the gender balance zeitgeist. They have, in a sense, been obliged to, by their need to empathise with their client. If the balance of genders at the top of a firm's client organisations changes, its ability to empathise with those clients can only be sustained if there's a corresponding change at the top of their own organisations.

We spoke to David Cruickshank, Chairman of leading professional services firm Deloitte in August 2014. He told us that 'Although we're a partnership, our governance structure is fairly akin to that of a major corporation. We have a board and board sub-committees. My role is to run the board, not the firm. David Sproul runs the firm. He's responsible to the board as Chief Executive.' Cruickshank said that particularly since the appointment of the distinguished economist Dame DeAnne Julius as an NED in 2011, alongside Deloitte's other independent non-executives, Sir Gerry Grimstone and Sir Michael Peat, 'it ... feels more like a public company board now than it ever has before.'

We asked Cruickshank whether he had had gender diversity objectives when he was appointed chairman in 2007. 'If I'm honest, no. But there were a number of situations prior to being chairman where the benefits of diversity were very evident. So in all of my client teams I had a mix of men and women, because I truly believe [mixed teams] can find a better answer for us, and the client. Men and women think and connect in different ways when they are dealing with client interactions, and that's usually very valuable. I guess I had that in my mind, when I got to the board. It wasn't part of my manifesto to seek more diversity, but as time went on during my first term it became more important. There was a very short period where we were down to one woman on our board and the dynamics really changed …The changed dynamic was mentioned to me by a number of male board members.

'There is something in the way a woman will build a case, or mount an argument. When there is a group of women, they tend to pass the baton one to the other when an argument is being built and so make their point more forcibly. When you have one, even if individually she is very strong, it doesn't seem to have the same effect. Men don't seem to operate that way. They'll build an argument on their own and present something they think is complete. It is so hard to articulate this; it is only when you see it in action. I remember one critical board subcommittee. There was me and two women in the room, and a man on the phone. I had a clear idea of what I wanted from the subcommittee. The two women convinced me and the male board member on the phone; they worked the argument together, and were right. Everyone was happy with the outcome. So there is something about the dynamics of a good gender mix and you can really feel it when it's not there.'

Deloitte had two female board members when Cruickshank began his first stint as chairman in 2007. When we spoke to him in August 2014 the UK Board of Partners included four women. If Board Secretary Caryl Longley is included, 5 out of 18 (28%) directors are women.

Top city law firms are very profitable organisations, but, perhaps for that reason (if it works, why fix it?), they're also extremely conservative, and no more so than in the area of gender balance.

Although the intake of associates at the UK's 20 largest law firms is more or less evenly balanced between the genders, less than 19% of the partners of top city firms are women, according to research by *The Lawyer* magazine cited in the FT in 2014.[6]

Women in the top legal jobs are even rarer. A recent survey by the US National Association of Women Lawyers found that only 4% of the 200 largest US law firms have female managing/senior partners. The number of female senior partners in the UK's top 20 firms was zero at the end of 2013.

It could be that women simply have less appetite than men for both the work and the wealth associated with partnership. The same *Financial Times* article referred to a survey by the London-based firm Eversheds, which showed 34% of young female lawyers regard law as a career for life, against 46% of young male lawyers; and only 57% of young female lawyers wanted to be elected a partner, against 77% of young male lawyers.

But the cause and effect could be the other way around. The reason why so many young female lawyers do not see the law as a lifetime career may simply be that they don't rate their chances of making partner very highly.

Things are changing. Large law firms are already struggling to find a sufficient number of suitable candidates for partnership, because, as Pui-Guan Man put it in an article in *Legal Week*, 'Long office hours and the need for almost surgical attachment to a BlackBerry or other smartphone mean even the lure of potential seven-figure [annual incomes] … is increasingly failing to persuade younger lawyers that … partnership represents the holy grail of their career[s].'[7]

This disenchantment with partnership in the lower ranks is evident in the modest number of promotions to partners in recent years. In 2014 there was a welcome 17% increase, to 432 new partners at the 27 of the top 30 UK firms that had announced their new partners by the end of May that year. But even this was less than 4% of the firms' existing partners before the promotions, suggesting, according to Pui-Guan Man, that elevations to partnership 'are not keeping pace with partner retirement or natural attrition'.

In these circumstances, large law firms are under pressure to boost the pool of partner candidates by, among other things, making sure their candidate pools are not artificially constrained by embedded prejudices about the gender of new partners.

This helps to explain why 129 (30%) of the 432 new partners in the UK's top 30 firms were women in 2014. A third of the top 30 firms announced promotion pools that were at least 30% female, including two 'magic circle' firms – Clifford Chance, where women accounted for 33% of the 2014 pool, and Linklaters, where women accounted for 43% of the pool.

The recent emergence of this gender–balance leitmotiv in large law firms is evident right at the top of some firms.

In January 2014 Penelope Warne was appointed the senior partner of London-headquartered, CMS Cameron McKenna, where Fiona Woolf, the Lord Mayor of London for 2013–14, was a partner. In May, 2014 Sonya Leydecker became co-chief executive of UK-Australian firm, Herbert Smith Freehills. In 2010, FTSE Programme alumna Monica Burch was elected senior partner of Addleshaw Goddard, which currently ranks 23rd in *The Lawyer UK 200*.

In January, 2015 we spoke to Simon Davies, Firmwide Managing Partner of Linklaters. We asked him about gender balance in the firm. He said 'a better gender balance is one of our global priorities. There's no silver bullet for significant sustainable improvements in this area, but we've taken a number of initiatives in the past few years and they're starting to make a difference. Last year 43% of all new partners were female. That was a major step forward for the firm. We have received lots of accolades as one of the best places to work for women. We're the first UK entity to receive the National Equality Standard.

'So in terms of gender balance, we have improved our position, and we have taken a number of initiatives to ensure that that position is sustainable. But we have more to do.'

To what does Davies attribute the large proportion of women in the firm's recent partnership round?

'Every year we try to elect our best. As a result of these efforts to achieve gender balance, we have a better cohort to choose from. A larger portion of female candidates are being nominated; and not at the expense of male candidates.

'I think the work life balance issue is gender neutral and I think managing work and personal commitments is vital, for everyone. The work here is very demanding and high-paced. We have high achieving people, and they are advising clients in a complex and challenging environment. We have many people who want to thrive in that type of environment. I don't think that it's deterring many people from partnership, but it's incumbent on the firm to support our people, so that the best feel comfortable with the balance they achieve. We spend a lot of time creating a positive culture. Flexibility is going to be important. We're going to have to become more flexible in many ways, ranging from deploying the appropriate technology, to having family-friendly, or career-friendly emergency support. I think these approaches are gender neutral – not only for women. We also have to listen to the needs of the younger generation coming through, so that we make this organisation fit for purpose, in the future.'

We asked how Linklaters's male lawyers are reacting.

'We've had instances when our actions have been mis-perceived. The way we've addressed that is through continuous communication. It's about explaining the reasons for addressing the gender imbalance, and making it clear this is about equal opportunity. I see this as an important cultural facet; an evolutionary development. It's the role of the leadership to clarify our vision and priorities and to explain the rationale. I see gender balance as part of Linklaters being a meritocracy. That means we must ensure that everyone has an equal opportunity to demonstrate his or her merit.'

Does Linklaters have internal targets for gender balance?

'Yes – our aspiration is that the Executive Committee and International Board will comprise at least 30% women by 2018 and in future all partner elections will comprise at least 30% women. To achieve that, the pipeline, or catchment group has to be greater than 30%' (see Chapter 10).

He sees four key benefits of gender balance: 'better opportunities for our people ... more innovative solutions for clients; potentially better financial results for our firm ... hopefully, we will leave a legacy for future generations of both genders to thrive.'

Other walks of life

No one can say with any confidence at what point the trend towards more gender-balanced boards will level off, and we do not believe it is sensible to have a precise figure in mind. As far as the 'big project' is concerned, the main objective is to increase the influence of women in the elites by assigning power, influence and leadership roles more evenly between the genders.

But some indication of where the 'S' curve might reach its plateau can be deduced from the gender balance in other walks of life.

Scientists

Science is an enterprise much like business in that it's conducted by many kinds of people, playing different roles, all dedicated to the goals of improving our understanding of the world and deriving from that increased understanding, innovative, more efficient and better products and services.

As Diana Garnham, Chief Executive of the UK's Science Council, put it in early 2014: 'Science is like an orchestra. It takes many instruments working together to produce a fine performance. At the moment ... it is the virtuosity of the soloists [academic scientists and researchers] being addressed and praised. Of course, they are essential to science and should be valued accordingly. However, we must at the same time recognise and encourage the many other types of contributory scientific talent and experience.'[8]

To address the narrowness of the conventional vision of scientists the Science Council compiled a list of the country's 100 leading practising scientists. Science Council member organisations and other associates were invited to nominate individuals for each of ten types of scientist

(Explorer, Investigator, Developer, Service provider, Monitor/Regulator, Entrepreneur, Communicator, Teacher, Business/Marketing, Policy maker) who were currently engaged in UK science, and to whom other scientists might look for leadership in their sectors or careers.

Of the 100 leading scientists so identified, 40 were women.

Charities

According to the 2014 analysis of the Charity 100 Index, published by Charity Finance, 35% of the trustees on Charity 100 boards were women, up from 31% in 2011. Three of the top 100 (Islamic Relief Worldwide, The Leverhulme Trust, Elim Foursquare Gospel Alliance), had no female trustees, however. Only 22 index constituents had boards comprising 25% or more women and only 16 had female chairs.[9]

Commenting on the 2014 Charity 100 Index analysis, former BBC News presenter Martyn Lewis, who became Chair of the National Council for Voluntary Organisations in 2010, said: 'There has been a wave of support for getting more women on top charity boards after the corporate sector report [Lord Davies's review] – but this has been relatively recent. I think everyone's getting the message now. But it will take time – you have to wait for vacancies to come up, and then apply a new approach to trustee recruitment.'

Film

Of the 18 films nominated for the coveted Palme d'Or at the Cannes Film festival in May 2014, two were directed by women.

'Only two female directors,' said English actor Keira Knightley in an interview in the *Sunday Times*, 'but you look at the film schools and it's 50-50, and you look at the short film prizes and it's 50-50. So what happens between the student, the short film and the [feature] … they're winning the same amount of prizes, so where are we losing them?'[10]

(There is as yet no consensus within the film-making profession or in publishers' 'style guides' on whether a female actor should be styled 'actor' or 'actress'. Some say that, if female doctors are styled 'doctors', it should be the same for thespians. Others say that, if female princes are princesses, why should it be different in acting? We have taken the view of African-American actor Whoopi Goldberg, who said 'An actress can only play a woman. I'm an actor – I can play anything').

According to a survey by Dr Martha Lauzen, Director of the Center for the Study of Women in Television and Film at San Diego State University, 7% of the directors of the top 250 films of 2014 were women, up one percentage point from 2013. Overall, women accounted for 17% of directors, executive producers, producers, writers, cinematographers and editors in 2014's top 250 films – an increase of a percentage point on 2013, but the same as the 1998 percentage.[11]

Knightley wants to know why, given the fact that women account for 52% of cinema audiences, there were so few women at the top of the profession. She suggested it might be because film financiers were worried that men would not watch 'girlie' films. Lauzen said that 'Women directors are regarded as "riskier hires"' than men, who may have only directed a pop video before being handed a blockbuster.'

It may be that women are also perceived as 'riskier hires' when it comes to executive board appointments.

Three challenges

There's no suggestion above that 40% is the 'right' proportion for science, or that 19% or 30% is right for law firms, any more than the 50% of permanent secretaries in early 2011 was 'right' for the civil service. If the Science Council's questions had been asked a year earlier, or a year later, it is highly unlikely that the same proportion of women would have been identified as the UK's leading scientists. It might have been more, or it might have been less.

The gender balancing process in large law firms is still at a very early stage, at least compared with large companies. There is no way of knowing where, or at what proportions of men and women, it will end up.

Whatever numbers or ballpark figures people have in mind, it seems likely that the 'big project' will require the boards of companies and other large organisations to move more rapidly towards balance between the genders in the coming years. It also seems likely that the trend will be accompanied by changes in work–life patterns – more job-sharing; early retirement; later retirement; gradual, rather than abrupt withdrawal from work (what Garrick Fraser, of Executive Alumni, calls the 'glide path'); more home-working; more self-employment; more entrepreneurs.

This proliferation of work–life patterns could create more choices for men and women and help to fill the pipelines of talent, energy and competence needed to drive the 'big project'.

After a decade of agonisingly slow but still significant progress towards gender-balanced boards in the UK, the next phase in the gender dimension of the 'big project' will be focusing on two main challenges: filling the pipelines from which female members of the new elites will emerge, and shifting the focus from the number of female directors (and their equivalents, outside business), to the number of senior female executives.

As we will see in Chapter 7, substantially increasing the share of FTSE 100 executive directors accounted for by women (from the March 2015 figure of 8.6%), is a much tougher challenge than meeting Lord Davies's target of 25% for boards as a whole. The Davies target is very likely to be met, with the help of the appointment of a large number of women as NEDs. For reasons we will explain, we believe the focus of attention now should move down the pipeline one level, to the Executive Committee (ExCo) and to the pipeline to it.

There is a third challenge, too.

It seems fair to say that the successes, so far, in bringing more women into the business and other elites have required women to do most of the adapting. To use a term popularised by Sheryl Sandberg, the chief operating officer of Facebook, women have 'leaned in' to hitherto male-dominated elites, more than elites have 'leaned out'.[12] The gap between organisations as they are now and the qualities they seek in senior executives on the one hand, and the qualities of women, as women, on the other, needs to be bridged by some 'leaning'. But the 'big project' requires organisations to 'lean out', and meet leaning in women halfway. To use the term we employ in Chapter 6, an organisation that 'leans out' to women is an organisation that changes the 'setting' at the top in ways that are designed to make it more attractive to women.

It seems to us that younger women, or 'pipeliners' as we call them in Chapter 8, reject Sandberg's 'lean in' proposal and are looking for more than token 'lean out' gestures. Their demands for balance in their work and home lives, previously issued more in hope than expectation, are becoming more insistent. They are less interested in careers in large organisations, where work–life balance is hard to come by. They want the organisations they work for to exhibit a concern for work–life balance issues that extend beyond a gracious licence to leave work early once a term to go to sports days.

In an article in the *Financial Times* a 20-something of unspecified gender explained why he or she had left a leading investment bank, after two years on the bank's graduate scheme: 'It wasn't that I couldn't cope. It's that I didn't want to cope. I didn't see why I ought to.' A 2014 survey by Deloitte found the fast-moving consumer goods sector had, for the first time, replaced banking as the favourite sector for business graduates. According to Simon Collins, UK Chairman of professional services firm KPMG, the so-called 'millennial generation', aged between 18 and 33, bring a different attitude to work: 'To motivate my generation was easy, you threw scraps of cash at us and kicked us. This generation is looking for meaning in life, which, candidly and shamefully, I don't think our generation was.'[13]

Two arguments

Some people have suggested that efforts to intervene in the market for directors, either through quotas or exhortations, will lead to sub-optimisation and a consequent reduction in our competitiveness in the global marketplace. At a time when Far Eastern peoples, in particular, are out-working and out-studying us and poised to 'eat our lunch', as *New York Times* columnist Tom Friedman puts it, we simply can't afford to burden ourselves with romantic notions such as the 'big project'.

Although the notion that we can choose a preferred balance between work and home life, share jobs, retire early or gradually, rather than abruptly, may be appealing, it is impractical in an age, like the present, of intensifying international competition. According to this view, seeking a better balance than the market produces between assignments of power and influence, and work and home life is like rearranging the deck chairs on the *Titanic*. As the 'tiger mother', Amy Chua, has warned us, if our children don't swot until midnight, and if we don't all work till we drop, our economies are going to be on the losing side in the coming world economic war.

We don't subscribe to this view. Working less and more flexibly is the reward for economic success, not a herald of economic failure. It is what economic growth is for. As the Asian economies approach western living standards their people will choose to work less and more flexibly, as we have done.

There is no correlation between the hours in a day people work and the performance of their economies. According to the Organisation for Economic Co-operation and Development (OECD), Britons worked, on average, 1,669 hours in 2013; less than the 1,788 and the 1,735 hours worked by the Americans and Japanese, respectively, but more than the 1,489 and 1,388 by the French and Germans, respectively.

The *Financial Times* reported in the summer of 2014 that the German engineering group Daimler had announced that the firm's 100,000 or so German employees could choose to have all their incoming emails automatically deleted while they are on holiday. The sender is sent back a 'Mail on Holiday' message and advised to contact a nominated alternative.[14] So no email messages on holiday, and empty inboxes on your first day back (see Chapter 11).

The challenge for affluent western economies is to work out how to use opportunities that have not hitherto been available, to change the ways we work, and the trade-offs we make between work and home life, and how to remove prejudices and other market inefficiencies that prevent talent, ability, and experience from moving to higher value uses.

This, too, is part of the 'big project': flexibility and choice, the removal of prejudices, and other obstructions to ease of movement in every direction; loosening the grip of the status quo and those with interests vested in it. We believe that the FTSE Programme is making a contribution to this project of transition and change.

The wider context

The 'big project' is our environment. We operate within it, depend on it and, in a small way, are helping to shape it. It includes, but it is not confined to, the achievement of a better gender balance in the top echelons of our society and economy, and its gender balance element is, itself, multifaceted.

An illustration of this multifaceted nature of the gender balance challenge is provided by the *Building on progress* position paper published by the Confederation of British Industry (CBI) in June 2014. The paper called on 'schools, businesses and government to work in partnership to boost gender diversity and to reduce the gender pay gap'. Beginning with schools, the CBI said 'occupational segregation' had to be reduced if the education system is to equip all young people to fulfil their potential. 'Too many areas of work ... are seen as male-dominated ... [the evidence suggests that] girls are actively or passively steered away from [careers] that would give them better access to higher pay and seniority.' The paper pointed out that of university places accepted in 2011 only 13% in engineering, 18% in technology and 22% in mathematics and computer sciences were taken by women. But women accounted for 89% of nursing places and 85% of education places.

Careers guidance is another suitable case for treatment, according to the CBI. Data collected by the 'employers' union', as the CBI is sometimes called, shows that only one in 20 employers believe that career advice is currently good enough, and nearly three-quarters say it must be improved. The paper proposes 'a nationally-mandated, locally-run system to support employer engagement in careers services' and to provide 'a formal framework within which the aspirations and ambitions of young women could be fostered with help that explains a clear path to their goal[s]'.

The CBI paper further urges its own member businesses 'to do their part to support schools' and says that 'the Inspiring Women campaign, led by the Education and Employers Taskforce, is a valuable example of a [national] … initiative to encourage women of all occupations to reach out to female students and share their experiences' (see box 'Inspiring Women').

Inspiring Women

The *Inspiring the Future: Inspiring Women* campaign was launched on 17 October 2013, with a 'career speed networking' event hosted by Miriam González Durántez, wife of the then Deputy Prime Minister, Nick Clegg. Also in attendance were BBC journalist and presenter Fiona Bruce; historian and broadcaster Bettany Hughes; Thea Green, CEO of Nails Inc.; Livia Firth, Creative Director of Eco Age; Mumsnet co-founder Carrie Longton; Carolyn McCall, easyJet's CEO; Heather McGregor, entrepreneur and *Financial Times* columnist; Dame Barbara Stocking, President of Murray Edwards College at the University of Cambridge, and former Oxfam CEO; and Dame Athene Donald, Professor of Experimental Physics at the University of Cambridge.

The campaign, run by the Education and Employers Taskforce charity launched in October 2009, aims to persuade 15,000 successful women to visit UK state schools to talk to 250,000 young women about the range of jobs available and how to acquire them. By mid-2014 some 8,250 women had been signed up to talk with girls.

Inspiring Women is part of the Education and Employers Taskforce's Inspiring the Future programme, which seeks out volunteers to talk to state secondary school pupils about jobs and careers. Since it was launched in 2012, 85% of state secondary schools have signed up to the programme.

In its use of successful women to advise and inspire younger women the *Inspiring Women* campaign resembles The Mentoring Foundation's Next Generation Women Leaders programme (see Chapter 7). Mentoring and mentoring-type relationships are common 'big project' delivery systems.

In sketching out its own perspective on the 'big project', the CBI is not motivated by a concern for social equity. It is concerned with encouraging more girls and women to take jobs in 'high value growth sectors' in which STEM (Science, Technology, Engineering, Maths) skills are required. The paper cites what it calls 'shocking' statistics: women account for 46% of the workforce, but only 15.5% of the STEM workforce, and barely 8% of engineering professionals. The CBI believes STEM skills are 'vital to the UK's ability to sustain and develop high value-added industries – they underpin the UK's future economic growth'. They're in short supply everywhere. And one way of increasing the supply, according to the CBI, is to increase the participation of girls in STEM subjects at school.

The Royal Society of Edinburgh estimates that doing so could add £2 billion a year to the UK's Gross Domestic Product.

It will not be easy.

Female participation in STEM subjects has recently increased up to GCSE level, but drops off sharply thereafter. Only 21% of physics and 39% of maths A level candidates were female in 2013, and the same proportions apply to university entrants. Part of the problem is cultural. A survey by the Institution of Mechanical Engineers found that two-thirds of people associate the term 'engineer' more with men than with women.

Citing the success of the targets set by Lord Davies in his *Women on Boards* review the CBI suggests that every school, sixth form, college and university should set and monitor targets for female participation in key subjects, such as physics. It believes this would 'help bring this issue into the spotlight, and sharpen minds to start making real progress that gives girls the start they need to succeed in areas of skills shortages'.

In addition to proposals for reducing gender-related 'occupational segregation', the CBI position paper included other gender balance proposals for government:

- Increase awareness about the options and benefits of *flexible working* and give firms clearer guidance on handling requests.
- Clarify *shared parental leave* legislation and reassure firms concerned about the impact on their existing processes and benefits packages. Allow the new system to settle down before changing it. Consider allowing employees to take their leave on a part-time basis, with the agreement of their employers.
- Increase *free childcare provision* for those most likely to be isolated from the labour market and support mothers returning to work before free provision is available. Ensure the type, as well as the amount, of childcare allows women to return to work. Provide 'wrap-around' care in schools through breakfast and after school clubs.
- Make reducing the *gender pay gap* a high priority, in much the same way that Lord Davies's review highlighted gender balance on boards.

The government also sees the 'big project' as multifaceted and is in broad agreement with the CBI's agenda.

At the launch of the *Female FTSE Report 2014* on 26 March 2014 the then Secretary of State for Business, Innovation & Skills, Sir Vince Cable, said the Davies target was well in sight but was 'part of a much bigger cultural change'. A year later, in the March 2015 Report, one of the Committee's main recommendations for sustaining the female pipeline was to 'change the predominant culture'.

Neither Cable nor the 2015 Report describe, in any detail, the nature of the cultural change required, but Cable noted that record numbers of women were in work and that the government had enacted legislation on shared parental leave and flexible working rights and planned to grant tax reliefs on childcare costs. The March 2015 Report refers to a culture of 'truly agile working', a reference to a more balanced work culture.

The correspondences between the government's and CBI's view of the gender balance challenge, and what needs to be done about it, and the conspicuous absence of any significant opposing views, shows that on this, at least, the country and its political and economic leaders are of one mind. The 'big project' is not controversial. The main obstacles to its success are not conscious opposition but inertia and market inefficiencies that are hard to correct.

Gender balance on boards and executive committees (and equivalents in non-business sectors) is only one part of the society-wide 'big project'. But it is an important part, not only for its own sake but also for its symbolism. Ordinary people see business leaders as members of the ruling elite, and the composition of that ruling elite (its mix of gender, ethnicity, etc.) as an indication of the appropriate assignments of power and roles in society at large.

Little 'big projects'

The government and the CBI see the 'big project' as a society-wide enterprise, but comparable multifaceted umbrella projects are also appearing within organisations.

In March 2014 António Horta-Osório, Chief Executive Officer of Lloyds Banking Group (LBG), unveiled the bank's 'Helping Britain Prosper Plan', a set of public commitments on areas where the bank can make a difference for customers, across households, businesses and communities.

The commitments, designed to support LBG's business strategy to be the best bank for customers, included helping customers get on the housing ladder, helping them save for later life, taking a lead on financial inclusion, helping businesses to start up and scale up, and reflecting at all levels of the company the diversity (gender, ethnicity, disability and sexual orientation) of its customer base and the communities it operates in.

The latter included the breathtaking commitment to reach the point before the end of this decade where women hold 40% of the group's top 8,000 jobs (see Chapter 9).

Summary

- The women on boards issue is not just about gender and numbers.
- Achieving a better gender balance on boards is part of a 'big project' involving reassignments of power and roles.
- Quotas and threats of quotas reflect the people's dissatisfaction with the status quo.
- Negotiation and conversation between genders and generations are better than quotas.
- Moves towards gender balance are evident in Whitehall, professional services firms, science, charities and film-making.
- Organisations must move towards gender balance more rapidly, shift their focus from non-executives to executives, and 'lean out' more to women.
- Working less and more flexibly is the reward for economic success, not a herald of economic failure.
- Gender imbalance runs deep; its origins lie, at least in part, in 'occupational segregation' in schools.

The Story so Far

In a joint foreword to Cranfield University School of Management's *Female FTSE Board Report 2015*, Vince Cable, UK Secretary of State for Business, Innovation and Skills, and Nicky Morgan, Secretary of State for Education, and Minister for Women and Equalities, struck a positive, verging on a celebratory, note: 'Since the publication of the Davies Review in 2011, we have made huge strides in gender diversity in our top companies. We have almost doubled women's representation and ended all-male boards in the FTSE 100. This is a credit to the leadership and determination of so many business leaders … With women's representation at 23.5% in the FTSE 100, we are so very close to the 2015 target.'

In a direct call to arms they continued: 'We are keen to show the rest of the world we can do this on our own without quotas and in doing so, we will achieve long-term sustainable change in the boardroom and wider workplace.'

They acknowledged that the end of a particular phase was in sight, but emphasised that more needed to be done. 'This is not gender parity, but it is a major milestone in a much longer journey.'

We agree. As Thomas Watson, founder of IBM, observed: 'Whenever an individual, or a business decides that success has been attained, progress stops.' It would be a pity if reaching Lord Davies's 25% target by the end of 2015 were to be seen as 'job done'. As we argued in Chapter 1, there's still an enormous amount to do. The pipeline of 'board-ready' women will have to become fuller if the proportion of women on FTSE 100 boards is not to drop back after 2015, and as far as contributions to what we call the 'big project' are concerned, the more difficult, but also more important challenge is to encourage companies to appoint more women to senior *executive* positions.

But directorships are directorships, and there is no denying that in the first decade and a half of the 21st century there has been a substantial increase in the numbers and proportion of women on the boards of our largest companies. When the Cranfield team published their first *Female FTSE Report* in 1999 women accounted for 6.3% of FTSE 100 directors. The 2014 *Female FTSE Report* showed that almost 21% of FTSE 100 board seats were held by women at the start of the year. The March 2015 *Report* shows that in a decade the figure has jumped by 12.6% points to 23.5%.

Progress hasn't been even, however. The percentage dropped in 2000 and again in 2006, and the steepest increase has been in the past three years, as the Davies deadline approached. Using a three-year moving average to even out the year-to-year fluctuations revealed relatively pedestrian progress between 1999 and 2010. It took well over a decade for the proportion of female FTSE 100 directors to double from 6.29% in 1999 to 12.14% in 2010. Between 2010 and 2015 the figure increased by another 8.4 percentage points to 20.5%.

Whether the sharp acceleration after the Davies Review in 2011 had anything to do with Lord Davies's end of 2015 deadline is hard to say, but it seems reasonable to assume that interested observers, who are by no means confined to Lord Davies (see below), have been exerting some influence on the Nomination Committees (NomCos) of FTSE 100 boards. With the undisguised threat of mandatory quotas held in reserve by the UK government, it would be surprising if the Davies target and deadline were not concentrating the minds of NomCos.

Other features emerged from a longitudinal analysis of Cranfield's *Female FTSE Reports* from 1999 to March 2015.

The analysis reveals that the average size of FTSE 100 boards fell throughout the period, but not dramatically. The average number of directors on FTSE 100 boards fell from 12.55 in 1999, to 11.17 in 2015; a reduction of 11%. But there are signs that board size has stabilised. It reached a nadir of 10.76 in 2010, but has risen since then.

This suggests the corporate governance reforms in the aftermath of the 2007–8 financial and banking crisis, which involved a certain amount of rationalisation, have now been completed, and board size at FTSE 100 companies is settling down to an average of about 11.

A more dramatic change occurred during the 1999–2015 period in the composition of boards, thanks partly to the recommendations in Sir Derek Higgs's 2003 'Review of the role and effectiveness of non-executive directors', and their incorporation in the Financial Reporting Council's subsequently updated UK Corporate Governance Code.

In 1999 over half of the average FTSE 100 constituent's board were executive directors (EDs). In 2015 barely a quarter of the average FTSE 100 company's board were EDs. Despite the reduction in the size of FTSE 100 boards, the number of non-executive directors (NEDs) has increased steadily, from 610 in 1999 to 838 in March 2015; an increase of over a third. The March 2015 Female FTSE Report shows that although the average size of FTSE 100 boards remained unchanged from 2014, the number of EDs fell from 291 to 279.

Since most appointments of women to boards are non-executive, this casts doubt on the claim that shrinking boards explained the slow pace of growth in the proportion of women on boards, particularly during the period 2008–11. The shrinkage of boards has been more than compensated for by the increase in the proportion of NEDs.

There are good corporate governance reasons for the sharp increase in the proportion of NEDs on FTSE 100 boards from 49% in 1999 to 75% in 2015. It is hard to escape the suspicion, however, that the chances of meeting the Davies target when it was set in 2011 would have been lower, had it not been for the rebalancing of boards in favour of NEDs.

Some corroboration for the conjecture is provided by the fact that the most rapid rate of increase in the number of FTSE 100 NEDs occurred after Lord Davies set his target in 2011. In the 11 years to 2010 FTSE 100 constituent companies appointed an additional 141 NEDs. In the four years to 2014 they appointed an additional 87.

The relatively modest increase in the average number of female EDs during the period also corroborates the suspicion that FTSE 100 companies would have been hard pressed to meet Davies's target, if the average proportion of NEDs on FTSE 100 boards had not risen so substantially.

In 1999 women held 13 FTSE 100 executive directorships, accounting for 16.5% of all FTSE 100 female directorships. By 2015 there were 24 female FTSE 100 EDs, an increase of 85%; but they accounted for barely 9% of all FTSE 100 female directors in 2015. This near halving of the proportion of female directors accounted for by EDs is perhaps the most disappointing aspect of what appears, at first sight, to be encouraging progress in recent years towards a better gender balance on the boards of our largest companies.

The fact that the number of female NEDs more than tripled over the 1999–2015 period should deliver considerable governance benefits. But that the number of female EDs rose by only 85% (compared with the 200+ % increase in female NEDs) over the same period is cause for less optimism about the improvements in the quality of management on which the business case for better gender balance on boards largely rests.

It is easy to attach too much significance to the relative paucity of female EDs, however. As we have seen it reflects in part a more general reduction in the number of EDs on FTSE 100 boards from 649 (an average of 6.5 per board) in 1999, to 279 (an average of 2.8 per board) in 2015. And this wasn't a 'Davies' phenomenon. Most of the fall in the number of EDs per FTSE 100 board occurred before the Davies Review in 2011. The average EDs per FTSE 100 board fell from 5.5 to 3.3 between 1999 and 2010.

That said, however, board experience of the ED, or the NED kind is valuable in its own right, and insofar as experience as an NED adds to a woman's credentials for an ED position, the sharp increase in the number of female NEDs could be seen as a valuable contribution to the pipeline for senior female executives on the board and, more importantly, on the Executive Committee. Time will tell.

The most encouraging message emerging from the statistics of women on FTSE 100 boards so far is that there is, as yet, little sign of the so-called 'golden skirts' phenomenon; the tendency, when there is pressure to hit targets, or satisfy quotas, for the same number of women to spread themselves across more boards. Golden skirts, the name given in Norway to women who hold several NED positions at the same time (see Chapter 1), often emerge after the introduction of statutory quotas.

It is still very early days, but the evidence so far suggests that the UK's self-regulatory approach to gender-balanced boards may be less prone to the golden skirts phenomenon than statutory quotas.

In 1999 women held 79 FTSE 100 board seats, but only 67 women were FTSE 100 directors. It follows from this that in 1999 the average female FTSE 100 director held 1.18 FTSE 100 board seats. The ratio (a good indicator of the golden skirts phenomenon) held remarkably steady throughout the 1999–2015 period, rising slowly to a peak of 1.23 in 2007, and declining thereafter to 1.13 in both 2014 and 2015. In the 2015 *Female FTSE Report*, a table of multiple non-executive directorships in the FTSE 100 shows that, of 212 female directors only 21 held more than one seat, of whom 20 held two seats and only one held three seats.

This decline in the average number of FTSE 100 main board seats held by each female FTSE 100 director shows that the increase in the number of FTSE 100 board seats held by women during the period is more than wholly accounted for by the rise in the number of women occupying them (from 67 in 1999 to 233 in 2015).

It is hard to say whether the slight fall in the average number of board seats held by each female FTSE 100 director is a result of the voluntary nature of the UK's approach, but it is reasonable to expect interested observers, such as the UK government, to observe more intently, and exert more pressure, when they are not rendered superfluous by statutory quotas.

One closely watched statistic, to which headline writers probably attach too much significance, is the number of FTSE 100 companies with no female directors. It is in this series where the impact of the Davies Review has been most dramatic. There were 36 FTSE 100 companies with no female directors in 1999, 42 in 2000 and 43 in 2001. Thereafter the number fell steadily to 21 in 2010. After the Davies Review in 2011, this dwindling group of women-free FTSE 100 boards shrank dramatically. In early 2014 there were only two FTSE 100 companies with no female directors: commodities production and trading group, Glencore Xstrata, first listed on the London Stock Exchange in May 2011, and copper mining group, Antofagasta, which first raised money on the London Stock Exchange in 1888.

Soon after the publication of Cranfield's *Female FTSE Board Report 2014*, Antofagasta announced the appointment of Vivianne Blanlot, a 59-year-old economist, and former Chilean defence minister, to its board.

Glencore Xstrata's chairman, Tony Hayward, announced at the firm's annual general meeting (AGM) in April 2014 that it would appoint a female director by the end of 2014. On 26 June, Glencore appointed Patrice Merrin, a former Canadian mining executive, as an NED.

Everyone was delighted. Business secretary Vince Cable called it an 'historic day for the FTSE and ... the reforms I've been pushing for to ensure that there is more diversity in the talent running our biggest companies'. He said the appointment had 'been long in the making but I congratulate Glencore today on hiring their first woman ... board director'.[1]

The appointment was gratifying for those advocating gender balance on boards for its symbolic significance; the last bastion of male-only boards in the FTSE 100 had fallen. It was also gratifying for another reason. Three years earlier, at the time of Glencore's IPO (Initial Public Offering) on the London Stock Exchange, Hayward's predecessor, Simon Murray, had scandalised the business press, the political establishment and the public by expressing the view that women were 'not so ambitious, in business, as men' and often liked 'bringing up their children and all sorts of other things'.

After the Murray gaffe, Patrice Merrin's appointment to Glencore's board was redemption of a kind.

Merrin's appointment created a potential liability for the FTSE 100 companies, of which there were 11, including Antofagasta, in March 2015 with only one woman on their boards. The opprobrium heaped on Glencore while it had a male-only board was a clear warning. In the event that their only female director left for any reason, such companies would be under considerable pressure when searching for a replacement to instruct their executive search consultants (headhunters) to submit women-only shortlists.

This pressure to replace a female director who leaves with a woman was acknowledged by Sir Philip Hampton, then chairman of the Royal Bank of Scotland Group (RBS). When we spoke to him in summer 2014 women accounted for a quarter of the RBS Group board. The board was thus in no danger of slipping back into the proscribed male-only state. 'Oddly enough,' Sir Philip told us, 'we very recently got very close to putting another woman on the board. So we're not thinking "we get to 25% and that's the job done" as it were ... So we don't have a cap. We do probably have, realistically, a floor ... if one of our [female directors] left we would be very very keen to make sure we kept to a 25% minimum' (see Chapter 10).

The pressure on companies with only one female director to specify women-only shortlists when their female director quits, would, of course, be far greater. But there are legal constraints here. When Vince Cable received Charlotte Sweeney's report on the workings of the headhunters' code (see page 43), he sought advice on whether a women-only short-list for a board position was lawful. The Equality and Human Rights Commission (EHRC) reported back on 23 July 2014. Its conclusion was unequivocal – it was not lawful to seek gender balances 'by longlisting or shortlisting only female candidates to the detriment of male candidates'.

The law can only deal with particular cases. It has nothing to say about overall aspirations for gender balance on boards. This being so, it is clear that for those companies wishing to remain in good standing, as far as a gender balance on their board is concerned, one female director is not enough.

The observers

In a letter to the chairs of FTSE 250 companies (the FTSE 100 plus the FTSE 250 comprise the FTSE 350, the UK's largest 350 companies listed on the London Stock Exchange) in January 2014 Vince Cable, Secretary of State for Business, Innovation and Skills (Dbis), and Lord Davies (author of the *Women on Boards* Review) said 'the UK's voluntary approach is under intense scrutiny. France, Italy and now Germany are introducing board quotas. The world is watching to see whether UK businesses can deliver real change ... using voluntary means.'

'The world is watching' is a familiar refrain in speeches, letters and comments issuing from Dbis. But pressure on large companies to improve the gender balance on their boards did not begin with Lord Davies's Review in 2011.

Catalyst, the US not-for-profit focusing on women in the workplace founded by Felice Schwartz in 1962, began tracking women on boards in 1975. As noted, Cranfield School of Management's International Centre for Women Leaders began publishing its annual *Female FTSE Reports* in 1999, the year in which Peninah Thomson, a co-author of this book, Elizabeth Coffey and Clare Huffington published *The Changing Culture of Leadership: Women Leaders' Voices* back in 1999.[2] Numerous books, articles and academic studies followed.

Roy Adler, professor at Pepperdine University in Malibu, conducted a study of 215 *Fortune 500* companies between 1980 and 1998.[3] He found the 25 firms with the best record of promoting women to executive positions were 18–69% more profitable than the median in their industries.

The analysis by Cristian Dezsõ, of the University of Maryland, and David Ross, of Columbia University Business School, of Standard & Poor's ExecuComp data on the largest 1,500 US companies from 1992 to 2006, found a relationship between firm quality, as measured by Tobin's 'Q' (market value, divided by replacement value of assets) and the proportion of women in senior management.

A 2007 Catalyst study found *Fortune 500* companies with more female directors than average performed better on three key measures than companies with fewer female board members.

In the same year a McKinsey & Company survey of 101 large companies in Europe, America and Asia found companies with three or more women in senior management outperformed those with none on nine criteria, and that performance improved most significantly when 30% or more of management committee members were women.

A 2009 report by Ernst & Young summarised all the research to that date, and concluded that there was a large, untapped potential for business in the under-representation of women. 'At a time when our global economy is facing its greatest challenge in decades', said the authors, 'we have to capitalise on the contributions women can make ... The learning that comes from a crisis is a terrible thing to waste.'[4]

The financial crisis added a new urgency to the debate about women on boards, exemplified by former Labour minister Harriet Harman's conjecture that if Lehman Brothers had been Lehman 'Sisters', we would not have got into such a mess.

Observations of this kind were not confined to outside observers.

On 20 October 2008, a few weeks after the sudden failure of Lehman Brothers had sent a shock wave through the world financial system, a letter appeared in the *Daily Telegraph* under the title 'Now more than ever we need women on boards.' It was signed by the following (some positions have since changed):

- Roger Carr, Chairman of Cadbury and Centrica;
- Dominic Casserley, Managing Partner UK and Ireland, McKinsey & Company;
- Peter Erskine, former Chief Executive of O2 and non-executive director of Telefónica SA;

- Sir Richard Evans CBE, former Chairman of United Utilities;
- Iain Ferguson CBE, Chief Executive of Tate & Lyle;
- Niall FitzGerald KBE, Deputy Chairman of Thomson Reuters;
- Sir Philip Hampton, Chairman of J Sainsbury and Vice President of the CBI (Confederation of British Industry);
- Philip Jansen, CEO Europe of Sodexo;
- Sir Rob Margetts CBE, Chairman of Legal & General Group;
- Charles Miller Smith, Chairman of Asia House;
- Sir Mark Moody-Stuart KCMG, Chairman of Anglo American;
- Richard Olver, Chairman of BAE Systems;
- Sir John Parker, Chairman of National Grid Group;
- David Reid, Chairman of Tesco;
- Sir Peter Ricketts, Permanent Under Secretary and head of the Diplomatic Service, Foreign and Commonwealth Office;
- James Smith, Chairman of Shell UK;
- Peter Sutherland KCMG, Chairman of BP.

All the signatories were or had been mentors of high-flying female executives in the FTSE 100® Cross-Company Mentoring Programme. With the shock of the Lehman Brothers collapse ringing in their ears they said it was 'essential to accelerate the progress of women into senior positions, given the UK's need to deploy the best talent available ... [and this need was] greater than ever in the current economic climate ... Women contribute to properly balanced boards and, from our personal experience, we are clear that their participation has a beneficial impact on the character and culture of the board.'

It is clear from this that a good two and a half years before Dbis asked Lord Davies to report on 'Women on Boards' a significant and growing proportion of Britain's most distinguished business leaders were 'on the case'. Not only were they urging their peers to move more urgently towards gender-balanced boards; they were also helping to supply the human wherewithal, by mentoring senior women from other companies in their corporate peer group.

The 2011 Davies Review fanned flames of a fire already lit.

Infrastructure

Since then, the fire has been spreading rapidly to all corners of the economy. New businesses, organisations and institutions are appearing to campaign for gender-balanced boards, and to help meet the inevitable increase in the demand for 'board-ready' women with information, education, sponsoring, networking and mentoring.

Prominent among the UK campaigning groups are 20-first and the 30% Club.

20-first is run by its founder Avivah Wittenberg-Cox, who is among the most innovative entrepreneurs in what amounts to a world-wide gender-balance mini-industry (see Chapter 5 on her contribution to women's networks). Each year 20-first publishes a Global Gender Balance Scorecard, for female membership of executive committees (ExCos), rather than boards. The focus on ExCo membership reflects our own belief that the next phase of the gender-balancing project must be to get more *executive* power into female hands (see Chapter 1).

Probably the most vociferous and effective campaigner for women on boards in the UK is the 30% Club, founded by Helena Morrissey, CEO of Newton Investment Management and, since June 2014, chair of the new Investment Association, which united the Investment Management Association and the investment affairs division of the Association of British Insurers. Launched on 9 November 2010 to coincide with the *Financial Times*'s 'Women at the Top' conference, the 30% Club campaigns vigorously for gender balance and stages free events 'to develop momentum and to evolve thinking around the issue'.

Campaigning organisations such as 20-first and the 30% Club are on missions to increase the demand for talented female executives and 'board-ready' women. Today's gender-balance industry also includes a large and growing number of organisations focused on the supply side of the markets for female executive talent.

Headhunters

The organisations closest to the interface between the demand side and the supply side of the market are search consultants. It is to them that NomCos turn when they want to appoint new directors. Search firms usually take their briefs from chairmen for NED appointments and from CEOs (chief executive officers) for ED appointments.

They are closest to the market, and have a crucial part to play in translating the wishes, aspirations and preferences of the board into candidates. When conducting his research Lord Davies was very conscious of the pivotal role of executive search consultants, and recommended in his *Women on Boards* Review published in February 2011 that executive search firms should draft a voluntary code of conduct, covering search criteria and best practice processes when making FTSE 350 board appointments.

The search industry responded promptly – a working group of search consultants was formed right away and produced a Voluntary Code of Conduct for Executive Search Firms in July 2011. The provisions of the voluntary code covered:

1. *Succession planning*: firms should help their clients develop medium-term succession plans, identifying the experience and skills they will need over the next two to three years. This will allow them to look at their whole board, and so specify candidates more flexibly.
2. *Diversity goals*: firms should look at board composition, and at the board's agreed goals on gender balance and diversity, more broadly, and establish with the client whether hiring a woman is a priority.
3. *Defining briefs*: firms should ensure that significant weight is given in briefs to skill, competence and ability, as well as experience. This is designed to extend the candidate pool beyond those with board experience or conventional careers.
4. *Long lists*: when presenting 'long lists' firms should try to ensure at least 30% of candidates are women. If they cannot, they should explain to the client why not.
5. *Demonstrating commitment*: firms should make their commitment to gender diversity on boards clear on their websites and in their

marketing, and are encouraged to develop relationships with future female candidates.

6. *Candidate support*: firms should offer appropriate support to candidates, particularly 'first-time' candidates, during the selection process, to prepare them for interviews and guide them through the process.
7. *Support selection*: firms should ensure clients always assign appropriate weights to competence, abilities and experience, and should advise clients on how to avoid unconscious gender bias during the interview process.
8. *Induction*: firms should advise clients on 'best practice' in induction processes to help new directors settle quickly.
9. *Embed best practice*: firms should ensure that best practices on helping clients improve board gender balance are recorded and shared, and compliance with the Code is well monitored.

By the end of 2013, 68 search firms had signed the code and pledged themselves to adhere to its provisions.

In a Dbis-commissioned review of the working of the Voluntary Code published in March 2014, review author Charlotte Sweeney reached a 'curate's egg' (good in parts) conclusion.[5]

She found some executive search firms took their commitment to the provisions of the code much more seriously than others: 'Some see their commitment as a differentiator in the market whilst some may see this as a profiling opportunity, or an annoyance.' Sweeney was surprised to find only a quarter of the signatories were 'actively promoting their involvement via their websites or other marketing materials', and only 12% were sharing information on the number of women on their long lists. She said that since this was 'one of the more visible requirements of the code one can only assume that delivery towards the other provisions is mixed'.

She made several recommendations, including:

• Search firms should discuss with the client each woman on the longlist and recommend at least one woman for inclusion on the shortlist.
• Search firms should record what happens at every stage of the search and hiring process, and share the information with the government as and when requested.

- Search firms should be more open on their websites, marketing literature and when talking to clients about their commitment to the code and to sharing data and successful case studies.
- FTSE 350 companies should demand statements in contracts that commit the search firm to comply with all the code provisions on an 'if not, why not?' basis.
- A database of 'board ready' women should be compiled for Lord Davies's Steering Group (of which FTSE Programme alumna Denise Wilson is chief executive).
- Investors should challenge businesses on their gender-balance plans. Lord Davies's Steering Group should provide investors with information on why gender balance on boards is important and suggest questions to ask companies and what to look for.
- The Equalities and Human Rights Commission should be asked to rule on the legality or otherwise of 'women only' shortlists (it did; see page 37).
- The Dbis website should publish the code, the signatories and reports on how it is working, and the code should be referred to on the Financial Reporting Council's (FRC) website and in the next edition of its Guidance on Board Effectiveness.

The Davies-inspired voluntary code for search firms, and Sweeney's Dbis-sponsored recommendations for strengthening it, reflect a new government conviction that the search industry has a vital role to play in achieving and maintaining gender balance on boards.

It would be wrong, however, to suppose that gender balance was not on the search industry's horizon before the 2011 Davies Review.

Many of the UK's leading search consultants are women, and many of them and their male colleagues were active participants in debates and discussions about women on boards long before 2011.

For example, Sapphire Partners say on their website: '[we] always include women on our shortlists, and over the last nine years, 65% of our placements have been women'. They contributed to the Davies Review, helped to draft the 'voluntary code' for search firms (see above) and were early supporters of the 30% Club.

Sapphire Partners publish a quarterly 'Movers & Shakers' survey of female executive appointments. The ninth survey, published in May 2014, recorded 140 appointments and 33 departures in the quarter to 30 April 2014. In the year to that date, 590 women were appointed to NED and executive positions at FTSE 350 companies, professional services firms and not-for-profits.

Commenting on the February–April 2014 survey, Kate Grussing, the firm's founder and managing director, said it demonstrated 'the growing ranks of extremely well qualified women in the UK being appointed to top jobs'. She was particularly encouraged by the 'broadening of backgrounds and new board appointments', and said any company that says it's having trouble finding well qualified women 'should look harder'.

Other notable headhunting contributors to the gender balance cause are Julia Budd and Laura Sanderson of the Zygos Partnership, Honor Pollok of CTPartners, Patricia Tehan of Lygon Group, Anna Rex of JCA Group, Katushka Giltsoff of The Miles Partnership, Tessa Bamford of Spencer Stuart, Philip Marsden, founder of Ridgeway Partners, Deborah Howard of Per Ardua and Carol Leonard of The Inzito Partnership.

Training and mentoring

Some search firms anticipated the sixth principle of the voluntary code: candidate support.

The executive search firm, MWM, founded by Anna Mann (previously a co-founder of the Whitehead Mann executive search firm), launched Women For Boards in 2009, 'aimed at helping rising female talent to secure their first Board roles on FTSE 250 or FTSE 350 companies'.

It has built a database of 'high-quality, high-potential women who are ready to take on their first Non-Executive role[s]'. The Women for Boards team work with FTSE 250 companies to identify suitable women to join their boards. Candidates shortlisted for NED roles are given the opportunity to be mentored by an experienced, female NED, to help them to contribute effectively. Mentors include Helen Alexander, Chairman of UBM and an NED of Rolls-Royce; Anna Ford, a former BBC TV presenter and NED of N Brown; DeAnne Julius, NED of Roche Holdings, Jones Lang Lasalle and Deloitte UK; and Johanna Waterous, Senior Independent Director at Rexam and NED of RSA and Morrisons.

Executive search consultancy Bird & Co. launched its Glass Ladder Programme in 2009, to prepare senior female executives for board positions. The ten-month programme uses mentoring, case-study-based group sessions and interactive learning sessions. Session leaders and mentors are drawn from a pool of active NEDs.

Elin Hurvenes founded The Professional Boards Forum in Norway just before Norway's enactment in November 2003 of a law requiring the boards of listed companies to consist of at least 40% women and at least 40% men (see Chapter 3). She brought The Professional Boards Forum to the UK with a fellow London Business School alumna, Jane Scott. The UK Professional Boards Forum acts as a shop window for 'board-ready' women by organising events that connect chairmen and CEOs of leading UK companies with female board candidates.

The first UK event was held in May 2009. At the time of writing in early 2015, 12 Professional Boards Forum events had been held in May and November each year.

Other individuals and organisations, too numerous to mention, have also made and are making valuable contributions to increasing the number of 'board-ready' women.

Education and 'groupthink'

In his post-crisis 'Review of corporate governance in UK banks and other financial industry entities' (HM Treasury, 2009), Sir David Walker (see Chapter 10) said in Annex 4 that 'board behaviour cannot be regulated or managed through organisational structures and controls alone'. It develops in response to current and anticipated situations, such as the 'strategic context, social influence and the dynamic of the group itself'.

Annex 4 distinguished between learnable behavioural abilities and 'intrinsic and innate' traits. Citing leadership research from the 1950s onwards, it said 'traits do not influence leadership ability as much as a person's ability to learn rapidly from and facilitate behavioural development in others', and recommended that executive and non-executive directors be 'schooled in group relations, power dynamics and the behaviours and processes' needed to maximize 'the intellectual capability of the group'.

In academic studies this is known as 'transformational' as opposed to 'transactional' leadership, which rewards good and punishes bad performance. Annex 4 said transactional leadership is 'predominant in the financial industry, where high risk, high pressure and high rewards dominate'.

Annex 4 argued that one way to minimise the risks of dysfunctional board behaviour was to train directors, particularly chairmen, in the art of 'transformational leadership', so that they can acquire 'highly-tuned facilitation and listening skills' and 'satisfy the group's emotional needs, whilst also holding the group to the work at hand'.

Another way is to change the people.

In contrasting 'transformational' with 'transactional' leadership styles, Sir David Walker's Annex 4 was drawing on academic studies using the so-called Multifactor Leadership Questionnaire. Most of these studies have concluded that female leaders are significantly more 'transformational' than male leaders.

According to these studies, the average male leader simply rewards and punishes appropriate and inappropriate behaviour. This is the 'transactional' style. The average female leader tries to motivate people by providing meaning, optimism and vision, and to encourage followers to question assumptions, create and innovate. She sees it as her duty to help her followers realise their potential. This is the 'transformational' style. 'Transactional' male leaders tend to focus on goals. 'Transformational' female leaders tend to focus on winning commitment to, and aligning people with, goals. The two styles have been depicted as the 'arrow' (the male goal-focus) and the 'spiral' (the female consensus-focus).

We're not entirely persuaded by this idea of gender-linked management dualism. What we have seen suggests, to us, that management styles vary too much from individual to individual, and from time to time in each individual, for such a distinction to be a reliable guide to a manager's behaviour. Moreover, the female consensus-focus and male goal-focus dualism takes too little account of the degree to which management styles are adapted to their environments; witness Sheryl Sandberg's 'leaning in'.

But although linking 'transactional' and 'transformational' styles to men and women respectively seems too much of a stretch, there's good reason to believe the potential synergy in the combination of different styles of management is more likely to emerge in gender-balanced situations because of a wider range of personalities. In other words, as we have said already, organisations are better run by men AND women than by men OR women.

There's also a growing belief that the problem of groupthink, to which Sir David Walker attributed some of the blame for the 2008 financial crisis in his Annex 4, is more likely to be avoided with more gender-balanced boards.

In an article in *Bloomberg Businessweek*, Sharon Allen, Chairman of the Board at Deloitte LLP, said that Sidney Lumet's 1957 film *Twelve Angry Men* demonstrated how groupthink can produce bad decisions and, in a jury, can lead to a miscarriage of justice.[6]

A jury of 12 white, middle-class, middle-aged men (a typical board of roughly the right size) discuss what appears to be an open-and-shut murder case. Groupthink would have led to a guilty verdict, but Davis, played by Henry Fonda, resisted pressure from the other jurors, which turned out to be based on prejudice and an eagerness to reach a quick decision, and took them on a journey of discovery that led to a unanimous not-guilty verdict.

A play based on Lumet's film (itself based on a US television play of the early 1950s) opened at the Garrick Theatre in London, early in November 2013. It received rave reviews.

If women improve management with their transformational style, and improve corporate governance with their resistance to groupthink, this must be reflected in how management and governance are taught in business and management schools. Education is a crucial part of the 'big project'.

Here too there are some signs that the necessary infrastructure is now emerging; witness, among others, Cranfield University Business School's International Centre for Women Leaders; London Business School's Women in Business Club, Henley Business School's Women as Leaders programme and Manchester Business School's Centre for Equality and Diversity at Work.

If the complementary quality of male and female styles in business is emphasised and recognised in business schools from the outset, less will have to be learned later on, and the pipeline from which board-ready women emerge will become wider and fuller. In the end, it's a matter of what is generally seen as normal and commonplace. In single-sex schools the common rooms are usually single sex too. When a school becomes co-educational, the style of teaching has to change, and the single-sex common room has to change to reflect the co-educational student body.

Investors

In May 2014 the Investment Management Association (IMA) published the results of a survey of its members' adherence to the Financial Reporting Council's Stewardship Code. Respondents to the survey, which together managed assets accounting for about a third of the UK equity market's capitalisation, were asked to say what were the most important issues in their engagement with companies.

'Strategy and objectives' was ranked first, 'board leadership' was next, then 'board and committee composition and succession' (which includes gender diversity) and then 'remuneration'. This marked a significant shift in priorities, following the preoccupation of institutional investors in recent years with remuneration. Four of the respondents said they were updating voting policies to take a stronger stance against companies with limited gender diversity.

An article on the survey in the Institute of Chartered Secretaries and Administrators' magazine *Governance + Compliance* reported that some investors had recently indicated 'they will vote against the re-election of the chair of the nominations committee of any FTSE 100 company which has an all-male board and intend to vote against the annual report and accounts of any FTSE 100 company that lacks a ... plan to ensure that a quarter of their board members are women – as recommended by the 2011 Davies report'. The article said that 'these voting initiatives may be extended to companies in the FTSE 250 also'.[7]

At the FTSE 100® Cross-Company Mentoring Programme's Colloquium at the Bank of England on 3 October 2013, Legal & General Group's CEO, Nigel Wilson, commented on 'the equality and diversity issues we are encountering as an investor [with £463bn under management, Legal & General Investment Management is one of the UK's largest institutional investors] in the course of our corporate governance work'.

Wilson said that L&G was opposed to quotas, because 'we don't want companies appointing women just to make up the numbers'. But L&G's investment division does expect the boards of companies it invests in 'to have clear action plans in place and this starts by knowing the facts' and seeing whether 'the plans are making a difference'.

L&G has declared, publicly, that its oversight of gender diversity will extend to AGM votes. As Wilson put it, 'we will be prepared to vote against Chairmen or chairs of Nomination Committees where a company has no female representation at board level, and no policy in place on diversity commitments'.

Wilson revealed that L&G had been talking to headhunters about the gender issue. L&G 'would like to see more open candidate lists and to encourage the recruitment' of those without board experience if they have 'the right experience for the company ... it's not always about going for the obvious candidate'.

He would also like to see 'much more engagement' from pension fund managers and 'proxy advisors', including Institutional Shareholder Services, Pensions and Investment Research Consultants, Manifest, Glass Lewis & Co. and the Association of British Insurers, and some indications of their policy 'for example, on flagging up diversity as a material factor in their research'.

Sir Win Bischoff, Chairman of the Financial Reporting Council, has doubts about the commitment of institutional investors to activism in this area. 'Investors should be encouraged to sign up to the Stewardship Code and abide by it. They won't all have the same concerns. Some will have concerns about succession planning and diversity. Others will be more concerned about transparency in the accounts. Still others will have greater concerns about "going concern" issues. Whatever their concerns, they should get engaged, not just be passive. They own chunks of these organisations. In the past they have taken the view that if they don't like what a company's doing, they can sell the shares. That's one way, but it is the worst default. We want people to get engaged and use their *nous*, and their perceptions of what the company's doing. We want investing institutions to engage with the company and talk about these issues.

'They have tended to do that more on remuneration, which is a high pro-file issue. Rather than just selling the shares they have stood up and said "we don't like this", presumably because they do quite like the shares, but they also think remuneration is excessive and have chosen to tackle the problem, rather than sell the shares.'

Sir Win says the reason why investors should be more interested in gender balance is that one of the main advantages of having women on boards is that they are more thoughtful about risk (see Chapter 10).

Not before time, the previously supine attitude to board diversity of institutional investors seems to be changing. Its direction of travel in the medium term is unlikely to change after the merger of the IMA and the investment affairs division of the Association of British Insurers, to form the Investment Association (which became effective in early 2015) and the appointment of the founder of the 30% Club, Helena Morrissey, as the IA's first chair.

The second division

Until now most of the 'women on boards' attention has been focused on the constituents of the FTSE 100. It is generally accepted that the business case for gender-balanced boards is equally cogent for smaller companies, but there are no targets for the vast majority of companies that are not FTSE 100 constituents, and the spotlight of publicity has yet to be turned on them.

To attribute the relatively low percentages of women on the boards of the 250 FTSE 350 companies not in the FTSE 100 (the FTSE 250) to their evasion, to date, of targets and spotlights would be an over-simplification.

The first point to note is that companies with market values close to the top of the FTSE 250 range are 'playing for promotion'. They want to be FTSE 100 companies and conduct themselves accordingly by adopting FTSE 100 policies, standards and systems, and behaving as if they're FTSE 100 companies. The Davies Review set no targets for FTSE 250 companies, but those seeking promotion to the FTSE 100 are aware of and influenced by, the FTSE 100 targets. In 2010, the year before Lord Davies published his review, women accounted for 7.8% of FTSE 250 directors. By 2015 the percentage had doubled to 18%, a greater proportionate change than that recorded by FTSE 100 companies (12.5% to 23.5%) over the same period (see Table 2.1).

Nigel Rich, CBE, the chairman of FTSE 250 constituent SEGRO, a property group formerly known as Slough Estates, suggests other reasons for the relative lack of women on FTSE 250 boards.

'Clearly the public and the political pressure was on the FTSE 100, because it is the most visible. This is the principal reason for the differences in gender balance between the boards of FTSE 100 and FTSE 250

TABLE 2.1 FTSE 100 and FTSE 250 gender balances, March 2015

	FTSE 100	FTSE 250
All directors	1,117	2,027
Average board size	11.2	8.1
% female	*23.5*	*18.0*
All NEDs	838	1,478
% female	*28.5*	*23*
All EDs	279	543
% female	*8.6*	*4.6*
All ExCo (2014)	1,317	2,367
% female	*13.7*	*17.7*

Source: Female FTSE Reports, Cranfield School of Management.

companies. But you also have to look at the mix of companies in the FTSE 250. I suspect that if you looked at the top 30–40 in market value, you would probably find they're closer to achieving what the FTSE 100 has achieved in the gender balance on their boards, whereas the bottom 30–40 companies are less advanced. I think that this is because there are companies within the FTSE 250 that are family dominated or entrepreneurially led that have relatively small boards.'

He also suspects, but he admits that it's hard to be sure, that because there's a shortage of 'board-ready' women, those that are suitable for boards can take their pick and tend to prefer to join the FTSE 100 rather than the smaller FTSE 250 boards.

The fact that FTSE 250 boards are significantly smaller than those of the FTSE 100 (averages of eight and 11 respectively) could also help to explain the gender-balance differences between the first and second divisions. There is not as much room on FTSE 250 boards for new female NEDs as there is on FTSE 100 boards. NEDS represent a slightly smaller proportion of FTSE 250 boards, but these boards are themselves 27% smaller than FTSE 100 boards. On average, they have room for an average of six NEDs, whereas the average FTSE 100 board has room for eight.

Ian Coull, then chairman of FTSE 250 housebuilder Galliford Try and former CEO of SEGRO, suggested other reasons for the difference in the gender balance on FTSE 250 and FTSE 100 boards.

'I struggle with this, I really do. I've given a lot of thought to it. Bear in mind that most of my career, as an executive, was with FTSE 100 companies, so I'm used to the FTSE 100 environment.'

He said that when he became chairman of a FTSE 250 company, '[it was] led by a very dynamic, very successful chief executive … You need a strong chairman to get the board to change its thinking, and to realise the benefits [gender diversity] brings. FTSE 100 companies are much more sophisticated companies and the people who lead them have a much broader perspective on how a good, successful company operates and sits in society.

'We realised at Sainsbury's [where Coull was a main board director and CEO of the group's property company] that, by encouraging our people to get involved in charitable activities, they became more engaged in the company. They were representing Sainsbury. If they were school governors, for example, they would have time off to do that and we would make donations to the schools. That strengthens the bonds between individuals and the company. On charitable days, for instance, the shop manager, two assistants, and six women from the checkout would go to do an old people's home garden. Because it was a completely different environment they would end up with a different leader. Often, one woman would show leadership skills we hadn't been aware of.'

A curious statistic in Table 2.1 that may or may not be significant is that in 2014 women accounted for a significantly larger proportion of FTSE 250 ExCos (18%) than for FTSE 100 ExCos (14%).

Building an ecosystem

An objective interim assessment of the 'women-on-boards' component of the 'big project' would be 'OK so far, but there's still a long way to go'.

The 'big project' isn't called 'big' for nothing. As we defined it in Chapter 1, it involves reassigning power, roles and wealth in our society and institutions in ways better adapted to the modern world than current assignments, and finding a balance between work and private life better adapted to the needs of the human spirit.

Even when focusing on one element of the 'big project' – the quest for gender-balanced boards – you can't escape the realisation that in a mature society it is very difficult to reassign power, roles and wealth. It is difficult not just because of the vast interests vested in the status quo. It is also difficult because it is very complicated, takes a lot of time and requires the construction of an elaborate supporting infrastructure.

As we have seen, such an infrastructure is under construction. The elements needed to support the new assignments of power and roles are being assembled. The belief in the need for such reassignment is growing among key groups (including headhunters and investors), education and training, including mentoring, tailored specifically for women are becoming more widely available, information is being gathered and analysed, and networks (see Chapter 5) are forming and growing.

In other words, the components of the ecosystem needed to support more women on boards permanently are gradually coming together.

Governments have roles to play in the women on boards component of the 'big project' as partners, catalysts, cheerleaders and goads. They can help overcome rolling resistance, clear the path and, most important of all, set an example in their own promotions and appointments, and their encouragement of flexible working.

But the drivers of change are the directly interested parties; the organisations themselves (including public sector organisations); their leaders, employees, suppliers, customers and owners, and the components of the infrastructure they're assembling around them to bring about what amounts to deep cultural change.

Summary

- Lord Davies's *Women on Boards* Review has proved a powerful stimulus for change.
- Board size has fallen; the proportion of NEDs has soared.
- There's no sign of a 'golden skirts' phenomenon in the UK.
- Headhunters have produced a voluntary Code of Conduct, which has been reviewed and revised.
- Numerous businesses have been established to prepare women for board positions.
- The dangers of groupthink can be reduced by changing the gender composition of the group and the way business is taught in business schools.
- FTSE 250 companies have different priorities from FTSE 100 companies, but are making progress towards more gender-balanced boards.
- The components of the ecosystem needed to support more women on boards permanently are coming together.

The Political Environment

In western societies on both sides of the Atlantic gender-balanced large company boards are increasingly being seen as symbols of the new enlightenment. Politicians of all colours and persuasions have become convinced that male-dominated leadership of large companies and other organisations is an anachronism in a modern democracy. It violates the principle of equality of opportunity and leads to sub-optimal allocations of talent, skill and ability.

It is widely recognised, however, that the wish for gender balance on boards isn't father to the fact. The predominance of men in the top echelons of business and other organisations is a consequence of centuries of organisational evolution and will not be easily or quickly corrected by competitive pressure alone.

Politicians keen to endow their countries with the attributes of a modern democracy, and conscious of the public's loss of faith in the ruling elites following the 2008 financial crash, are becoming impatient, and resorting to interventions to speed up the process of gender balancing.

In Europe, governments have adopted two main approaches: statutory quotas for the proportion of women on boards or supervisory boards (if the governance system is two-tier), and exhortation, backed up by the threat of quotas, if self-regulation doesn't correct gender imbalances on boards sufficiently quickly.

Before briefly reviewing the positions in several countries, it is important to note that corporate governance systems vary. In the European Union (EU) corporate governance codes recommend unitary boards in nine countries, dual boards (management and supervisory) in ten countries and hybrid systems in which companies can choose unitary or dual systems in the remaining nine countries. Gender-balancing laws and regulation for boards so far passed or proposed in Europe are mostly aimed at supervisory boards and non-executive directors (NEDs) of unitary boards.

Much has been made of the differences between unitary and two-tier boards; probably too much. As we saw in Chapter 2, FTSE 100 boards have been shedding executive directors (EDs) steadily and, in the process, becoming more like the supervisory boards of the two-tier arrangements common in continental Europe. This can be seen as an example of 'convergent evolution'. In nature, the evolution of the cetaceans (dolphins and whales), has 'converged' on the pattern of the fish, because both have had to adapt to the same environment. Similarly, corporate governance systems have converged on the two-tier system, the place of the management board in a unitary system being taken by the Executive Committee (ExCo).

The board and the ExCo in an ostensibly unitary system effectively comprise a two-tier system, with the board taking the place of the 'supervisory board' and the ExCo acting as the 'management board'. The two main differences are that ExCo members don't have the same legal duties as directors, and a few executives (not so many these days; see Chapter 2) sit on the supervisory board.

In this chapter, we will summarise the 'women on boards' positions in three large European countries: Italy, Germany and Spain. We will then look at the position in France in some detail, as a case study for legal quotas, glance very briefly at recent developments in Japan, discuss the philosophical antipathy to statutory quotas in the US, and end with an assessment of the unique approach being adopted in the UK.

Italy

Italy's new prime minister Matteo Renzi demonstrated the political hunger for the attributes of modernity in February 2014, when he announced a thoroughly modern government. The average age of his cabinet was 48, and half were women. It is hard to exaggerate the symbolic significance of the composition of Renzi's new cabinet in Europe's most gerontocratic, male-dominated economy, where, until quite recently, 80% of the directors of listed companies were over 55, and barely 6% were women.

Less than two months after being signed in as prime minister, Renzi announced new appointments to the boards of three of the country's largest state-controlled companies. They included the appointments of three women to senior non-executive positions.

Italy's 'iron lady' Emma Marcegaglia, the 49-year-old joint CEO of the Marcegaglia steel group and former head of Confindustria (the employers' association), was appointed the president of oil and gas giant Eni, Italy's largest quoted company. Olivetti's president, Patrizia Grieco, was appointed president of Enel, the electricity utility. Luisa Todini, a director of state broadcaster RAI, was appointed president of the postal service, Poste Italiane, which would be privatised later that year.

The appointments of female presidents to Poste Italiane, Enel and Eni came at a time of intensifying pressure on Italy's big, listed companies to appoint more women to their boards. Italy had enacted a boardroom gender quota in 2011, requiring listed and state-owned companies to have at least 33% of each gender on their boards (the law applies to both boards of companies that have opted for a dual structure) by 2015. The law applies when a company re-elects its board(s). On the first re-election after August 2012 there was an interim target of 20% of each gender. The 33% quota applied on the second and subsequent re-elections.

The policing authority for the law is the regulator of the Italian Stock Exchange, CONSOB. If it has reason to believe a company is non-compliant, it issues a warning and demands full compliance in four months. If at the end of that period the company remains non-compliant, a fine of up to €1m can be imposed. Subsequent failures to comply may lead to the dissolution of the board(s).

The impact of the quota law began to become apparent in the spring of 2012, when the car maker, Fiat, brought 113 years of male-only boards to an end by appointing two female directors. Fiat's sister company, Fiat Industrial, luxury spectacles maker Luxottica and tyre-maker Pirelli also appointed women to their boards at their spring 2012 re-elections. By 2014, according to the *Female FTSE Report, 2015*, the proportion of women on the boards of Italy's top 19 companies was just over 20%.

Germany

Germany's centre-left Social Democrats (SPD) won a concession from Chancellor Angela Merkel's conservative Christian Democrats (CDU) during their negotiations, in November 2013, to form a coalition government. Notwithstanding the CDU's hitherto adamant opposition to statutory quotas, the parties agreed to introduce legislation requiring Germany's listed companies to assign 30% of the seats on their supervisory boards to women from 2016.

Exhortation had been tried in 2001, when voluntary targets for the proportion of women in top management positions were set. They had had little effect. As the issue began creeping up the electorate's agenda, another attempt to exhort Germany's large listed companies to appoint more women to their supervisory boards was made in 2011, with another set of voluntary targets.

The rate of progress increased, but at 12% the proportion of women on the supervisory boards of listed German companies remained well below the EU average.

The SPD had long been pushing for supervisory boards consisting of at least 40% women, but until that pre-coalition horse-trading in November 2013, the conservatives had continued to resist statutory quotas, despite the failures of fixed voluntary targets. 'It is a toad that we are going to have to swallow,' said the CDU's Michael Fuchs after the coalition negotiations. 'There are companies where that's going to be difficult.'

It was expected that under the new law, companies that were unable to appoint women to at least 30% of board vacancies by 2016 would be required to leave those seats vacant.

According to the 2015 *Female FTSE Report*, women accounted for 16.6% of the directors of Germany's largest 44 companies in 2014.

Spain

Spain's Congress of Deputies passed a law in March 2007 that obliged Spain's largest companies to appoint boards incorporating at least 40% of each gender by 2015.

The law is a good example of political modernisation of the kind discussed at the beginning of this chapter. It was enacted during Spanish Socialist Workers' Party leader Jose Zapatero's first term as Prime Minister of Spain. It was a manifestation of his 'female-friendly policies', exemplified by his first cabinet, over half of whom were women.

It is not a quota law with teeth, comparable to Norway's or those discussed above, because the only sanctions are a legal obligation to 'comply or explain', and the government's declared intention to take compliance, or otherwise, into account when assigning certain public contracts. But the law has had an effect. Estimates vary a little, but the proportion of women on the boards of Spain's large listed companies increased from roughly 9% in 2009 to about 15% in 2013. As at 2014, according to the *Female FTSE Report 2015*, the level of female directors of Spain's top 20 companies stood at only 15.5%.

CNMV, Spain's financial securities regulator, has included, in its code of corporate governance, the recommendation, on a comply-or-explain basis, that when companies appoint directors they should consider women with appropriate business backgrounds.

France – quota case study

Exhortation and self-regulation was also tried in France, but here too it was insufficiently effective to prevent the introduction of statutory quotas.

In late 2009, 100 or so members of the French parliament tabled an 'economic equality' bill, which proposed quotas for women on both executive and supervisory boards. On 20 January 2010 the bill was adopted by the Assemblée Nationale.

The introduction of the economic equality bill and the belief that it would be enacted triggered a surge of self-regulatory activity. The proportion of women appointed to the boards of France's CAC 40 companies (the equivalent of the FTSE 100) was less than a fifth in 1999. In 2010 the proportion soared to 50%, which increased the proportion of female directors on CAC 40 boards from 11% to 16%.

Realising that even this was insufficient to prevent the enactment of the bill, the French Association of Private Companies (AFEP) and the Movement of French Companies (MEDEF) got together in April 2010 to urge their members to appoint more women to their boards, and added recommendations for voluntary targets to their Codes of Corporate Governance. The revised AFEP/MEDEF code recommended that French boards should consist of at least 20% of each gender within three years and 40% within six years.

It was too late. By now the political momentum behind the economic equality bill was irresistible. The bill was passed by the Sénat, on first reading, on 27 October 2010. The decree giving effect to the Copé–Zimmermann law (named after sponsors Jean-François Copé and Marie-Jo Zimmermann) was signed by France's President, Nicolas Sarkozy, on 27 January 2011.

The new law made compulsory the voluntary AFEP/MEDEF targets of at least 20% of women and 20% of men on boards within three years and 40% within six. Companies with no female directors were obliged to elect at least one woman within six months of enactment or as soon as there was a board opening, whichever came first.

The law came into effect on 1 January 2014. The proportion of men or women on boards after that date can't be lower than 20%, rising to 40% after 1 January 2017. Non-compliance will lead to a freeze of directors' fees and the annulment of all male board nominations until board composition complies with the law.

The law also requires the chairman to report to the Annual General Meeting of shareholders on the composition of the board and on the application of the principle of gender balance.

The law now applies to boards of directors and supervisory boards of all French companies with 250 or more employees and turnover of €50m or more a year, including government-owned companies.

The Copé–Zimmermann law has propelled France from an 'also ran', in terms of the modernisation of its economy, to (by one account at least) the world leader in moving to a gender-balanced business elite.

According to a study by Washington-based Corporate Women Directors International (CWDI), published in 2013, the average percentage of female directors among the 17 French companies in Fortune's *Global 200* was 25%, compared with 21% at the 57 US *Global 200* companies and 15% for the *Global 200* as a whole. According to the 2015 *Female FTSE Report* women account for 28.5% of the directors of France's top 58 companies.

We talked in autumn 2014 to Véronique Préaux-Cobti and Marie-Claude Peyrache, co-founders of BoardWomen Partners, a French cross-company mentoring programme partly based on the FTSE Programme. They told us how the Copé–Zimmermann law was working in practice.

In their view no significant gender-balancing of boards would have occurred in France without the Copé–Zimmermann law: 'Before the law the percentage of women on CAC 40 boards was 14%, so it increased from 14% to 30%. In the SBF 120 it rose from 11% before the law to 30%. We are certain that without the law, there wouldn't have been a strong effort.

'A large majority of CAC 40 CEOs were against this law. They would have preferred "guidelines" rather than quotas; this was why AFEP-MEDEF published their code. Today, most of them acknowledge that without the law the situation wouldn't have changed. This is clear if you look at executive committees [ExCos], where the law doesn't apply. In 2002, women accounted for only 7.1% of CAC 40 executive committee members, and the figure for the end of 2012 was 7.5% – it moved by only 0.4% in 11 years. This year [2014] the figure for CAC 40 ExCos is 10.3%.'

Préaux-Cobti and Peyrache are not sanguine about the use of law or fear of the law to boost the number of female *executive* directors (EDs): 'For NEDs, it's OK; it's going with the law. But for EDs it is still not moving. We don't think it will be possible to have a law for EDs – too complicated. There is pressure from government, which has passed a law covering aspects of equality: pay, parental leave, etc … The law urges firms to promote equality in management and to sign equality agreements with trades unions. But there's no regulation, as such.'

The BoardWomen Partners co-founders don't seem too concerned about the 'golden skirts' phenomenon. They pointed out that of the 28 women who joined CAC 40 boards in 2013, only eight were already on a French board, and of the 22 women who joined CAC 40 boards in 2014, only six were already on a French board. They are much more concerned about the number of foreign women joining the boards of French companies. Nearly 60% of the women who joined CAC 40 boards in 2014 were foreigners.

The situation is more encouraging in the SBF 120, the constituents of which appointed 27 new French women to their boards in 2014 (of whom seven were BoardWomen Partners mentees). Peyrache and Préaux-Cobti are in no doubt that, without the Copé–Zimmermann law 'the 27 French women would never have joined a board. They would be hidden – no one would know of them, because no one would have looked for them. Now they are visible – people know them. Some of our mentees who joined SBF 120 boards three years ago are ready to move to CAC 40 companies. A new pipeline has been created.'

The teeth of the Copé–Zimmermann law – non-compliance is sanctioned by a freeze of directors' fees and the annulment of all male board nominations until the company complies – had yet to be tested when we spoke to

Peyrache and Préaux-Cobti. 'We're not yet there,' they said. 'The law came into effect on January 1, 2014 and companies had another six months to comply. So the deadline [for the initial 20% target] is the end of June.' As far as they could see, one CAC 40 company and three or four SBF 120 companies seemed likely to be non-compliant by the 30 June deadline.

'It's complicated,' they said. 'We don't think those companies know they failed to meet the target. The problem is that when the board is, for instance, eight people, 20% is 1.6, but of course it can't be 0.6 of a person, so the effective target is two.'

In effect, the law requires companies to round up to the nearest whole person.

Overall CAC 40 and SBF 120 constituents were comfortably compliant by June 2014. Women accounted for 30% of CAC 40 board members and 29% of SBF 120 board members. Some 90% of CAC 40 firms had three or more female directors, and 72.5% had four or more. Four-fifths of SBF 120 companies had three or more female directors and almost half had four or more. All SBF companies had at least one woman on their boards.

Some companies are under the impression that the compliance job is almost done. Thanks partly to the requirement to round up to the nearest whole person, the 20% interim target has been more than met, and there are only 10 percentage points to go for CAC 40 (11 percentage points for SBF 120) companies to hit the target of 40% by 1 January 2017.

But Préaux-Cobti and Peyrache believe such optimism is misplaced. 'The CAC 40 companies have recruited about 100 female directors in four to five years. They need to recruit another 70 before the end of 2016 to meet the 40% target by January 1, 2017. But that takes no account of the 10 or so women likely to leave CAC 40 boards in each of the next three years. So the real target is another 100 or so female CAC 40 directors in the next three years.'

This is the quantitative challenge.

Préaux-Cobti and Peyrache expect the qualitative challenge to be even tougher, because the low-hanging fruit have been picked. 'If you look at the type of women joining CAC 40 boards today, you see more than half are foreign. It's not a French pipeline. And if you look at the profiles of women joining French boards, you see they are the same as they've always been – there has been no broadening of criteria. Chairmen and CEOs are still looking for the same kind of people. And when they go abroad it's the same thing. Today they are finding them, but maybe not tomorrow.

'French companies were among the first to appoint foreign women to their boards. Today, companies from many countries are looking for foreign board candidates. The pipeline of foreign women with the necessary qualifications could soon dry up. We need to broaden the profile.

'It's going to be a struggle [to hit the 1 January 2017 target of 40% of each sex on company boards] and the struggle starts now. We are halfway. The next three years will be much more challenging.'

In addition to feeding the pipeline, broadening the criteria firms apply when searching for a new director increases diversity on the board and changes board behaviour. The BoardWomen Partners founders said: 'We can't speak about management, but perhaps we can speak a little about governance. We have some mentees who have joined boards. They tell us that if you have three or four women on a board there are some significant changes. Until now men have appointed people like themselves, with the same type of profile, same education, same type of career. So sometimes some of the questions were not being asked. Then women arrive with no history, different profiles, especially if they are foreigners, and don't mind asking obvious questions, because they're not going to be judged the same way. Sometimes they can ask the simplest of questions and realise no one actually knows. So that makes for new dynamics on boards. It's different.

'Have CEOs seen any change in governance? Generally, the answer is "no, not much", because "I was used to seeing women, so no change" or "it's not because she's a woman". But the opinion of our former mentees is that "when we're in sufficient numbers, we can see that it is really different". Some CEOs say there are changes, but not many. Maybe they don't want to admit it. When talking with CEOs we have found this is not an easy question.'

We asked Peyrache and Préaux-Cobti whether they felt the balancing of the genders on boards was an isolated development, or an aspect of a wider reform of French institutions.

'It's not an isolated development, because in France we have a new law covering many aspects of gender equality.' They were referring to a law approved, by a majority of 359 to 24, by the French National Assembly on 28 January 2014.

The equality law is the most comprehensive in France's history. It covers a range of issues, including paternity leave, the portrayal of women in the media, wage equality, gender balance on corporate boards and the banning of 'Mini-Miss' child beauty pageants. There is also a clause that removes a requirement that women seeking to terminate unwanted pregnancies must prove they are 'in distress', and theatres, sports federations, chambers of commerce and farming associations will all be required to appoint equal numbers of men and women by 2020.

The political classes are also covered. At a time when only 27% of France's 577 members of parliament and 14% of the country's 36,500 mayors are women, existing fines for political parties that fail to field women in elections will be doubled.

'So it's a movement in France – a trend,' Préaux-Cobti and Peyrache said. Is business leading or following the trend, we asked. 'A bit of both,' they replied. 'It depends on the factors you look at. If you look at general wider factors, such as dual careers, companies are behind, because they have yet to adapt to dual careers. But if you look at the fact that women are still doing 80% of home and family work, society is behind industry.'

One much-discussed obstacle to an increased participation of women in the workforce, the cost of childcare, is lower in France than in the UK. 'It's easier for women to work in France,' Préaux-Cobti and Peyrache admitted. 'There's no social pressure not to work, as there is in Germany. Over 90% of [French] women between the ages of 25 and 55 work. You can find someone to look after children. It is normal. We don't say it's easy, but it's more accepted.'

This casts doubt on the argument often heard in the UK that a lack of affordable and flexible childcare provision is responsible, in part, for the lack of women coming up through the organisational ranks. Despite their tradition of cheaper and more extensive childcare provision, and their equality legislation, the French suffer from the same problems of under-representation of women at the top of their institutions as do the British.

Préaux-Cobti and Peyrache believe that in France, as we believe is the case in the UK, one aspect of the society-wide 'big project', exemplified by the equality law and the Copé–Zimmermann law, is the transfer of power between the generations as well as genders. They also detect, in France, signs of a gentle push-back. 'In many companies we work with some men are saying "I'm the wrong age, nationality and sex so I have no future in this company." Men are saying it's impossible – that they are a sacrificed generation for boards. We say, OK, we are going for 40%. If you consider you are sacrificed because you will only have 60% of board seats, that is your problem. But the feeling is there.'

The founders of BoardWomen Partners concluded their interview with some comments on the impact of the programme on France's evolving business culture: 'We think that the programme has contributed to a change in the minds of mentors and of women in large enterprises who wouldn't have thought of joining boards without the programme. It's not supplying all the new women joining boards of course, but it has contributed a large group of women. It is one of the routes for bringing new women onto boards. We've also noticed a change in the attitudes of mentors. Some were very reluctant, at first. One we know well said to us recently "the meeting was so interesting". We couldn't believe it. His attitude to the programme has changed completely. It isn't only helping mentees; it is also about making mentors more sensitive to the issue.

'Some mentors who were sceptics at first are contributing far more now, and are getting more involved. At the beginning, they weren't convinced at all – physically present, but not contributing. They thought: "I've been a mentor. I've put a mentee on the programme. I've contributed. It has cost a lot of money and time." Today they really have changed, the reserve has gone – they feel they've been part of something positive and significant.'

Whatever view one takes about the merits or otherwise of statutory quotas it seems clear that, in France at any rate, they have been instrumental in promoting gender balance on boards; in identifying and making visible a new generation of 'board-ready' women and in helping the male-dominated French business elite get used to women on boards, as well as learning to appreciate the value they can add.

European Union

The European Commission (EC) is of the view that a failure to take full advantage of the skills of women, who account for almost two-thirds of EU university graduates, 'constitutes a waste of talent, and a loss of economic growth potential'.[1]

The EC says the failure is exemplified by the fact that, according to its *Database on women and men in decision-making*, less than 18% of the directors of the EU's large, listed companies were women in October 2013.

The EC's assertion that 'the intense debate' on the gender balance on boards issue was 'initiated by Vice-President Viviane Reding' is debatable, but it is clear Reding (EU Commissioner for Justice, Fundamental Rights and Citizenship) and the EC see gender balance on boards as an area within their prerogative, and thus a suitable subject for a Directive.

In 2011, the EC called for 'credible self-regulation by companies to ensure better gender balance in companies' supervisory boards'. When little progress was evident a year later, the EC's directive generating process swung into action. A draft law was published in September 2012, which would have put EU-listed companies under a legal obligation to have at least 40% of their non-executive board positions held by women or men by 2020.

Objections by member states, including Germany, the UK, Sweden and the Netherlands, led to a revision of the draft law, substituting what the EC called a 'procedural quota' for statutory quotas. The revised draft was published on 14 November 2012. It set the same target of at least 40% of non-executive directors of each sex on listed company boards by 2020, and obliged companies that failed to reach that target to introduce new selection procedures for board appointments that gave priority to qualified female candidates. If other qualifications are equal, firms should appoint the candidate of the under-represented sex.

The main idea is that no woman should get a job on a board because she is a woman, and no woman should be denied a board job because she is a woman.

The law was passed by the European Parliament on November 2013. At the time of writing in March 2015 it was still being considered by the EU's Council of Ministers. It only applies to supervisory boards or non-executive directors of publicly listed companies. But there is an additional 'flexi quota', which obliges companies to set their own targets for the representation of each gender among executive directors by 2020, and to report annually on progress made.

The proposed Directive is a temporary measure. If approved by the Council, it will expire automatically in 2028.

In its final form the gender balance on boards directive is a pale shadow of Commissioner Reding's original law, which had statutory quotas. But, as is often the case with EU law, there will be boxes to be ticked and compliance costs to incur, because, in the event of its failure to hit the 40% target by 2020, it will be up to the company to show that its selection processes are gender neutral.

Japan

In January 2014, Japan's Prime Minister Shinzo Abe proved himself a new enlightenment 'moderniser' by setting a goal to increase the percentage of women in executive positions in the country's listed companies to at least 30% by 2020, and urging every company to have at least one senior female executive. At the time, women held less than 2% of senior executive roles in Japanese listed companies and only 15% of its listed companies had any senior female executives.

When announcing his new gender-balance policy Abe said that 'women are Japan's most underused resource'. He announced plans for a set of government measures designed to stimulate progress towards his goal, including tax incentives for companies, another 250,000 day care places over the next few years and longer maternity/paternity leave to encourage young mothers to return to work. Barely a third of Japanese mothers are currently in the workforce. Roughly 70% of Japanese women stop working after their first child.

A year later new government figures showed that women held a record 8.3% of managerial positions in Japan in 2014. Another sign that Abe's so-called 'womenomics' campaign was gathering momentum was the appointment in March 2015 of Haruno Yoshida as the first female executive of Japan's powerful business association, Keidanren.[2] The 2015 *Female FTSE Report* reported that women held only 3.3% of the directorships of Japan's largest companies.

The US

Not so long ago the US led the world in the proportion of women on the boards of its largest companies. In recent years, however, it has been overtaken by a group of quota-powered European countries, while its own proportion of women on the boards of large companies has remained static.

Catalyst's figures published in December 2013 show that women held 16.9% of *Fortune 500* board seats compared to 16.6% in the previous year. The figure has hovered around 17% for several years.

There is plenty of lobbying for gender-balanced boards by Catalyst and other campaigning groups, such as the Thirty Percent Coalition (seeking

30% of women on large company boards by 2015), 2020 Women on Boards (seeking 20% of women on big company boards by 2020) and The Alliance for Board Diversity, but their exhortations are aimed at companies and their investors, not at the government.

Neither political party proposes statutory quotas.

The nearest approach to regulation in this area was the Securities and Exchange Commission (SEC) approval of a rule in December 2009 requiring all listed companies to disclose whether, and if so how, their Nomination Committees (NomCos) considered diversity when identifying candidates for board seats. If the NomCo or board has a policy of this kind, the rule obliges the company to state how the policy is implemented and how the board assesses the policy's effectiveness.

The SEC rule, which became effective on 28 February 2010, doesn't define 'diversity'. That's up to the company. It seems fair to say that the rule has had little effect, and been more honoured in the breach than in the observance.

There has been some discussion, in the US and elsewhere about why the idea of statutory quotas has failed to take root in the US.

One suggestion is that they would breach the Constitution's 'Equal Protection' clause, as interpreted in *Regents of the University of California v. Bakke* in 1978, when the court found that the use of racial quotas in the admission process of a public university was unconstitutional, and in *Mississippi University for Women v. Hogan* in 1982, when the court judged a women-only admissions policy at a state nursing school to be unconstitutional.

The lack of significant lobbying for quotas by women themselves in the US is attributed to 'skepticism [that] quotas are effective at fixing the systemic problems that lead to unequal representation in the first place' and 'a worry the measure could paint brilliant candidates as obligatory hires'.[3]

Another suggestion is that statutory quotas for anything violate a deeply felt national antipathy to federal or state intrusion into the workings of markets of all kinds. The laissez-faire principle is seen, by many

Americans, to be one of the main pillars on which US economic might rests. The idea that government, at the state or federal level, should presume to dictate to shareholders the kinds of people they can choose to govern their companies is anathema to American liberals.

This argument is not as persuasive as it seems at first sight. It is overt, dirigiste intervention that Americans object to. They do not mind a bit of 'nudging' here and there. Anne Alstott, Taxation Professor at Yale Law School, has pointed out that federal and state governments often intervene indirectly in US markets through subsidies and tax incentives.[4] (This is the instrument Shinzo Abe is using to tap 'Japan's most underused resource', noted earlier in this chapter.)

Siri Terjesen, Ruth Aguilera and Ruth Lorenz argue that three main factors determine whether or not a particular country adopts quota legislation.[5]

1. The extent of 'gendered welfare state provisions' (also known as 'maternity leave and childcare') to enable women to work.
2. The presence or absence of a 'left-leaning' government.
3. Inertia in policy development; for example a national distaste for violations of the laissez-faire principle.

The first and third seem plausible predictors of whether or not a particular country opts for statutory quotas for women on boards. Maternity leave and childcare provision are much more generous in Europe than in the US, and Europe's social democratic traditions are much more fertile ground for the use of legislation to correct social injustices and imbalances than American liberalism. But, as noted, generous childcare provision wasn't enough, on its own, to stimulate progress towards gender balance on boards in France.

The second factor is less persuasive. Shinzo Abe is no left-leaner (far from it) and neither is the Conservative Nicolas Sarkozy, the former French President who signed the decree that enacted the Copé–Zimmermann law. Norway's trail-blazing quota law was initiated by Christian Democrats, but may never have reached the statute book had it not been for the support of Conservative Trade and Industry Minister Ansgar Gabrielsen.

The impression we are left with when talking to our mentors on the FTSE Programme is that the same is true in the UK. There's nothing party political or socially 'progressive' about their enthusiasm for the gender-balanced board. They favour them because they believe them to be better boards. It's a commercial argument.

Divided loyalties

Not for the first time the UK is being pulled in two directions by the gender balance on boards issue.

On the one hand the laissez-faire philosophy it shares with the US sets it against statutory quotas in principle. On the other hand, the traditions of social democracy the UK shares with its European neighbours inclines it towards statutory intervention.

The result has been a compromise; the use of the fear of quotas to create an environment that stimulates vigorous self-regulation.

The government was very aware that, in choosing a hybrid policy of this kind, it was opening itself up to criticism from both the old and new worlds, and that it would get the worst of both worlds.

At the launch of the *Female FTSE Report 2014* on 26 March 2014 the Secretary of State for Business, Innovation & Skills (Dbis), Vince Cable, said that 'The British way of doing it is a voluntary, business-led approach', and quotas were unnecessary 'because the voluntary approach is working.'

As noted in Chapter 2, he and Lord Davies said, in a January 2014 letter to the chairs of *FTSE 250* companies, 'the UK's voluntary approach is under intense scrutiny. France, Italy and … Germany are introducing board quotas. The world is watching to see whether UK business can deliver real change in this area using voluntary means.' At the launch of the *Female FTSE Report 2014* he said the British approach 'relies on a change of culture, not regulation or coercion. We've chosen the voluntary approach in the UK, and we've got to make it work. A great deal is at stake …'.

The jury is still out on this classic British compromise. In terms of numbers, it seems to be working as well as the statutory quotas in France, Italy and Germany, in that Lord Davies's target of 25% women on FTSE 100 boards by the end of 2015 seemed, at the time of writing, likely to be met. There is also some evidence to support Cable's implicit assertion that the 'voluntary approach' is more likely than 'regulation or coercion' to bring about 'a change of culture' (see Chapter 11).

For instance, the so-called 'pipeline problem' – the lack of women coming up through organisations to the board candidate level (see Chapter 7) – seems to be attracting more attention in the UK than in France, where statutory quotas apply only to boards.

Another indication that the UK's approach is changing attitudes as well as numbers is the attention attracted in the British media by the annual *Female FTSE Reports*, and the celebrations that followed Glencore's loss of its status as the only FTSE 100 company with no female directors (see Chapter 2).

Cultural change, and its contribution to filling the pipeline, are important, because, as the French case study shows (see page 65), the 'women on boards' project is a treadmill. Women leave boards too. You have to run fast just to stand still. And once all the 'quick wins' have been grabbed and global pipelines have been tapped, the treadmill tilts and it gets harder and harder to make progress.

We expect that many years from now the gender-balanced board will be unremarkable, and women will occupy more or less half the board seats of the average company, year in, year out. The only reliable way to get to that position is through prolonged cultural change. It is still early days, but we believe the UK's voluntary approach offers an opportunity to touch places deep in the culture that the statutory approach cannot reach.

Some American liberals may argue that the UK system is a statutory system in all but name, because it depends for its effectiveness on an overt threat of statutory quotas; in other words, that it is a statutory system masquerading as a voluntary system.

We do not see it that way, because we know that the epiphanies and processes that have got us so far can trace their origins back to long before statutory quotas began to be discussed.

But this should on no account be taken as a criticism of the model developed and managed by Vince Cable and Lord Davies. We think it is both an elegant and effective approach. Unlike most government reviews and inquiries, it did not begin and end with Lord Davies's 2011 *Women on Boards* Review. It has a permanent steering group run by FTSE Programme alumna Denise Wilson, which gathers information and is assembling a database of board-ready women. Its creators speak regularly on gender diversity and disseminate its messages to, for example, FTSE 250 companies and the executive search firms. It has become a fixture of the UK environment, and the environment is the better for it.

It is a new kind of quasi-interventionist government initiative, and has been attracting attention. As we saw in Chapter 1, the Confederation of British Industry (CBI) suggests the Davies model could be used to set and monitor targets for female participation in STEM (Science, Technology, Engineering, Maths) subjects at school, and to set and monitor progress towards targets for reducing gender pay gaps and improving ethnic diversity at the top of our institutions.

The fact that the British model seems to be working suggests to us that as far as the gender balance issue is concerned, the cultures of the political and business establishments are better aligned in the UK than in some other countries.

Summary

- Unitary boards are effectively two-tier boards in disguise.
- The French experience suggests high childcare costs aren't a major obstacle to achieving gender balance on boards.
- Quota laws are becoming commonplace in Europe.
- Quota laws are tougher than they seem, because companies must round up to the nearest whole person.

- Quotas are not to everyone's taste, but they do bring more women to the top.
- Neither political party in the US proposes statutory quotas.
- The 'women on boards' project is a treadmill. You have to run fast just to stand still.
- The UK's voluntary approach can touch places in the culture a statutory approach can't reach.

4

chapter

Cross-Company Mentoring Works

Hitting a target is one thing. Cultivating an environment in which targets are superfluous, because they have been exceeded and there are no signs of regress, is quite another.

We are not against targets. They can add momentum to a trend. When they are public and progress towards them is closely watched, they create environments that favour growth. They stimulate, motivate and direct. They keep trends in the variables they are designed to stimulate in the forefront of minds and near the top of priorities and agendas.

António Horta-Osório, CEO of Lloyds Banking Group (LBG), knows and does not hesitate to use the rhetorical power of targets. As noted in Chapter 1, LBG has publicly committed itself to reach the point before this decade is out where women hold 40% of the group's top 8,000 jobs. Talking in October 2014 at The Mentoring Foundation's annual Colloquium, he said: 'My management team will tell you that I am fond of making public commitments. In my experience, it helps to focus minds and achieve results! Since there is no hiding place once you have made such a commitment in public' (see Chapter 9).

The public commitment is reminiscent of the speech by US President John F. Kennedy when launching the Apollo space programme in May 1961. He said: 'I believe that this nation should commit itself to achieving the goal, before this decade is out, of landing a man on the Moon and returning him safely to the Earth.'

But the targets themselves achieve nothing. It is what they induce people to believe and organisations to do that changes things.

Kennedy had little appreciation of the technical difficulties, but his vision created a reality. A few months later a janitor working at a National Aeronautics and Space Administration (NASA) facility was asked to describe his job. He said: 'I am working to put a man on the moon.'

Actions designed to improve the gender balance of boards and their equivalents in other organisations can take many forms, and can be aimed at a wide variety of variables and trigger points. They can address gender imbalances at every level of the organisation, from initial hiring to the board (see Chapter 7).

Since it was launched in 2003 the FTSE 100® Cross-Company Mentoring Programme has sought to improve the gender balance on the boards and board equivalents of large organisations, including the constituents of the FTSE 100 Index but not confined to them.

Its model, which has been emulated throughout the world, is to ask the mostly male chairmen, or chief executives or equivalents, of large organisations to act as mentors of women at the so-called 'marzipan' level, immediately below the board, or board equivalent at other large organisations.

Although there's no way of knowing how well the women who had been through the FTSE Programme from its launch until February 2015 would have done had they not been through it, the programme's alumnae as a group have achieved considerable success.

Achievements of FTSE Programme alumnae – quantitative

Excluding current mentees, a total of 103 women have completed one- or two-year mentoring programmes organised by The Mentoring Foundation between the launch of the programme in 2003 and 31 January 2015. Another 62 mentees were being actively mentored at that date.

Between them they've amassed 182 promotions or appointments during or after their participation in the Programme. These advancements have included promotions to senior executive jobs, including 'C-level' roles (CEO, CFO, COO) in countries, businesses or subsidiaries; appointments to executive committees (ExCos) and to boards, or their equivalents, as executive or non-executive directors; and appointments outside their own sectors. The total does not include three national honours, one French and two British, awarded to FTSE Programme alumnae.

As one would expect, the rate at which alumnae have been appointed and promoted has been growing as the programme has matured and its alumnae ranks have grown (see Table 4.1).

It is hard to categorise these promotions or appointments with any precision, because titles vary from organisation to organisation and it is often unclear, unless you work in the organisation, what a particular job title

TABLE 4.1   FTSE 100® Cross-Company Mentoring Programme, alumnae appointments/promotions, June 2005–March 2015

Year	Appointments/promotions
2005	2 (6 months)
2006	9
2007	6
2008	12
2009	9
2010	22
2011	20
2012	25
2013	24
2014	40
2015	13 (3 months)
Total	182

Source: The Mentoring Foundation.

signifies. Moreover, some appointments were to senior jobs at divisions or subsidiaries of large organisations that are, themselves, considerably larger than other organisations represented in the list.

Notwithstanding these classification difficulties, we felt that it was worth trying to give a very rough idea of the pattern of these 182 appointments and promotions of FTSE Programme alumnae by dividing them into eleven categories (see Table 4.2).

It was not our intention at the outset to stray beyond our initial defined operating territory of FTSE 100 constituents, but a number of senior people in the UK civil service became interested in what we were doing and asked us whether they could join the Programme. We agreed and have had no cause to regret that decision. The addition of senior civil servants

TABLE 4.2 FTSE 100® Cross-Company Mentoring Programme, appointments/ promotions by category, June 2005–March 2015

	Appointments /Promotions	Number	%
1.	Executive directors and executive committees of FTSE 100 companies	21	12
2.	Non-executive directors of FTSE 100 companies	9	5
3.	Executive committees of FTSE 101–350 companies	4	2
4.	Non-executive directors of FTSE 101–350 companies	32	18
5.	Directors of listed foreign companies	6	3
6.	Executive directors of non-FTSE companies and not-for-profits	10	5
7.	Non-executive directors of charities, building societies and not-for-profits	17	9
8.	Trustee of top four bank pension fund	1	1
9.	Promotions in own or to another company	61	34
10.	Non-executive directors of public sector organisations (e.g. NHS trusts, government departments)	8	4
11.	Appointment to other government roles (e.g. United Nations committees, regulators)	13	7
	Total	182	100

Source: The Mentoring Foundation.

has enriched the Programme and, as a by-product, improved the quality of communication between the private and public sectors in the UK.

The 'public sector' appointments of FTSE Programme alumnae have included an ambassador, two permanent secretaries, two Cabinet Office jobs, executive and non-executive appointments to NHS trusts, senior roles at the Bank of England, the CEO of an industry regulator and two senior roles at the United Nations.

There has been movement between the categories too. Civil servants have been appointed company non-executive directors (NEDs), and company executives have been appointed to non-executive roles in the public sector. This is as it should be. Able, talented people in senior positions at private and public sector institutions should be mixing more, and learning to understand one another better.

The variety and intermingling reveals something else – that 'board-ready' women are not merely ready to serve on company boards. As talented and able people emerge from their pipelines at the top of their organisations, and begin looking left and right, they realise they have become candidates for leadership roles in many different kinds of organisation.

Many FTSE Programme alumnae have had more than one promotion or appointment since joining the Programme. Table 4.3 shows the numbers of alumnae who have been appointed/promoted more than once since they joined the FTSE Programme.

It might seem at first sight as if these multiple appointments are evidence of the 'golden skirts' or 'going plural' phenomenon; the attempt to meet targets or quotas by appointing each of a limited number of 'board-ready' women to two or more company boards.

These numbers do not support that inference. As we have seen, many alumnae promotions/appointments have been to organisations outside the company sector and don't, therefore, qualify as components of portfolios of corporate board seats. There are some FTSE Programme alumnae who seem to be opting for 'portfolio' careers, but

TABLE 4.3   FTSE 100® Cross-Company Mentoring Programme multiple appointments/promotions to March 2015

No. of Appointments/ Promotions	No. of FTSE Programme Alumnae
2	17
3	11
4	5
5	4
6	1
7	1

Source: The Mentoring Foundation.

not many. As we saw in Chapter 2 the average number of FTSE 100 board seats held by each female FTSE 100 director is only slightly more than one.

To summarise – about two-thirds of alumnae promotions/appointments have been either within or into the company sector. The rest are spread among government, the UN, the professions, not-for-profits, universities, regulatory bodies and industry associations. In all, 85 FTSE Programme alumnae (some 83% of the total) have either been promoted or appointed to senior positions, many of them more than once.

We can't prove it, but we believe the FTSE Programme has contributed to the successes of its alumnae. Many alumnae agree.

Achievements of FTSE Programme alumnae – qualitative

A career, like a life, consists of a sequence of experiences; some good, some bad, some strange, some interesting, some frustrating, some transitory, some unforgettable. Among the most important of these career experiences are the consequences of chance encounters and conversations with people beyond your métier, or walk of life. We see the facilitation of 'off piste' encounters and conversations such as these as the essential task of The Mentoring Foundation.

The conversations that take place during a FTSE Programme mentor and mentee pairing are often off piste. They are almost invariably between men and women (because the mentee is always a woman and the mentor has almost always been a man, although this is changing), and they are always between people from different organisations, working in different sectors and at different stages in their careers. These are not people who would, ordinarily, spend time with one another. The prolonged conversation during a FTSE Programme pairing is unusual, for both mentor and mentee, and is memorable for both parties for that reason.

The testimony of mentors and mentees suggests this conversation is also instructive, enlightening and, in some cases, life-changing. It will not always be followed by the advancement of the mentee's career. Occasionally, the outcome is the mentee's realisation that the price of advancement is too high, and there are aspects of her life she values more than a successful career (see Chapter 6).

Such an outcome is not what The Mentoring Foundation was set up to achieve, but we believe that any outcome leading to an improvement in a mentee's understanding of what is important in her life is a successful outcome.

The vast majority of FTSE Programme mentees have responded to the Programme in the ways we would have hoped, however.

When talking about the Programme, all express appreciation of, and gratitude for, the opportunity it gave them to get to know, and to be known by, distinguished and successful mentors. As was only to be expected, however, mentees valued the Programme experience for many different reasons.

Increased self-confidence has been one benefit.

Angela Pearson, a Partner at the international law firm Ashurst, said that her confidence had grown as a result of her participation in the Programme. She said it was an important factor in her subsequent election to the Ashurst board. 'Being part of the Programme gave me the confidence to reach for what a year ago would have seemed like an unattainable goal. My mentor has been a fantastic sounding board and given me great advice and encouragement. He had confidence in me at times when I was having trouble finding it within myself. I have always felt privileged to be part of the Programme; a member of a very special club. I am now further proof that it achieves great results.'

Joanna Mackle, Deputy Director, The British Museum, said the most important benefit for her was the nature of the relationship she built with her mentor: 'My mentor has allowed me, through his listening, to speak. He says to me: 'Joanna, I hear all that you say but none of it is in your CV!' With him I did a lot of work on that. He is affirming, and tells me I have a lot to offer, which is very empowering. He is also introducing me to important connections, such as other chairmen and headhunters.'

The affirmation provided by mentors and the transformational nature of their conversations are highly prized features of the Programme for many mentees. Sharon White was appointed Chief Executive of OFCOM during her time on the Programme. She said: 'In my nearly 25 years of training and development in the civil service, the last 18 months working with my mentor have been the most precious, the most interesting and the most challenging. He shifted my way of thinking; we had different sorts of conversations.'

Diane Varrin Eshleman, Chief Procurement Officer at Barclays, concurs. 'The most important benefit for me has been the interaction with my mentor. We've shared and compared the trajectory of our respective careers. We have had fascinating discussions across a broad range of topics – from the future direction of the economy to the disruptive impact of new technologies and the evolution of corporate governance. At a personal level, I've benefited greatly from the advice and sponsorship of my mentor as I look to shape the future direction of my career.'

Elizabeth Corley, CEO of Allianz Global Investors, spoke of how her mentor encouraged her to stay focused on her broader ambitions: 'I could have conversations with my mentor that I couldn't have with anyone in the company. This was particularly valuable. If it hadn't been for my mentor, I would have lost sight of those broader goals beyond my executive career. I would have been consumed by the passion for the business transformation. I can't imagine where I would be now without my mentor. Having a mentor made the difference: without him I'd have made the list of things to do, but never have got round to them.'

During her time on the Programme, Corley was appointed an NED of Pearson.

The opportunity to focus on broader career objectives was mentioned by Ruth Cairnie, former Executive Vice President, Strategy & Planning at Royal Dutch Shell. She described how her mentor 'gave me a multi-directional nudging in the right direction, and he made me think about my own marketing plan for myself'. After joining the Programme, Cairnie retired from her executive position at Shell and was appointed to the boards of ABF, Keller Group and Rolls-Royce as an NED.

Eva Eisenschimmel, then Group Marketing & Brands Director for Lloyds Banking Group, described her meetings with her mentor as 'a joy for me. I look forward to them, prepare as much as possible and always benefit from our discussions. I find myself replaying our discussion for some days afterwards and working through the best application of his comments. My mentor often surprises me with his perspective – I relish that lack of predictability – and I appreciate his genuine interest in supporting me.' Since the Programme Eisenschimmel has been appointed Chief Marketing Officer at Regus.

Looking back on her mentoring relationship, Sarah Breeden, Director, International Banks, Bank of England, recalled how the relationship gave her the confidence to move forward independently as the relationship drew to a close: 'He has almost taught me enough so that I don't need him. At the beginning, I was learning every time, but the relationship teaches you how to do it for yourself. Is this what you call moving from unconscious incompetence to conscious competence? It's an affirmation rather than a nudge. It's a transfer of knowledge.'

Alumnae also look back on their mentoring experience as periods of personal enlightenment.

Andrea Blance, former Strategy and Planning Director of Legal & General Assurance Society, said her mentor had given her 'thought-provoking and incisive advice in many areas, ranging from effective networking and general career advice, to helping me be "more strategic" when I present to our board'. Deborah Bronnert, now Chief Operating Officer at the Foreign & Commonwealth Office, said she had gained from her mentor 'invaluable insights into leadership and impact at the very highest level', which she subsequently used in her work in the Foreign Office.

Emma FitzGerald said the Programme 'has given me an opportunity to really gain an independent perspective on my leadership style and advice on how to present this authentically'. She received 'sound advice on the due diligence you must do before signing up as an NED, and constant reinforcement that the key decision point must be whether the chemistry with the board is right, and whether you believe you can learn something from them, as well as contributing yourself'. Whilst participating in the Programme she was promoted to Vice President, Shell Global Retail Network and appointed to the boards of Cookson Group (now Alent) and the Windsor Leadership Trust. She is currently CEO of Gas Distribution, National Grid.

Lynne Weedall said that the Programme had helped 'lift my head out of the day job, and look beyond the here and now into the future'. She was appointed to the board of Opportunity Now, Business in the Community's gender diversity campaign, during the Programme. Since completing the Programme she has been promoted to Group HR and Strategy Director at DixonsCarphone Group, and been appointed an NED at Greene King and the West London Mental Health Trust.

Several mentees spoke of the ways in which their networks had been enriched by the Programme.

Eva Eisenschimmel shares the view of other mentees that developing networks through their mentors is something that arises naturally over time as the relationship progresses: 'I have been careful not to ask for any action by him, but as our relationship has developed, he has volunteered to make introductions and to urge reluctant headhunters to fix meetings, when I was otherwise struggling. This was something I had not expected and yet I prize highly.' Alison Horner, Group Personnel Director of Tesco, also describes how her mentor 'put me in contact with lots of people. The Programme came at a good time. He has helped me to sort out my priorities.' This sponsorship, while highly prized, is rarely the core of the mentoring relationship. It develops as the two parties get to know each other.

The networking with other mentees through events organised by The Mentoring Foundation is frequently cited by mentees as a valued component of the Programme. Elizabeth Lee, General Counsel and Executive Board member at Close Brothers Group, says of the Unilever Mentee Network for Mentees and Alumnae of the Executive Programme (see Chapter 5): 'I think the network is superb; that is a very big plus for me. Nobody seems to need to score points off each other. I really appreciate the relatively informal side to the meetings; the networking and discussion.'

For Helen Burton, a Partner at Ashurst, the wisdom of her mentor and the shared experience with fellow mentees and alumnae were important factors in helping her move to the next level of her executive career. Since joining the Programme, Helen has been appointed Global Head of Financial Institutions and Funds for Ashurst. 'I can honestly say that the wisdom, insight and confidence that being part of your scheme has given me, helped me approach the request to take on this role with a lot more enthusiasm (as opposed to terror) than may have been the case if I hadn't had the privilege of benefiting from my mentor's wise words and also had the support of the mentee network.'

One issue we were particularly curious about was the impression we had gathered that some senior women were thinking about issues that transcended their careers. They were saying to themselves, in effect: 'OK, I have this position. I'm on top of the job – I'm not complacent, but I'm not struggling. What should I do with it now?'

We spoke to Clare Francis, Managing Director, Global Corporate Banking, at Lloyds Banking Group (LBG), in September 2014. She had been mentored by Patrick O'Sullivan, chairman of Old Mutual Group, and by

Sir John Sawers, then Chief of the UK's Secret Intelligence Service: 'Before my current position, I'd been very fortunate in having a variety of roles across continents. I have managed the Global Corporate business within the Commercial Banking division at Lloyds Bank for the last couple of years. This involves managing the bank's overall relationship with some of the largest companies in the UK, and the role spans international geographies. I am a banker through and through and what concerns me today is that we all belonged to an industry that was trusted, respected and integral to the success of the country and economy. Unfortunately, we find ourselves not in that position today and my personal view is a strong economy requires a strong banking sector and vice versa. I often ask myself "what role can I play personally to restore some normality to the relationship?" The mentoring network that I have established has allowed me to identify and execute simple strategies to contribute to making our sector great again.

'I believe strongly in client-centricity and how banks should be set up to serve their clients. This approach has been coupled with prudent risk management. In fact, I was running the risk management team in the dealing room at HSBC when the pound dropped out of the ERM [Exchange Rate Mechanism] in 1992 – this taught me a great deal about how to deal with big market events and how best to equip clients with the "right" solution through challenging and turbulent times.

'One of the main challenges we face relates to how we work together better with the relevant stakeholders, including regulators and the media, to restore trust in the eyes of the people that matter, our clients. All of these experts have to get together and be more collective in our thinking to stimulate growth and drive prosperity – good progress has been made, but there is still room for improvement.

'I was asked to lead the client growth committee for the Association for Financial Markets in Europe, which was a privilege. This has centred on listening to clients and working with some great people across the whole industry to understand how we act on what our clients are telling us and develop the right strategies for change in the future. In December 2014, I delivered a speech at the European Parliament about financing growth – this simply would never have happened a few years ago.'

But Francis insists that, as her positions have become more senior her values and beliefs system have remained unchanged.

'Like many in this industry, I have to think through how I can best utilise my value and belief system on a larger scale and adapt it to what I have learnt. Client knowledge; delivering to clients' needs; risk management; doing things safely and commercially; all underpinned with a need to act with integrity. In the current environment, I think demonstrating and embedding these values have become a prerequisite – as an industry we need to promote these more than ever.'

We asked her what had led her to decide to act on a bigger stage: 'With the help of the FTSE Programme I have acquired a network of mentors. It is not just the mentors, although they have been brilliant; it is how I have been able to leverage the mentoring to provide me with the space to think more innovatively. Now, internally within LBG, I have António [Horta-Osório, CEO of LBG] as my mentor from a business perspective. He has tremendous ability to develop differentiating strategies while being focused on the long-term, adapting to the economic fundamentals operating within a tighter and changing regulatory framework – this is just one area we have focused on and our sessions continue to teach me a great deal.'

Francis implied that some of the value she obtained from mentoring stemmed from fortunate circumstances: 'I had been mentored by Patrick [O'Sullivan, chairman of Old Mutual Group] and he had been a fantastic sounding board. His wide experience across many forms of leadership have helped me greatly. I also had the opportunity of going to see Sir John Sawers. I was not 100% convinced quite how that was going to work for him or for me. I didn't know what to expect. The fantastic thing was we clicked straight away, and he was incredibly open. We talked about what I was trying to achieve within an industry that was experiencing a difficult time.

'Sir John challenged me on how I could extend my network to sectors outside banking to provide enhanced value to my clients – with areas such as government and the media, to name but two. This is where the idea of expanding the scope of the Lloyds Bank Business Leaders Summit started. It has become our annual summit for senior British business executives. At our last summit, the CFO of a real estate company replied to the question I asked "What is a good subject for our next business leaders?" by saying "The subject you must cover is how Lloyds Bank will help clients understand more about financial security and fraud." Until then I had talked about the macroeconomic environment, financial risk management and how customers raised capital. I had not associated security and fraud with the boardroom agendas of FTSE listed companies – I had left that to another department of the bank. There I was being thrown a good idea from a great client and I had just acquired a valuable mentor in Sir John. That made me think "a bank's role in society is to be able to make our customers feel secure". So I thought about cyber threats; the increasing issues relating to fraud and how the team and I could better support our clients in facing these challenges. Whilst these issues are taken very seriously within the Bank, I had not discussed them with many of the CEOs and CFOs who I have met. Now my team are brainstorming about how we best explore these themes, and they will feature as a focus area at our Business Leaders Summit next year.'

We suggested that this was a way of bringing another part of her belief system into play; making the institution a safe place.

'Yes, but I was also trying to predict what my clients may need in the future. This plays to my client-centric beliefs. How does an organisation put its clients at the heart of what it does? How does it help them in their management of risk? How do we assist them with growth for the future? This is how we restore credibility to an industry that has lost its way.'

We asked her if she had raised this idea with Horta-Osório.

'António is thoughtful about this every day, just on a bigger scale. He has been very supportive, not only of how I develop my area within the Bank, but also in how we ensure key relevant themes that make a difference to our clients are always at the forefront of our minds. This is essential across our group and industry.'

A high-level network

In due time, it may turn out that the network of alumnae the FTSE Programme has incidentally created is among the Programme's most valuable legacies.

It's a group of able and successful women who have become, through their mentors, very well connected with and accepted by the still male-dominated ruling elite. Group members share something akin to an *esprit de corps*, as indicated by consistently good attendances at Unilever Mentee Network meetings (see Chapter 9). There is not a 'queen bee' among them. Far from being jealous of their rarity and inclined to pull up the ladder behind them, as queen bees of old were said to do, they are, in their own words 'lifting while rising'.

As a group, Programme alumnae remain interested in, and committed to the achievement of, gender balance in the top echelons of management. They see themselves as the vanguard of a new generation of senior female executives and leaders, who know the value created by women at the tops of organisations, and want more of them.

When we decided to launch our Pipeline Pilot Programme in 2012 and we asked a few Programme alumnae whether they were interested in being mentors of female executives two or three levels below the board, they readily agreed. They had had a helping hand through the FTSE Programme and were eager to extend the same help to those who were coming up behind them (see Chapter 7).

It works for mentors too

As noted above, the prolonged conversation during a FTSE Programme pairing is unusual for both parties, and memorable for both parties for that reason.

But for so many of our mentors to agree to take on a second, third or fourth mentee, it would not be enough for such conversations to be memorable. They're busy people. They must believe the time they spend mentoring for the Programme is time well spent.

While writing our last book (*Women & the New Business Leadership* – Palgrave Macmillan, 2011), we asked a number of our mentors to say why they joined the Programme.

The short answer was that all agreed with Niall FitzGerald, KBE, one of our first mentors and now on his third mentee, who said 'The world would be a better place with more women in senior positions.'

All agreed the presence of women on boards improved the quality of boardroom debate. Some acknowledged the possibility that, if there had been more women on the boards of our large banks the financial crisis of 2007–8 may have been avoided, because bank boards would have been less afflicted by the psycho-toxin of groupthink.

The dangers of groupthink were mentioned by most mentors. They saw diversity as a way to reduce the risks of groupthink in a new era in which traditional certainties and the old assumptions about the system's resilience had proved to be mistaken.

Some of these captains of industry said all-male boards created an abnormal and undesirable behavioural context. Women were said to be better listeners than men, and to improve the social dynamics of a board; to have a keener sense of personal responsibility than men; to be more willing to compromise; to think more deeply about other people; and to bring a wider, more balanced and fairer perspective to the boardroom.

Women were also said to have a better understanding of why someone holds a particular view, which can be very helpful on a board, and to be good in areas that were becoming more important in corporate governance, such as sustainability, cultural and social issues and fairness.

Sir John Parker spoke of the synergies of gender balance, and said its value lay not so much in women as the differences between men and women.

These views, expressed half a decade ago, seem so enlightened, and so strongly felt, that it is easy to forget they were the views of senior members of the business establishment.

Some will be inclined to dismiss these gender characterisations as stereotypes. But stereotypes are simple and unchanging. The views of the business elite about gender-balanced boards are complex and have been evolving.

We spoke to mentor Sir Philip Hampton in July 2014. He said: 'an all-male group will talk differently. They'll have different conversations. The casual chat will be different. Women change male behaviour. Not always. You can get into simple gender stereotyping here, like "the women are always calming influences. They're not. They can be tough, demanding, challenging, aggressive influences as well. But the behaviour of men is modified by [the presence of] women; you're likely to have a more balanced consideration of things with mixed gender meetings.

'You need the right amount of diversity. It is much more difficult to get the right amount of diversity, when you exclude 50% of the population. Women look at situations and issues differently. They have different insights, and they lack some other things that men have. We bring different things – to some extent we have different chemistries in our bodies. We also have different experiences and expectations in our lives. You are always going to bring elements of that into a boardroom.'

Niall FitzGerald was in broad agreement when we spoke to him in July 2014: 'The basic reason why this [a better gender balance on boards] is necessary is that we need to be able to tap into the other 50% of the talent that is available, and we need gender diversity for its own sake. Diverse groups tend to produce richer outcomes. They tend to cope with crises better, when they bring in a broader range of perspectives. A diverse universe is more robust and sustainable.'

At the time of writing in January 2015, there were almost 70 mentors on The Mentoring Foundation's roll (not including mentors on the *Next Generation Women Leaders Programme*). Of these, four were women.

The full list is shown in the Appendix.

We are particularly grateful to our 'serial' mentors, many of whom have been actively involved with the Programme for several years (see Table 4.4).

TABLE 4.4   The FTSE Programme's serial mentors

Name	No. of Mentees
Baroness Hogg, former Chairman, Financial Reporting Council	4
Dennis Holt, Chairman, Beazley	4
Sir Rob Margetts, CBE, FREng, Chairman, Ordnance Survey	4
Sir Mark Moody-Stuart, KCMG, Chairman, UN Global Compact Foundation	4
Sir Richard Olver, FREng, Former Chairman, BAE Systems	4
Sir David Reid, Chairman, Intertek	4
Sir Richard Broadbent, KCB, Chairman, Tesco	3
Dominic Casserley, CEO, Willis Group Holdings	3
Iain Ferguson, CBE, Chairman, Wilton Park, former CEO, Tate & Lyle	3
Niall FitzGerald, KBE, Chairman, The Leverhulme Trust	3
Nigel Rich, CBE, Chairman, SEGRO	3
James Smith, former Chairman, Shell UK	3
David Tyler, Chairman, J Sainsbury	3
Marcus Agius, Chairman, PA Consulting Group	2
Andrew Beeson, Chairman, Schroders	2
Sir Win Bischoff, Chairman, Financial Reporting Council	2
Clement Booth, Chairman, Allianz UK Global Investors, Member of the Board of Management Allianz SE	2
John F. Brock, Chairman & CEO Coca-Cola Enterprises Inc	2

(continued)

TABLE 4.4   Continued

Patrick Burgess, MBE, Chairman, Intu Properties	2
Dame Alison Carnwath, Chairman, Land Securities	2
Spencer Dale, Chief Economist, BP	2
Douglas Flint, CBE, Group Chairman, HSBC Holdings	2
Sir Peter Gershon, CBE, FREng, Chairman, National Grid	2
Sir Philip Hampton, Chairman, GlaxoSmithKline	2
Anthony Hobson, SID, James Dyson, former Chairman, Sage Group	2
Glyn Jones, Chairman, Aspen Insurance Holdings	2
David Kappler, Deputy Chairman, Shire	2
Irwin Lee, Vice President UK & Ireland, Procter & Gamble	2
Strone Macpherson, Chairman, Close Brothers Group	2
Sir John Peace, Chairman, Standard Chartered	2
Ian Powell, Chairman & Senior Partner, PwC LLP	2
Don Robert, Chairman, Experian	2
Sir Simon Robertson, Deputy Chairman, SID, HSBC Holdings	2
Lord Stuart Rose, Chairman, Ocado Group	2
John Stewart, Chairman, Legal & General Group	2
Graham van't Hoff, Executive VP, Shell Chemicals	2

Source: The Mentoring Foundation, March 2015.

The FTSE Programme in context

The Programme is not the answer to the gender imbalances at the top of our largest organisations, but the evidence suggests it is part of the answer. The generations and genders represented by each member of the mentoring pair know it works. If their organisations didn't also know it worked, they wouldn't be continuing to support it and to recommend it to other organisations.

Mentors and mentees email, phone and send each other texts, but the essence of the relationships is a series of face-to-face, one-to-one meetings stretching over one or two years. As we have seen the relationships are normally followed by alumnae appointments or promotions, although we cannot, of course, prove a causal link.

We believe there are five reasons for the success of the Programme:

1. The unusual nature of the pairing, and the face-to-face, one-to-one format, mean both parties take the mentoring process very seriously.
2. Considerable time and thought are devoted to the matching of mentor and mentee.
3. The Mentoring Foundation monitors and fine-tunes the process, as necessary.
4. The cross-company feature ensures that there are no conflicts of interest; the encounters take place on neutral ground and are unaffected by internal politics.
5. The cross-industry feature provides different perspectives of interest to both parties.

The Programme's mentoring model focuses on the relationship rather than on goals or outcomes. The mentor and mentee decide their own terms of reference, within Mentoring Foundation parameters. We do not specify or prescribe. We favour fluid, evolving relationships and we interpret the terms 'mentor' and 'mentoring' very widely.

Much has been said and written, in recent years, about the alleged difference between 'mentors' and 'sponsors'. It has been suggested that mentoring is all very well, but what women need are powerful patrons 'to inspire them, propel them and protect them through the perilous straits of upper management'.[1]

We see this as a distinction without a difference.

The sponsorship advocates focus mainly on internal programmes, where mentors are colleagues and sponsors are senior people in the same organisation. The mentors in cross-company programmes, such as the FTSE Programme, lack sufficient influence in their mentees' organisations to be effective sponsors, *in those organisations*. But this is only a problem if the goal is to achieve promotions within the mentees' organisations. The goal of the FTSE Programme is not to help the mentees to get on their own boards – although sometimes they do – but to help them get on other boards, win promotion or otherwise advance their careers.

Moreover, if the mentor in a cross-company programme is sufficiently senior, he or she will have considerable indirect influence in the mentee's organisation through his or her membership of networks of which senior people in the mentee's organisation are also members. This is one of the advantages of the cross-company model. It introduces mentees to networks that include, but are not confined to, their own organisations.

It is the relationship that matters, not the name people attach to the protagonists' roles. The support provided by one individual to another in the latter's efforts to achieve his/her goal or realise his/her ambition can take various forms. At different times and in different circumstances the supporter may play different parts, or several parts at once. We see supporters and their roles as lying on a continuum ranging from, at one end, no support at all, where people are alone and must find ways to their goals unaided, to, at the other end, what would usually be seen as excessive support and be described pejoratively as 'nepotism' or 'cronyism'.

Between the extremes lie many roles: adviser, advocate, champion, coach, confidant(e), counsellor, fairy godmother, friend at court, guardian angel, guide, guru, mentor, patron, sponsor, tutor, well-wisher. During a mentoring relationship, the mentor may play several of these roles at one time or another. He or she would not feel obliged to confine himself or herself to the role prescribed by a strict interpretation of the word 'mentor.'

Whether you call an individual's supporter a mentor, sponsor, guru or patron, the more senior and influential the mentor/patron, the better for a mentee/protégée, not because, or not only because the mentor/patron will be more experienced and knowledgeable, but also because the mentor/patron has more power to change the environment in ways that favour the mentee/protégée.

In one-to-one support relationships supporters play many parts. It is what they can and are willing to do for those they support, not how they are described, that really matters.

We would be the first to acknowledge, however, that the FTSE Programme is small and bespoke, with limited scalability. The success of The Mentoring Foundation's Next Generation Women Leaders Programme (NGWL) shows that the same principles can be applied successfully to lower levels in organisational hierarchies (see Chapter 7), but the NGWL Programme is also, by its nature, small and bespoke.

But could some of the design features that have contributed to the Programme's success be incorporated in an inherently more scalable programme? Could a larger, less bespoke, pared-down version also contribute to filling up the pipeline from which 'board-ready' women emerge?

We may soon see.

Following a six-month pilot scheme, the 30% Club and EY (formerly Ernst & Young) launched a cross-company mentoring scheme aimed at women in 'mid-career' (aged between 28 and 38) in September 2014. Although press releases and announcements about the scheme did not mention the FTSE Programme or the NGWL by name, the scheme appears designed to complement The Mentoring Foundation's programmes.

Its declared aim is to extend cross-company cross-sector mentoring which 'until now has been reserved for senior executives' to mid-career women, and to 'complement other schemes in the marketplace ... where cross-company mentoring is usually only available to very senior women.'

Feedback from the pilot scheme corroborated our own findings about the value of cross-company, cross-industry mentoring. 'Having the opportunity to be mentored by someone external to my company and from a different industry has been a great experience,' said one of the pilot programme mentees. Another said it had helped her 'get a perspective on my organisation; sometimes you can get caught up in the internal culture and forget to sense-check what happens in the bigger outside world'.

The sponsors say that they're addressing 'the issue of scalability in mentoring ... with the ... objective of reaching hundreds rather than tens of women as is the case currently'. They hope the scheme 'can be beneficial for, ultimately, thousands of women'.

Each mentoring assignment lasts ten months (feedback from the pilot suggested six months is too short) from September to the following July, compared with the FTSE Programme's more usual 24 months. But in some respects the format is similar to that of The Mentoring Foundation programmes.

It is cross-company, and cross-sector. Participating organisations provide mentors and nominate mentees – organisations can nominate up to ten female mentees and ten mentors per 'cohort'. The number of mentees and mentors nominated must be equal. Networking events are held before, during and after each scheme year.

The main difference, which was inevitable in an attempt to address 'the issue of scalability', is in the seniority of participants.

The mentee target group is women between 28 and 38, 'identified as high potential and who would benefit from mentoring at the current stage of their career[s]'. Mentors can be male or female (our NGWL mentors are all female) and, at launch, were senior executives; at Executive Committee level or a level below the Executive Committee or senior partner level.

Another difference from The Mentoring Foundation's more bespoke programmes is that the 30% Club/EY scheme uses an online system, to facilitate the matching of mentors and mentees. (The use of online systems to address the scalability of mentoring is interesting. It could be a step towards something akin to the Massive Open Online Courses, known as MOOCs, aimed at unlimited participation, with open access via the web, that have emerged in education in recent years.)

We wish this experiment well. Any attempts to make available, to a wider group of younger women, the proven benefits of cross-company and cross-industry mentoring is welcome.

For our part we see our smaller, more bespoke schemes as still the best way to help senior female executives take the final few steps to the board, the ExCo or their equivalents.

Patrons and protégées

The Mentoring Foundation's programmes and the 30% Club/EY programme are expressions of a general and time-honoured principle; that those who have gone before are best placed to help others make the same journey.

As António Horta-Osório put it, at The Mentoring Foundation's 2014 Colloquium, 'sharing career journeys and experiences of colleagues at all levels of the organisation can have a very powerful impact. For example, it may encourage women to apply for roles they might previously have perceived as being incompatible with family life' and encourage women to apply for jobs when 'they don't necessarily have every one of the elements on the person specification'.

The Lloyds Banking Group CEO said LBG had a coaching programme for female executives 'so that they have the right support in place to progress their careers. This is the hurdle from which women all too often pull back, and there is much evidence that their less well-qualified male counterparts will often persevere.' There is also a Women in Leadership

Programme for mid-level managers 'to further strengthen the pipeline'. The participants are supported by senior sponsors, 'whose role it is to actively work with their sponsee to develop their careers.

'We know too', he said, 'that an individual's experience is largely coloured by [his/her] line manager' and it was therefore essential 'that line managers understand what behaviours we expect from them and act consistently'. Support for line managers, at LBG, includes 'unconscious bias training'.

He is leading by example. He mentors three senior women within the group, and a fourth outside for the FTSE Programme (see Chapter 9).

LBG's multi-programme approach to meeting its ambitious target for female executives is more than mere 'box-ticking'. The target is a self-imposed challenge that requires a comprehensive response.

Mentoring is networking

Mentoring, particularly cross-company, cross-industry mentoring is a form of networking. It connects mentees to the higher level networks of their mentors and, as we shall see in the next chapter, to the network of alumnae that has coalesced around the Programme.

This has proved to be one of the Programme's most valuable outputs for mentees. It is hard to exaggerate the significance, for the cause of better gender balance on boards, of the existence of a vibrant, and still growing, high-level women's network, with a large number of female ExCo members, executive directors and NEDs at its centre.

It is a visible and accessible manifestation of the gender-balance zeitgeist; a collective role model for women everywhere, and clear evidence that progress is being made in the gender balance part of the 'big project'.

Summary

- Targets, by themselves, achieve nothing. It's what they induce people and organisations to do that changes things.

- The FTSE Programme's alumnae as a group have an impressive list of achievements to their names.
- The Programme covers professional services firms and Whitehall, as well as companies.
- Outputs valued by mentees include increased self-confidence, their relationships with their mentors, broader horizons and enriched networks as well as promotions and appointments.
- We describe five reasons for the FTSE Programme's success.
- Sponsors versus mentors: this is a distinction without a difference.

5
Network Capital

A much-discussed problem area for some women, as they endeavour to reach the top echelons of organisations, is 'networking'. Women are said to be less adept at networking than men, to dislike it or to find it distasteful, to have no time for it and to be effectively denied access to high-level networks that have tended historically to be male orientated.

The fact is, however, that in the absence of a perfectly efficient market in talent, skills, abilities and experience, some networking is essential.

Assigning power and influence when promoting people, or appointing directors, is a risky business, because a bad appointment can do a lot of damage. Organisations mitigate appointment risk by doing the equivalent of 'due diligence' on candidates. Those responsible for promotions and appointments can support formal due diligence with information on people they have met through networking and have been impressed by, or who are known and rated highly by people they know, and whose judgements they trust.

Networking is a slippery concept. It embraces 'schmoozing', a word that can mean different things in different contexts, but conveys the impression of alcohol-lubricated, off-site small talk between suppliers and existing or prospective customers or clients. It may or may not include, or be augmented by, communication by email and the social media. It can also be a form of 'politicking', in which many women believe their organisations indulge far too much.

When closed, elitist groups confine their assignments of power and influence within such groups, networking becomes indistinguishable from the anti-meritocratic vices of nepotism, cronyism and the so-called 'old boys' club'. In business 'crony capitalism' is seen to be inefficient, because it prevents the best-qualified people from being appointed to positions of power and influence, is unethical, and sometimes, in some places and circumstances, illegal.

Confucius saw *guanxi*, the ancient system of Chinese networking, as an invaluable social stabiliser. These days the word is synonymous in China with corruption: bribes, back-handers, turning blind eyes and close, corrupt relationships between business people and local communist party officials. The extraordinary wealth and power of China's so-called 'princelings' (sons and daughters of high-ranking party officials) are often said to be based on their membership of closed elitist networks.

But although networking has a 'dark side', exemplified by cronyism and corruption, a certain amount is, as we have said, essential.

The 16th-century physician Paracelsus said: 'The poison is in the dose.' He was referring to the medicinal properties of mercury and opium, but it is also true of networking. If it is substituted for the market, it can be toxic. When it simply compensates for market inefficiencies, it can be very useful.

The same goes for the politicking facilitated by networking. It is unrealistic to expect large integrated organisations, such as FTSE 100 or *Fortune 500* companies, to be politics-free zones. When many gather together to pursue a common purpose, such as creating value for shareholders, 'office politics' are inevitable, and ambitious people must engage in them. There are no perfect meritocracies and no perfect markets in management talent and ability. To assign or acquire power, exert influence or solicit support for a candidate or a course of action, you have to engage in political activity.

As long as the networks in which politicking occurs are 'open' and as long as they complement, rather than replace, the markets for talent and ability, there's nothing to object to. Networking is an investment in social capital, designed to reduce the risk that the talent and abilities of the investor will go unnoticed. As long as networks remain open and don't develop into the pathological forms latent within them, they can improve the efficiency of markets for executive talent.

The problem for ambitious female executives is that the networks they need to join are not completely open. They are not hotbeds of nepotism and cronyism, but many of them still bear the imprints of their male-only origins. Some are very old, consisting of alumni of elite 'public schools', colleges or gentlemen's clubs, and over the years have acquired qualities that reflect and are exclusive to the gender of their members.

Before considering what can be done about this problem, let's look a little more closely at the phenomenon of networking.

Unpacking networks

The first thing to notice about social networks is their shape and how it differs from the official shape of organisations. Networks are cellular, rather than hierarchical. Interaction is horizontal, rather than vertical. There's a presumption, in networks, that all members are equal. Members cannot, of course, entirely shed their positions in hierarchies outside the network, but conversations in the network are generally expected to be peer to peer.

The second thing to notice about networks is that, because members may each be a member of several networks, they are interconnected to a greater or lesser extent. Joining one network should give you access, in principle, to your fellow members' other networks.

The third thing to notice about networks is that they're literally everywhere. Apparently hierarchical organisations couldn't operate effectively without informal networks working across functions and management levels. All executives work horizontally and diagonally as well as vertically; and they know that of all the meetings they attend the most productive are those where status and position are put aside and conversations are peer to peer.

People often obtain jobs through their membership of networks, and the chances of promotion can be improved by networking. Salaries, bonuses and management performance are related, to some extent, to networking activity. Because networks host conversations between a wider and more diverse group than intra-departmental or functional groups, they stimulate innovation and promote information-sharing.

Networks that extend beyond the organisation often play a key role in creating career opportunities, 'opening doors' and facilitating important work and life transitions.

We're all 'networkers'. We couldn't operate effectively if we were not.

Dimensions of networking

Networks can be classified, categorised and described in all sorts of ways.

No two members of the same network will see it in exactly the same way. Some may see it as a source of valuable counsel; others as a trustworthy sounding board of like-minded people; others as a way of keeping their 'ears to the ground'; others as a source of new ideas, models and approaches; others as a source of recognition or support; and still others as a meeting place where the talk is interesting and where a chance encounter could lead to an unlooked-for opportunity.

A network can be thought of as a thing in itself of which a member is a part, or more subjectively, as a personal marketing asset for members that extends their area of engagement and opportunity into areas that would otherwise have been out of reach.

A network has breadth, depth and height.

Its 'breadth' is determined by the diversity of membership: people who are senior to you, your peers and people who are junior to you; people who work elsewhere, in other departments or functions, or at other sites, offices, subsidiaries or companies; people who work in other industries or countries; people who work in other economic sectors (public, private, non-profit, academia, etc.); and people who are members of other professions.

A network's 'depth' is determined by the types of relationships it harbours. There may be a core network of founders who meet often, surrounded by a larger number of less active associate members. A large, planetary network needs a core of some kind, and a schedule of regular events, if it's to survive. Networks that outlive their usefulness soon dissipate.

The 'height' of a network is determined by the power and influence of its members. If your objective is to be appointed to a board it stands to reason that it would be helpful to belong to a high-level network, the members of which include chairmen, C-level executives, members of board Nomination Committees (NomCos) and headhunters.

From the individual's point of view the value of a network, and of the networking required to remain an active member, depends on how likely it is that the networking will contribute to achieving the individual's goals. Short-term goals, such as winning new business and maintaining good relationships with customers or clients, will be served by one kind of network. Long-term goals, such as gaining promotion, moving to another organisation or being appointed to a board, will be served by another kind of network.

Networks and networking hold promise but offer no guarantees. The undisputed father of modern advertising, John Wanamaker, said that 'Half the money I spend on advertising is wasted; the trouble is I don't know which half.' The same is true of networking, which is a form of advertising. You have to invest time and opportunity costs in networking, knowing that much of that investment will be wasted.

It's a mistake to be too calculating about networking. You need to get 'into it', as they say; to learn to enjoy it for its own sake. And you must recognise that the underlying agenda in networking is reciprocity. As you sow, so shall you reap. As Adam Grant puts it, it's 'Give and Take'.[1] Information, influence and insights in your gift are exchanged for the same currencies in the gifts of other members.

Much has been written over the years about how to get the most out of networks and networking. This is not the place to summarise the literature, but it is worth noting a few themes and tips that crop up regularly.

- Transmit as well as receive. Be active. Get yourself noticed.
- Do your homework on fellow members.
- Keep in touch; make a point of contacting everyone in your networks at regular, if infrequent, intervals.
- Hone your social skills.
- Be selective. You have a limited amount of time you can devote to networking, so make it count in networks with high potential value.
- Take some risks and play your hunches. Careers are shaped by chance encounters. A network that seems of little immediate relevance could produce unexpected opportunities.
- Bring your best game, which is your true self, to networking. Try to forget you're in marketing mode.
- It helps if you actually *like* people.

In a 2012 *Harvard Business Review* blogpost, Athena Vongalis-Macrow advised those trying to decide if one particular network was worth joining to ask four questions about it.[2]

Who is in the network? The ideal combination of qualities provided by a network's members are those of the polymath or 'pack rat' (an obsessive collector of ideas and tools for thought), the librarian and the Good Samaritan. If the network consists of and is built on the relationships between talented, knowledgeable and supportive members, it is probably worth joining.

How well does the network connect? A network's strength depends on the frequency and quality of the communication between members. It is a plus point for the network if interactions are consistent and professional and are characterised by integrity, courtesy, respect and, when necessary, confidentiality.

Is there functional communication? We all have days of frustration and disappointment at work. A network is valuable if it is a place where you can express such frustrations and 'let off steam'. Care and concern create network value, because they cultivate trust and provide support.

To whom are you talking? Networking with senior members of networks helps to strengthen and extend your personal network.

'Your time is valuable', said Vongalis-Macrow: '... networking can be hit and miss if you cannot assess the value of a network first. Before you start networking, find out about the network and how it can help you move toward your goals.'

Networking is career-enhancing. No-one with ambition can afford to refrain from it. It is an integral part of the system that assigns roles and allocates human resources.

Women and networks

A study by law firm Trowers & Hamlins and headhunters fdu group found women over the age of 35 'network' (defined as face-to-face meetings, excluding email, Facebook, Twitter, etc.) significantly less than men in the same age group.[3]

Over 240 professionals took part in the 2013 survey and 84% agreed networking was important for their career development. The figure for women alone was 87%. And yet, on average, men networked almost twice as much as women. A quarter of women said they networked at least once a week, compared with 46% of men. Almost a third of the women in the 35+ age group networked less than once a month.

Among 25–34 year olds the networking gender split is more even. Of the men and women in this age group, 29% and 30% respectively said they networked once a week or more.

An obvious inference is that as well as being an important age for career development, the mid-30s is also, these days, an important time for child-bearing and thus maternity leave. This conjecture is confirmed by the survey's finding that 51% of fathers but 24% of mothers network once a week, or more. Many mothers cited family commitments as the reason for networking infrequently. Networking consumes out-of-working-hours time. It seems discretionary, but is actually essential for career development.

Two other interesting findings were that women were just as likely as men to network in bars and had no strong preference for single-sex networking events. It is not clear whether these findings hold true throughout the age range.

The survey did not corroborate the widespread suspicion that women are deterred from networking by the male-orientated nature of many networks. It found, for example, that professional women were just as likely as men to network in bars and at sporting events.

Tania Tandon, 'employment' partner at Trowers & Hamlins, concluded that whatever the reasons for the much less frequent networking of women over the age of 35, the survey suggests they have more to do with 'mothers and fathers making choices at ... a critical time in their careers than about established barriers and prejudices'.

Others take a different view.

In her article in the Royal Society of Arts' quarterly magazine in 2010, Frances Rosenbluth, a professor of international politics at Yale University, said that women were 'better connected overall' than men, thanks largely to their liking for social media, such as Facebook and Twitter, but 'their networks typically fail to reach the boardroom'.[4]

They tend to network laterally with friends and peers, rather than verti-cally. Rosenbluth suggests that the reason why the laterally connected networks favoured by women don't reach the boardroom is that lateral connections thin out in the higher echelons populated mostly by white men. Men's networks are more vertically connected, and are better at carving out routes up hierarchies. As Rosenbluth puts it: 'Facebook and Twitter don't pack the same career punch as the golf course and the gentlemen's club.'

She says women are under-represented in professions that depend on continuous client contact, such as the law and investment banking, because the professional networks in which these contacts are made and maintained are built outside working hours when mothers are at home. Men accumulate more network capital than women because they start to acquire it early, when working and networking long hours.

To correct the imbalance, Rosenbluth suggests that foundations and civic groups could make compensatory investments in female network capital, by financing networking opportunities for women.

In considering the contribution that networking can make to career development it is first necessary to distinguish between two types of network: internal networks, which are often employer-sponsored and financed, and wider, more personal, external networks, formed by individuals.

Internal women's networks

In recent years, internal women's networks have become fixtures in large organisations. In the early days, they were seen as crucial innovations that could mark a decisive turning point in the quest for a better gender balance in the higher echelons of management.

A 2004 study by UK think-tank Demos (Girlfriends in High Places) found that such networks can promote diversity by challenging invisible structural obstacles to the promotion of women. In addition to giving women a more powerful collective voice, supporting their development and being an autonomous power base from which to seek information, exert influence and challenge policies and decisions, women's networks were said to be good places in which to develop networking skills. Demos found that the leaders and active members of women's networks became better known in their organisations, and a third of the women Demos talked to felt they had gained added confidence from their involvement in their women's networks.

Since then, a certain amount of disenchantment has set in.

In a *Harvard Business Review* blogpost Avivah Wittenberg-Cox warned that internal women's networks 'inadvertently … marginalize women into a separate group from the one currently in power'. She gave a less than flattering potted history of an apocryphal network:

'A group of men who decide (or are told by government) that they need more women in their teams turn to the few women in senior roles and task them with finding a solution. The women, delighted with this glimmer of interest in their fate, duly throw themselves (in their free time, on top of their day jobs) into launching [an] … unfunded corporate women's network and draft a business case on the corporate advantages of gender balance. A senior woman is put in charge and sent to every external conference as a corporate representative. This results in a women's conference with lots of motivational speakers and a few male "champions" to encourage the girls. Sound familiar?

'At first, everyone is happy. The women are delighted to have some time to themselves. As one senior woman in a Magic Circle law firm told me, "It's the only place where we can … be ourselves." The men are delighted that they are "doing something" for women.

'But after a few years, the ladies grow embittered, pointing out how little progress has been made in the actual balance of leadership. The gentlemen reaffirm that, despite "all that they have done for women", the ladies still aren't able to make it.

'This sidesteps the real issue: that the men currently in power may not actually have the skills and knowledge to effectively manage across genders (not to mention across nationalities, the other global elephant in the room). Women's networks and activities end up as politically savvy deflectors for blame.'

Wittenberg-Cox concluded that 'women's networks were used, more to placate women than to promote them' and that until 'male-dominated and masculine-normed leadership teams decide to proactively change the balance by pulling women into power, most corporate women's networks will remain nice places to hang out – and a noose for the gender-balance effort to hang itself on'.

To prevent an internal network from becoming increasingly isolated and ineffectual she has three prescriptions:

- Use women's networks to lobby. Get members to sign a petition asking the Executive Team to accept accountability for gender balance – with targets, key performance indicators (KPIs) and a budget. Evaluate managers on performance in building balanced teams. 'So, for example, at Facebook, Sandberg wouldn't be tasking women to "lean in", but rather evaluating the majority of men on their ability to promote balanced teams.' Switch the focus from the candidates to the management skills needed to develop balance.
- Turn women's networks into what Wittenberg-Cox calls 'balance networks' including men and women. She cites HSBC, in London, as a pioneer of such 'balance networks' that 'learn about the differences between male and female employees, customers, and careers'.
- Get men to lead the quest for balance – identify male leaders brave enough to impress on other men the need for balance and perceptive enough to understand the required skills. 'Some of them are even starting to go public like Warren Buffett, John Chambers at CISCO or Paul Polman at Unilever'.

Wittenberg-Cox believes that 'women are working far too hard at an issue actually beyond their power to solve. Corporate leaders must recognize that additional women-dominated efforts are not the way to get companies to take the gender issue seriously.' She says the solution is 'action by those in leadership positions'.[5]

We take a more sanguine view of internal women's networks, because we have seen how they help members hone their networking skills, make connections in the formal organisation and expose junior and middle managers to senior role models.

But we recognise there are downside risks.

The network's isolation from the organisation could make it a safe haven for some women, and weaken their engagement with the formal organisation. Some women may become accustomed to exercising power and exerting influence collectively through the network, and cease to challenge decisions and debate issues as individuals. And there is a danger, as Wittenberg-Cox warns, that the women's network may be seen by the leadership as a ticked box; an end in itself rather than a means to the end of a better gender balance.

All things considered, however, we believe large organisations are better off with women's networks, than without them – for a while, at least, until the processes that populate the higher echelons of organisational hierarchies become gender-neutral.

External women's networks

Wittenberg-Cox is not against women's networks per se. As founder of one of Europe's largest external women's networks (Professional Women's Network, or PWN Global, as it is now known – see page 116), how could she be? She says 'external women's networks serve many vital purposes, including lobbying, information sharing, education and mentoring'.

One of the most striking features of the change in the environment for ambitious women over the past decade has been an extraordinary proliferation of external women's networks. They range from a host of local groups, such as Women Outside The Box, a network club for freelancers, entrepreneurs and corporate women in Bristol; Norwich Business Women's Network for businesswomen in Norwich and Norfolk; Highflying Divas, a mentoring forum for professional women working in Essex and London; Networking Women, for women running small businesses in Wiltshire, Oxfordshire and Gloucestershire; Forward Ladies, for women in business in the North of England; and Women in Business NI, for businesswomen in Northern Ireland (part of the Women in Business 'federation' of networks see page 117), to national and international networks.

The National Women's Network was established in London in 1981 by Irene Harris. At that time there were no clubs for women in senior management. The day the network was born Irene and a distinguished companion, Odette Hallowes, the French wartime resistance heroine who received the George Cross in 1946, were refused a drink at the bar of the In & Out Club for servicemen.

The network was rebranded in 2011. It holds monthly meetings and organises workshops, discussion groups, seminars and annual events in prestigious venues, with distinguished guest speakers.

The City Women Network was founded in 1978 by American and British women – mostly bankers, accountants and lawyers, working in senior jobs in the City of London. It's 'a selective network basing entry on candidate seniority and professional merit'. The original aim was to establish a women's peer network 'to combat the effects of the Old Boys' Networks that dictated the City culture' and to help 'the entry of women into previously male-dominated professions and business functions'.

It arranges events each month, which range from social evenings to professional talks; offers networking opportunities with speakers and peers; provides opportunities for building business and social relationships; publishes a quarterly newsletter, *Connections*; and has close links with PWN Global and The International Alliance for Women.

It has over 250 members and a growing corporate membership.

The Professional Women's Network or EuropeanPWN, as it was first known, was launched by Avivah Wittenberg-Cox in Paris, in 2003. It was later rebranded EPWN, and in 2014, after the launch of city networks outside Europe, the organisation assumed its current name of PWN Global.

It is larger now, but in spring 2014 PWN Global was a federation of 24 city-based professional networks in Europe, South America and the Middle East, with one common objective: 'to provide women with the tools, networks and support resources they need to assume leadership positions'. Of its 4,000 or so members over half are or were corporate executives.

The Women in Business Network was launched in January 2005. It is a membership organisation for female entrepreneurs and executives seeking new business opportunities through word of mouth. At the time of writing in spring 2014 it had over 1,300 members. More of a federation than an integrated network, it consists of local and profession-specific groups to ensure members receive 'targeted help'.

The Athena Network, founded in the UK in 2005 by Jacqueline Rogers and focusing exclusively on female executives and entrepreneurs, 'provides a platform for members to share knowledge and experience across a diverse range of industry sectors, and to collaborate for mutual success'. It has over 2,600 UK-based members in 30 regions.

Following its expansion into Asia-Pacific in 2011, the Athena Network now offers members 'international collaboration opportunities', and 'a rapidly growing online community'.

Founded in 1999, Everywoman is a membership organisation dedicated to the advancement of women. Members include companies wishing to develop and retain a pipeline of female leaders, and women looking to advance in their organisations or develop their own businesses.

Building network capital

The Mentoring Foundation, the owner and operator of the FTSE 100® Cross-Company Mentoring Programme, has taken up Dr Rosenbluth's suggestion that foundations could make compensatory investments in female 'network capital' by financing networking opportunities for women (see above).

It became clear to us in conversations with mentees that there was a strong wish among mentees to keep in touch with each other after their mentoring, and so form a network of alumnae.

We explored the possibility with our network of FTSE Programme participants and were delighted when Michael Treschow, Chairman of Unilever and a mentor on the Programme, told us that the company was willing to sponsor such a network.

The Unilever Mentee Network was launched in May 2011. Mentees and alumnae of the FTSE Executive Programme now meet four times a year at Unilever's headquarters in London for a morning of discussions and networking.

In his inaugural address to the alumnae, Unilever's CEO Paul Polman said: 'When the crisis is highest, the opportunity is greatest. You have all the respect and credibility out there. This is the moment to be a little more courageous and to make a step change.'

Inspired by Polman's polemic, the Mentee Network participants drew up a mission statement:

> *Supporting the vision of more balanced boards*
> *through personal action and group contribution*

Four specific activities have been identified for implementing the mission:

- Supporting and promoting each other (including information sharing and influencing).
- Supporting and promoting the talent pipeline (helping to bring through the next level of talent).
- Preparation and development for board-readiness (equipping themselves).
- Communications and profile-raising.
- Helping the *FTSE 100® Cross-Company Mentoring Executive Programme* to grow.

Discussions that led to the formation of the Mentee Network and to the subsequent drafting of its mission statement, and the emphasis the network's members have placed on the talent pipeline, inspired and helped to shape another Mentoring Foundation project; the Next Generation Women Leaders Programme (see Chapter 7).

Executive Programme alumna Carole Machell is Head of International Business, Corporate Banking, at Barclays. She says the Unilever-sponsored mentee network helps 'to glue it together and drive more action. By giving ... mentees a chance to talk together and profile experiences, we inspire and motivate each other to do more. We're grateful for the opportunities that the Programme is giving us and talking about this encourages us to reach down, and help women at an earlier stage.' Machell believes that 'Without this opportunity to network and compare notes we would do less, in isolation.'

Other forms of network capital have been seeded by the Programme.

From 2011 to 2013, The Mentoring Foundation's annual Colloquium on the FTSE Programmes was hosted by Sir David Lees, former Chairman of the Court of the Bank of England, at the Bank's Threadneedle Street offices. The Colloquium is a closed event for mentees, mentors and friends of the FTSE Programmes. Its purpose is to update those attending on how the two programmes are going, share ideas and insights, and provide an opportunity for networking. Participants at the 2013 Colloquium, including over 70 mentees and alumnae and more than 50 chairmen, chief executives or managing partners, were addressed by the then new Governor of the Bank of England, Mark Carney.

The 2014 Colloquium was held at the Inner Temple in London. It was chaired by Sir Michael Rake, chairman of BT Group and the then President of the CBI. He shared the platform with The Rt. Hon. Lady Justice Hallett DBE, Member of the Court of Appeal, with responsibility for diversity in judicial appointments; Niall FitzGerald KBE, Chairman, The Leverhulme Trust; Lord Davies of Abersoch, CBE; António Horta-Osório, Group Chief Executive, Lloyds Banking Group; and Nigel Wilson, Group Chief Executive, Legal & General Group.

Another network capital spin-off from the Programme is a series of dinners or 'in conversation' events over canapés and drinks hosted by mentors with small groups of mentees and alumnae. Settings are informal and the Chatham House Rule applies to allow frank exchanges of view. Hosts have included Niall FitzGerald KBE (Chairman of The Leverhulme Trust); Sir John Parker (Chairman of Anglo American); Sir David Reid (the then Chairman of Tesco); Don Robert (Chairman of Experian); John Stewart (Chairman of Legal & General Group); David Fass (CEO EMEA of Macquarie Group); Sir Peter Gershon (Chairman of National Grid); Douglas Flint (Chairman of HSBC); Simon Davies (Firmwide Managing Partner of Linklaters) (see Chapter 1); Gavin Patterson (CEO of BT Group); Richard Davey (CEO of Amlin); Carl-Henric Svanberg (Chairman of BP); Glyn Jones (Chairman of Aspen Insurance Holdings); and Ian Powell (Chairman and Senior Partner of PwC).

We have also been collaborating with the Deloitte Academy to offer Executive Programme mentees and alumnae an opportunity to enrol on the Deloitte Academy's Navigating the Boardroom: Women on Boards Programme. The course offers a mixture of education and networking events designed for women with board potential. Some of our mentees have enrolled on the Programme.

The most important source of new female network capital associated with the Mentoring Foundation Programmes is, of course, the mentoring itself. It creates new network capital by strengthening a mentee's net-work with the addition of her mentor and, insofar as her mentor sees fit, by giving her access, through her mentor, to top-echelon networks that would otherwise have been beyond her reach.

Networking opportunities that suit women and are tailored for them have increased significantly in recent years, but compared with that of men, the networking 'infrastructure' for working women is still at an early stage of its development. This may help to explain why there are still so few women in the higher echelons of management and why there are still so few women in the pipeline leading up to those higher echelons.

When all is said and done, however, the goal isn't to increase the quantity and quality of the networking infrastructure tailored for women, but to fuse together female and male network capital into a single infrastructure equally accessible to both genders.

Networking – case study

Different people adapt to networking in different ways and develop different networking styles (some are sociable, some are serious, some are focused, some 'go with the flow', for example). They have different objectives, different expectations, different strategies and different priorities.

The best approach to networking depends on an individual's 'set' and the network 'setting' (see Chapter 6). Each individual finds his or her own way. You can't generalise, but the experience and subsequent reflections of one FTSE Programme alumna, Marianne Culver, the former Director of Global Supply Chain for Premier Farnell and now Managing Director, UK & Ireland, for TNT Holdings, will help to illustrate the stages that women new to high-level networking may go through.

Soon after she joined the FTSE Programme, Culver told us how her mentor encouraged her to change how she viewed and practised networking: 'I should have done this 10 years ago – I should have behaved more like a man. My mentor said to me: "This is what a man would do. He would be thinking about this and would be thinking about that." It wouldn't even occur to me to plot in that sort of very specific way. Most of my male counterparts would be networking. They'd be playing golf and I'd be thinking you know "when have they got time to do that? I haven't got time …"'.

Culver's job was demanding and involved a lot of travel. Combining it with a family had always meant that time was scarce and she had not previously felt she had enough time to think about developing her long-term career. Discussions with her mentor persuaded her to reassess her approach: 'I don't want to be sitting here in another six months thinking "I haven't done any networking yet". Throughout my career people have been incredibly willing to give their time when I asked for help. I had a very good relationship with the chairman of my previous parent company, but I have hardly seen him in ten years. Why didn't I bother to maintain that connection? Because I had young children and because I was very busy with my job, rather than my career.'

She knew she needed to increase her visibility with those who make hiring decisions for board positions. She said it was another world of which she had never previously been part, partly because of her education and industry, but mostly because she had not done enough networking earlier in her career.

'There is a group of people who are members of various boards, who know each other. I just feel very remote from that. My mentor's helping me bridge that gap. I don't know these people, and I don't know how I'd get to know them if my mentor didn't help me.'

We talked to Culver again several months later. By then, she had a plan for her networking. She had saved time in her working week by changing her leadership style – delegating more effectively and giving her career development a higher priority. She described how she had taken advantage of the networking opportunities offered by the FTSE Programme to develop relationships with other mentees and mentors.

'I'm starting to understand how the spider's web of connections works. It's not going to secure me an NED position. This is all about profile. I'm not thinking for a minute that knowing somebody is enough to get me an NED position. I don't believe that's how it works. But if you've got a reasonable network and I do have now, a much better network than I did four months ago, you're simply more visible.'

Over a 14-month period Culver's view of networks, fellow networkers, and her own networking activity was transformed. She has become proactive and confident. She no longer sees networking as an exclusively male activity. She sets a much higher priority on making and using new connections. She knows that it's not the be all and end all, but she recognises networking is helping to establish her as a visible and credible candidate for board positions.

'The Programme has changed my way of thinking. I'm taking my career seriously and doing something about it. My mentor is behind all of this, guiding me, but the baton of responsibility has passed to me.'

Not rocket science

As noted at the beginning of the chapter, networking is a slippery concept. Pedants object to the word itself, on the grounds that it is the present participle of a non-existent verb. They insist that the word 'network' is a noun, and they dislike the modern practice of corrupting English by turning perfectly respectable nouns into verbs (other common examples are 'access', 'impact' and 'source').

Some who are less fastidious about the language also object to the use of the word because of its implication that 'networking' is, in some important sense, different from socialising or interacting with other people. We all have groups of people, including friends and relations, whom we see a lot of and talk to frequently. When we see them, or talk to them, are we 'networking'? When we first meet a stranger at a dinner party with whom we later do some business should we, in retrospect, regard the dinner party as 'networking'? If you meet people in a pub and the 'craic is good', as the Irish say, is that 'networking'? If not, does it become so if you enjoy the craic with a stranger you find you like and with whom you have a rapport, and then later she or he recommends you for a job?

When 'networking' is seen as an activity distinct from other kinds of social interaction there is a danger that some people will decide that they're not good at it, or dislike it, or that it is too high a price to pay for advancement. If networking is just work-related socialising, why do we need another name for it?

We speak of 'networking' as 'putting yourself about a bit' among those who may be able to help you realise your ambitions, or whom you may be able to help realise their ambitions. It's a social activity, and there is nothing difficult about it. It's not rocket science. It's something you do anyway. The only difference is that it takes place in a work-related context.

The reason why it's useful and can be career-enhancing is that it allows people to put faces to names and personalities to CVs (of the kind NomCo members read through when selecting a shortlist of candidates for a board appointment).

In your work life you have two personae; your real flesh-and-blood personality who walks, talks, smiles and comes across as charming, smart, witty, serious, able and perceptive; and your résumé, which is just a map of your route, to date, through your working life.

The map is not the territory. At the margin, when two résumés tell roughly the same story, a NomCo member is likely to favour the one to which he or she can put a face and a personality.

Summary

- Networking has a 'dark side', but it's essential.
- Networks are cellular, interconnected and ubiquitous.
- Networks have breadth, depth and height.
- Women network less than men and tend to network laterally rather than vertically.
- There is a danger that internal women's networks may come to be seen as ends in themselves.
- The objective is to fuse male and female networks together.
- Networking is not rocket science.

6

When is the Price Too High?

As able and aspirational executives move up their organisations, they glance upwards, from time to time, through the reducing number of levels between them and the top level, and wonder what it would be like to be on the Executive Committee (ExCo) or the board.

As they get closer to the top their understanding of the nature of the work up there improves, and they begin to see the benefits and the costs of high executive office more clearly.

The attractions of high office are in the eye of the beholder, but one can imagine some of the more important ones: the allure of the view from the top must be powerful in many cases – wider horizons (economic and industry views no longer confined to, or obscured by your organisation); recognition of your worth; realisation of your potential; the power at last to apply your ideas about how things ought to be done, rather than implementing the ideas of others. At the top, you see further and feel part of something larger. You're a 'player'. It's more exciting, more challenging, less limited and much more rewarding, both materially and psychologically.

But there are also costs.

Old frustrations are replaced by new responsibilities. Pressure of work becomes more intense, and requires more sacrifice of home and family life. The politics in the upper reaches of the organisation become more intrusive. Your decisions carry more weight and affect more people. Your mistakes have greater consequences. And there is a contingent liability for your self-esteem: you will have further to fall if you fail.

As we saw in Chapter 2, the scepticism of younger people about the quality of life at the top is not confined to the company sector. These days law firms are also struggling to persuade young lawyers that a partner's life is a good life.

How each able and ambitious executive weighs up these benefits and costs, and trades them off against each other, and what conclusion he or she reaches about whether or not the benefits of making it to the top outweigh the costs, depend on the executive's 'set' and the organisation's 'setting'.

Set and setting

Your 'set' is multifaceted. It consists of your general outlook or world view; your basic beliefs; your sense of self and of your role in the world; your perceptions of your own strengths, weaknesses and potential; your hopes, fears, hungers, appetites and emotions; your interests and priorities; and the tools for thought you have accumulated over the years, with which you analyse, interpret and inwardly digest what is going on around you.

The 'setting' is an organisation's culture, behavioural norms (the way it does things), ethos, traditions, conventions and ambience. Some aspects of the setting are written down in values and mission statements. Others are less explicit, but no less important – the attitude to work, including the extent to which quantity (hours) is used as a proxy for less easy to measure quality; values attached in practice (rather than merely espoused) to diversity, integrity, honesty, candour and teamwork; fairness (in promotion, recognition and rewards); tolerance of the different, the unconventional and the unorthodox; the attitude to competition and rivalry within the organisation; the extent to which roles and positions are assigned according to political skill, rather than managerial merit; and so on.

The setting is an expression of an organisation's deep culture. It gets purer, more powerful and more distinctive as you climb up the hierarchy, because those whose sets are incompatible in one way or another with the setting are ejected during the climb. Only those with sets compatible with the setting can make it all the way.

The self-sustaining and self-reinforcing nature of organisational settings, derived from the progressive weeding out of people with incompatible sets, makes organisations prone to groupthink: the tendency of those with similar sets to adopt similar outlooks, and to maintain the setting (with which their sets are compatible) by excluding dissenting voices.

The danger of groupthink on boards is now widely recognised. More non-executive directors (NEDs) and more diversity (including gender diversity) are generally seen to be effective protections against it.

But the organisational 'setting' still exerts a powerful influence on executive selection; still deters those with incompatible sets from putting themselves forward for selection for high office; and allows groupthink to flourish below the board, where there are no non-executives and insufficient diversity to protect managers from groupthink effectively.

The three conceivable solutions are easy to specify, but very hard to achieve: individuals change their sets and adapt them better to their setting (Sheryl Sandberg's 'lean in'); organisations change their settings to accommodate a wider variety of sets ('lean out'); or a combination of leaning in and out that effectively leads to a convergence of sets and settings.

Opinion is divided on the practicality of these solutions, because there is no consensus on the extent to which sets and settings can change or be changed.

There's a belief within many modern organisations that the setting is sacrosanct. Individuals must adapt their sets to their setting, because the setting is immutable. It is what it is. The individual must take it or leave it.

It may be conceded that the setting can be changed a little at the edges, but it will be affirmed that the principal features of the setting have shaped and been shaped by the organisation's business model, and can't be changed without compromising the integrity (and so reducing the competitiveness) of that model.

The widespread belief in the immutability of settings has led to a common belief in the top echelons of UK management that it will be much harder to achieve a proportion of 25% women on ExCos than it has been to achieve a proportion of 25% women on boards.

The view from the top

We sought the views of some distinguished businessmen, all of whom are very good friends of The Mentoring Foundation, on how to boost the proportion of women among senior executives and on ExCos.

Sir Philip Hampton doesn't believe it is as important to achieve a gender balance among executive directors (EDs) as it is to achieve it among the board as a whole. 'It's great if you get female CEOs or financial directors (FDs) who are, therefore, on the board, but to me that is not the main issue, because there are so few posts; there are just a few hundred people in the whole country who would be CEOs, or FDs of the larger businesses. But it is disappointing that we have so few women in top management, and the ExCo especially. That's where the new focus should be.'

But he thinks that achieving a better gender balance on ExCos is a more difficult challenge than achieving a better gender balance on boards: 'If you get top performing people on the ExCo, you eventually want them to become the CEO, or FD. And I think that is always harder. I never thought it was hard to find excellent women to join boards as NEDs, and bring their experience and wisdom from various fields to a board discussion – there are plenty of women who can be very good non-executives. With executives, it is harder, because of how people run their family lives. It is easier for a non-executive, because, by definition, it is a part-time job and you can do other things including caring for family or children or the elderly; so many women can make that compatible with how they still live their family lives. Making a full-on executive position compatible with how women want to live their lives is still a real strain for many women and companies can't always provide a solution to that.

'I'm not sure this is a company, or board thing. Actually a lot of it is personal; how women can combine what they see as their other responsibilities with an executive job. You can't have part-time top executives; it doesn't work for the business. So the only way it can work is if women don't have other responsibilities and can give their time whole-heartedly to their executive duties, or when they share their other responsibilities with their partners. And of course there are some relationships where that happens, but not many, and doubtless not enough. As I say, there is a limit to what a company can actually do about that.'

It seemed to us that Sir Philip, knowing that he was straying onto controversial ground, was choosing his words carefully here.

'I've thought a lot about this, because I do think businesses have to be quite uncompromising about the time and dedication needed for the top jobs, and I don't think you can have these top jobs as part time. It's not fair on the organisation, and there is a limit to how much people can really work from home; you have to be there and so on. I think the thing we're weak at, and I don't see why it cannot be addressed more effectively, is understanding that there might be a period in a woman's life as it were, whether it's three years or ten years, when she goes away, has children and then comes back.

'And actually if a woman's away from the ages of 30 to 36 (for the sake of argument) well, she's not washed up at 36! She's still got a huge amount to offer. And if, by then, there is the family help, and it's not necessarily hugely expensive help at least for senior professionals, or if the kids are at school, women can come back, be effective and progress (maybe they don't come back full-time to start with). By the time they're 45 they've spent another ten years building their careers. So when the kids don't need looking after, women may have another ten years to become CEO or achieve other top positions.

'Getting women back when they have still got a lot of gas in their tanks – I don't see why we need to be bad at that, but we are.

'If you go back to some of our early conversations; it was getting women on boards to be role models. It is important that women can get to the top of the business. That's great, and I think that has been happening. But the best role model is still the woman who has really succeeded at an executive level. That'll be where the role models start to become very powerful. So I think if we can do this – if we can get more women into the top positions and get to an understanding of family life, and other responsibilities – I think it will become self-sustaining.

'But I don't think we've got there yet. I think that the Americans are getting there; they're ahead of us on this. We see that within RBS. Half our board, and half our senior management in America are women. That's a 20,000 workforce. We're about 30% in this country. There are quite a lot of American families who have made the woman the principal breadwinner; the man deals with the children, or the elderly parents, and works from home. There are increasing numbers of jobs where working from home is a reality either for the man or the woman, though, as I say, not for the most senior jobs.'

John Stewart, Chairman of Legal & General Group, agreed that getting the proportion of female EDs on FTSE 100 boards up from the current 8.6% (according to Cranfield's *Female FTSE Report 2015*) and of women on ExCos up from the 2014 figure of 14% will be much harder than getting the proportion of women on boards up to Lord Davies's 25% target.

'I think the real problem is in executives. In my experience women have much more interesting lives. They are less job-focussed. They balance their lives. So it's not so much the "glass ceiling", as a self-imposed ceiling. A woman looks up and asks herself "do I want that job?", because of the hours, etc. that the current holder does and says "I don't want that". So part of that is having to address other issues, not just the obvious ones like child care. Male role models have to behave in a family-friendly way. Let me give you an example. I was probably the wrong type of CEO, because I travelled on the weekends, so that I was there on a Monday morning, wherever I needed to be. I was lucky that my successor was in his early 40s when he was appointed. He had a young family, and he promised that he would keep that family life in balance with business life. This is part of the key.'

We asked him whether any of his senior male executives at L&G were exhibiting family friendly patterns of behaviour.

'Yes they are; not exclusively, but they are aware of it. They are family people so they have a reasonable balance. Let me give you a typical answer (but it's symbolic); if the boss says "I can't make that meeting on Wednesday afternoon, because it's sports day" that says that the sports day is more important than the meeting and so gives permission to everyone else to attend sports days. This will matter a lot more to women, than men. It's about balance.'

Stewart also agreed with Sir Philip that large companies needed to try harder to persuade women to come back, after taking a break.

'You must keep a connection at all levels. This is not just senior executives. You need to keep close, while women are on leave; stay in close touch, and be flexible in how you re-introduce them. It might be a job share or part-time and then eventually through that transition period they will become a top executive again, but that will be over a decade.'

We asked Stewart whether he had any suggestions about how we could improve the Next Generation Women Leaders Programme (NGWL), during the development of which L&G played an important role.

'I think that the biggest single thing you could do is to increase the critical mass this way, because in my experience younger women are just as talented, but they underestimate their abilities. They need some sort of programme to give them confidence; to make them believe they're good. They need to believe it. The second thing is that, very generally speaking, women think quite differently. They use persuasion much more than instruction. You need about a third of any group to be female, to get a critical mass. That's why Lord Davies is talking about 25%; not quite a third, but pretty close. At 5% or 10% or 15% you're struggling. You have a dominant culture that's male. If you get to about a third or at least a quarter you get different styles. We need volume. If we can get more talented women feeling confident, and joining the important committees when they're younger they will come back more confident after maternity leave.'

He agreed with us that, given all the initiatives, campaigning and exhortation in the UK over the past decade designed to improve the gender balance on boards, it was surprising, in a way, how lacking in self-confidence many female executives remained.

'Apart from a few individuals who are outstanding, we haven't even got close to achieving that.'

Sir Win Bischoff, Chairman of the Financial Reporting Council, was chairman of Lloyds Banking Group (LBG) until April 2014. We spoke to him in June 2014. He agreed the focus now should be on ExCos.

'Firstly, I think we have a very good chance of meeting the Davies target of 25% [women on FTSE 100 boards] by December 31, 2015. As for executive directors, I think that's the wrong measure, because in this country, as has been the case for many years in America, we're moving to fewer EDs. If you, for example, only had one ED on the board it's much more likely to be a man. So, we should look at the Executive Committee, rather than the EDs. That's certainly the way the Americans would look at it; at the ExCo, or the Management Committee; those who report to the CEO. Are women breaking through into that area? Of course, it takes much longer. As Chairman, you can appoint female NEDs, but as CEO you can't just appoint anyone [an ED]. You have to justify it more to your colleagues, and there must be a proven record of achievement. If women are not properly mentored and taken through it they can't show the [required] level of achievement. It is a much more complex thing.

'So I would look at the ExCo, or those who report to the CEO. It's a different measure. Because there are so few EDs, meeting targets for them could take forever.

'As you know at Lloyds Bank we made a commitment to have 40% women among our top 8,000 executives [by 2020]. You can talk about these things, but you only get there if you make a numerical commitment, like Lord Davies, and the 30% Club. I have also asked the 30% Club to consider whether [its members] are willing to say that in ExCos it should be 30%, by 2020 [close to Stewart's suggestion of 33% by 2024]. That seems a long way off, but if we got that, I think most people would be very pleased. We think we will get close; although we may not quite get to 30% by 2015. I think we'll hit the Davies target [25% women on the board], but why not also aim at something that can be a feeder [to the board]?

'[At LBG] we gave ourselves five years to get to 30% NEDs. We gave ourselves six years to get to the target [women accounting for 40% of top 8,000 executives]. Will [LBG] achieve it? I don't know, but we had to have a target to work towards; something to aim at. And something to be discussed with the CEOs who have more of a role to play [in promoting executives]. The Chairman does have a role to play, in succession planning and so on, but that is very much on a case-by-case basis.

'It's a joint effort. It's also an attitude. The first thing is to get women onto the selection lists; that's very important. Second, which I think is also hugely important, and António [Horta-Osório, Lloyds Banking Group's CEO] has embraced this; if a woman doesn't get a job for which she was shortlisted, you have to know why she didn't get it and what you're doing as the selection panel to make sure she gets the job next time. What are the gaps and what are we doing to help her forward? Putting her on a short list is all well and good, but if she isn't getting the job, you must prove how you can help her get it. This principle has been adopted by Lloyds.'

Former Unilever CEO Niall FitzGerald KBE believes that there are two related obstacles to getting more women on to ExCos: there are too few women with successful careers as executives coming up through the pipeline, just at a time when companies are looking in particular for more people with operating experience.

'These two problems are coming together. Why is that? In my view there are three main reasons: one is that it is harder for women, particularly women with family responsibilities, to make a commitment to a full-time executive job; it is very demanding and there's a lot of international travel. We all talk about it being a level playing field, but the fact is it isn't level, because the woman, in any relationship, is doing more of the nurturing and the caring. It's just how it is. You can try and pretend it's not that way, but that's silly. So it is tougher for women. The environment we expect them to operate in [the "setting"] has not yet changed to be more flexible and be more facilitating. It was an issue that I was endlessly told about at Unilever [where he was CEO from 1996 to 2004], and tried to do things about. I said "it's all very well to be committed to this, but unless we have created an environment that makes it easier for women to function equally with men …".

'What is that environment? It must be less of a lads' culture, and less dependent on having to leave on Sunday afternoon for Brazil, to be there on Monday morning. It's fewer breakfast meetings and there's a series of things that have become the norm, in terms of how businesses operate. They may not necessarily be effective, but they have become the norm and that makes it more difficult.

'The point is now I'm not going to commit the resource to make the investment I need to make in women, in salary, training, and so on and so forth, if I have an environment in the company that obliges her to leave half her talent in a jar outside the door. So I'm not getting access to all the talent I've hired. She has to leave half of herself outside the room either because the environment inside the room is not conducive to her being able to be herself, or the way in which we operate and manage the business and the demands we make, don't allow me to tap into 100% of her business talent.'

We asked FitzGerald whether he thought large companies were trying to enable women to bring all of themselves into the room: 'I think some are and some aren't. It depends on the people at the top. Let me make it very personal for the moment. When I had this little girl 13 years ago [his daughter] I made it clear to the company that I was now going to want to spend more time with her. As CEO of Unilever, I said: "I will not accept meetings and travel programmes you have arranged that require me to leave on Sunday. I won't arrange trips that bring me back on Saturday morning. I don't accept that I have to have meetings over breakfast – because I want to have breakfast with my daughter."

'I said that for me. And, like greased lightning it spread through the business. People, women in particular, said "well, if Niall is saying that, then we can as well". So what I was doing for selfish reasons suddenly had much more effect on the pace of change, than anything else. Now you can't always rely on that of course, but it is about trying to ensure senior people in the business understand the environment. Another thing I did that had some success, not as much as I would have liked, but it started along a road, is that I insisted that every one of the senior executives in the leadership team, starting with me, had a female mentor; someone who would sit with me regularly and teach me about being a woman in Unilever.

'So now I am the mentee, and you are helping me understand what it is like to be a woman in this organisation, what things are really getting in the way of your functioning. My decisions on policy and process are informed by that understanding. I do not know how many companies do that; I doubt there's that many.

'It's not taking soundings. It's a mentoring relationship, where I have to feel safe. I mean I'm the CEO of the company; I'm not used to saying to people "I don't know" or "I don't understand". I must feel completely secure and safe in having this conversation with a mentor who is a 27-year-old woman.

'Having established that, we then had periodic meetings of all the mentors and mentees (the senior leadership team) together.

'Not everyone was willing. Some went along with it because the CEO said they should, and he asked you every now and then how you were getting on. And you knew that every six months, you would all meet together and you would be put on the spot.

'Why don't we get more women to the executive ranks? I think there are four reasons. Firstly, it's much more demanding, and there are more demands than women are prepared to accept. Second, we still have in most companies an environment, and a way of operating that is simply not conducive to getting the best out of women; we don't have the necessary degree of flexibility. Third, the demands, such as travel or overseas secondments ("Please go to Hong Kong for the next two years"), are much more difficult for women to accommodate generally.

I am not saying it's easy for men, but it's easier. The fourth reason we are making less progress [in the executive ranks] is that it's less visible. I can look at an Annual Report, and say "Mr. Chairman of Company X, you have no women on your board. What are you doing about it?" If you only have one or two women on your board, they are not visible at the executive level.

'There's a supply and demand issue, too. There has been a burst of activity over the last few years that has kind of hoovered up all the available women onto boards. A lot of those have come from the professional services firms; lawyers, accountants, and people from finance firms. There's a limit to how many people from those kinds of background a chairman wants on the board nowadays; above all he or she wants people with operating experience. The danger is that, because women aren't coming up through the executive levels at the right pace, people will compromise more than they should. And that sets the whole process back.

'I go back to advice that I've given to a number of women who have been successful, in part by taking this advice: "forget about the FTSE 100". If I'm looking at someone I want to bring onto a FTSE 100 board as an NED, one of the things I want to feel is that they have non-executive experience. The FTSE 100's the top of the pile. My advice is: "don't worry about the size of the company, get your experience on a board, whether it's 250 or 500, it doesn't matter. You are building up a résumé of experience, which will prepare you for the next step." I don't think enough attention has been paid to getting women on [the boards of smaller companies], less in the spotlight where they don't feel the same pressure.

'A woman I had worked with in the past – she was a senior marketeer at Unilever – had breast cancer and decided she didn't want a full-time executive career. She had three girls between the ages of 12 and 15, and came to talk to me about what to do with her life. We discussed a portfolio career. Her first reaction was "am I not too young for that?" She was in the second half of her 40s. I told her it wasn't a question of age, but of what she wanted to do with her life at that point in time. If she decided that actually portfolio work would suit her, then age was neither here nor there. But she now needed to focus on getting the experience, to be credible. I introduced her to a few headhunters on the understanding that she would be modest in her ambitions to begin with. They got her onto the board of a FTSE 250 company quite quickly. She's now got three NED positions, and is being considered for the board of a FTSE 100 company. And all in two years. It is about accumulating experience and assembling the building blocks.'

We asked FitzGerald where he thought the 'project' that began with Lord Davies's *Women on Boards* Review should go from here.

'The updating of the Davies report should of course comment on the progress made on boards, but to be of real value, it should be re-orientating itself and seeing what's happening in executive teams. We don't need statutory quotas, but regulation encouraging people to be transparent about numbers in executive teams would be really useful. How many of your top 100, or top 200 people are women? I'd want to have much more transparency on the executive pool and much more monitoring by self-interested shareholders, as to whether the company is tapping, as effectively as it should, the 50% of talent that happens to be female. I'd want to know that. Companies don't need to be told [with legislation] how many women to have on their executive teams. It's simply knowing how many, and then I can make my own judgement.'

Changing the setting

Gender balance among executive directors isn't a big issue for Sir Philip Hampton, because there are so few ED posts nowadays, but he has been disappointed by the paucity of women on ExCos, where 'the new focus should be'.

He believes it will be difficult to make progress, 'because of how people run their family lives'. Making executive roles 'compatible with how women want to live their lives is still a real strain'.

Hampton doesn't believe the setting can be changed to relieve this strain. Companies have to be 'quite uncompromising about the time and dedication needed for the top jobs'. They can't be part time, because 'it's not fair on the organisation and there is a limit to how much people can ... work from home; you have to be there'. He says such jobs can only be done by women 'if they don't have other responsibilities, and can give their time whole-heartedly to their executive duties'.

This is in line with the views of Kirsty Bashforth, the Group Head of Organisational Effectiveness at BP: 'As female executives, we must not be naïve. I don't believe you can become the CEO of a major corporation and work two days a week – let's get real! Running an organisation takes hard graft, a lot of smarts, quite a lot of charisma, and you can't do that, if you're remote or work when you feel like it. I don't like the attitude: "Who's your female role model? Well, it wouldn't be her because she works all hours of the day and night." I went to a very revealing, and enlightening meeting in October [2014]. It was so refreshing when a couple of female CEOs stood up and said "I do my job because I love it, and I'm better at it because I love it. I probably put in an inordinate amount of time to do it, because I love it. Am I knackered? Yes I am, actually, but you know, I still love it! This is what I've chosen. I'm alive, stretched and challenged."

'I was disappointed when a few women said: "Isn't that awful? What a dreadful role model, saying she's a bit tired. How is that supposed to inspire us?" I get fed up with that, because the women have to play their parts. If you want to be a senior executive, whether you're a man or woman, its hard graft, you're out there, you have a persona and you have to manage it, because otherwise someone else will manage it for you. And you'll have power, whether you like it or not. You can't just exert influence quietly in the background.

'I am passionate about this. I get fed up with naïve women who say "I just want to be nice, and I just want to work part time and be this lovely woman who just glides through life, and that's my role model." The world doesn't work like that. It just isn't like that.

'I would like to hear more female executives saying "yes I have to juggle a bit, but I choose to juggle – this is what I've chosen to do." Everybody's way is different. There is no right answer.

'If you want to be part-time that's fantastic, just like I want to be full time. I make some choices too. Call me a bad mother? No, I love my children and my children love me. I'm still married to the same man. For some, it works. For some it doesn't. You can't "have it all", whatever that means. You make your choices. If they don't work for you, make some new choices. As long as they're right for you and the people you're close to, who's to say if it's right, or wrong?'

But although Sir Philip shares Bashforth's view that compromises are unavoidable for those aspiring to the top executive jobs, he recognises that the best role models for a young woman are women who have succeeded as senior executives. Given the incompatibility of most female sets with the settings at the top of most organisations, where, one wonders, could these role models come from? Sir Philip derives an answer to this question from the fact that a person's 'set' changes with age and stages of life.

When the setting doesn't change, sets that became incompatible may become compatible again later. This is what Sir Philip seems to be proposing to improve the gender balance among senior executives and ExCos; women with incompatible sets leaving and then returning years later with sets more compatible with the setting.

John Stewart of Legal & General sees the female executive problem in a similar way. He says women have more interesting, more balanced, less job-focused lives. They may look at the setting at the top and decide the price demanded (long hours, high pressure, lots of travel and total commitment) is too high.

But Stewart's solutions differ from those of Sir Philip.

He agrees that efforts must be made to keep in touch with women on leave, and 'be flexible in how you re-introduce them'. Unlike Sir Philip, however, he does not seem to believe that the settings at the top of organisations are immutable. He thinks they can be made more compatible with the sets of women who would otherwise leave, in cultural as well as practical ways, such as better childcare. Leaders can behave in a more family-friendly way, as did Stewart's successor as CEO of National Australia Bank.

If the CEO says he can't make the meeting on Wednesday, because it is sports day at his son's school, it says the sports day is more important than the meeting, and gives everyone a licence to attend sports days. 'This will matter a lot more to women, than men,' said Stewart. On the face of it, this seems a minor concession, but it is hard to exaggerate the impact on the organisation's behavioural norms, or setting, of the behaviour of its leader.

Stewart believes there is a gender balance point, which he puts at about 30% women, beyond which the previously dominant male culture begins to change for the better.

He acknowledges that it will be hard to get there on ExCos, but he says companies deal with many hard challenges in business 'so they must deal with gender balance, just deal with it'.

Sir Win Bischoff seems to imply that settings are mutable. He says it is important to get women on shortlists, to find out why women don't get jobs for which they are shortlisted, and to decide what the selection panel is going to do to ensure they get the job next time. 'Putting [a woman] on a shortlist is all well and good, but if she isn't getting the job, you must prove how you can help her get it. What are the gaps, and what are we doing to help her. This principle has been adopted by Lloyds.'

Niall FitzGerald's diagnosis of the female executive issue is much the same as Sir Philip Hampton's and John Stewart's. He says fewer women than men are willing to make the sacrifices that are needed to get to the top. 'I'm not saying it's good or bad. I'm saying it is a fact.'

The problem is compounded, in his view, by the fact that companies are looking for new directors with operating experience, which is the area where gender-balancing initiatives have, so far, had the least impact. The reason for this is that it's 'tougher for women, particularly women with family responsibilities' to commit to a full-time executive job; 'it's very demanding and there's a lot of international travel'.

FitzGerald's prescriptions resemble Stewart's, in that he believes that 'settings' can be changed. 'The environment we expect [women] to operate in has not yet changed to be more flexible.' He says it must become 'less of a lads' culture' and less dependent on having to leave on Sunday afternoon to be in Brazil on Monday morning. He sees no place for breakfast meetings, or other aspects of settings that are traditional, but may not be 'very effective'.

This challenges the conventional view that organisational settings are the creatures of business models and cannot be changed without reducing the organisation's competitiveness. FitzGerald suggests, on the contrary, that settings are just collections of habits and customs, some of which have outgrown their usefulness and would be counterproductive, irrespective of their impact on gender balance among top executives.

He goes further, by suggesting that settings incompatible with the set of an able woman oblige her 'to leave half her talent in a jar outside the door'. In other words, women who adapt their sets to an immutable setting cannot be themselves, and so can't contribute all their talent to the business.

FitzGerald's prescriptions for changing the setting are similar to Stewart's. When his daughter was born in 2001, he made it clear to his colleagues that he would be spending more time with her. He told them not to arrange meetings or journeys that required him to leave on Sunday or return on Saturday morning. He said breakfast meetings were out, because he would be having breakfast with his daughter. This declaration changed the setting. It spread through Unilever 'like greased lightning'. People said 'if Niall is saying that, then we can as well'.

According to Stewart and FitzGerald, therefore, the organisational setting can be changed. Sir Philip appeared to be less sanguine about this, but that might be because, when we spoke to him, he was chairman of a bank. It seems probable that the extent to which settings can be changed varies between sectors. With global capital markets open 24/7, it could be that settings in global banking, for instance, are less changeable than settings in other industries, because they are more closely integrated with the business model.

Ian Coull, former chairman of FTSE 250 house builder Galliford Try, thought this was the case in his industry. 'In the construction business it's hard for women to excel on the operational side. Those who do come into the built environment tend to come in as architects. The people who come up on the operational side of the business tend to be project managers – big boots, high-vis jackets and helmets. Not many women come through that process' (see Chapter 7).

But although sectors may vary in the mutability of their corporate cultures and settings, people who leave, because they're unable or unwilling to adapt their sets to the settings at the top of their organisations, represent an enormous loss, whatever the sector. It is impossible to measure, because there is no way of knowing how the organisation concerned would have fared, had they stayed. It's indisputable, however, that able and ambitious executives who quit because they can't or won't adapt their sets to the local setting, take with them, when they go, valuable assets in the form of their knowledge, experience, skills and talent.

In other settings some of those who leave might have turned out to be C-suite material.

There seems to be a strong business case, therefore, for investing in efforts to keep some of the value that would otherwise be lost by adapting the setting to the sets of able people who don't like, or don't think they are suited to, the kinds and quantity of work and the way of doing things on their ExCos and boards.

Lord Davies said as much at The Mentoring Foundation's Colloquium in October 2014. He warned that companies were asking for trouble if they failed to create working environments at the top of their organisations better suited than current environments to the needs and demands of the younger generation. It's not just a question of gender. The winners in the war for leadership talent will be those companies that refuse to take their settings for granted, and make considerable efforts to 'lean out' to able and talented people who don't like the look of current leadership roles.

A matter of balance

We shouldn't expect too much leaning out. As Sir Philip and Kirsty Bashforth point out, top positions are very demanding, whatever the gender of the holders.

But neither should organisations take their settings for granted.

As The Agile Future Forum says: 'In terms of technology, changing customer demands, demography and globalisation, a number of shifting trends have created new challenges and opportunities for organisations. As the external context becomes increasingly complex, traditional models of work will come under strain … more agile models of work will be required as the need for agility becomes a key focus of the modern competitive company.'[1]

Fiona Cannon OBE, Group Director, Diversity & Inclusion at Lloyds Banking Group, found that models of work appear more mutable, the more you look at them. During the year following the announcement, in January 2014, of LBG's goal of having 40% women among its top 8,000 executives by 2020, she found that 'some very senior people were working in different ways that we never knew about' and 'I've since been made aware of job-sharing agreements between very senior executives and also some that were working part-time too' (see Chapter 9).

Actual ways of working may differ from apparent and official ways as people adapt their immediate settings to suit themselves. It's known as 'job crafting'. That there are limits to 'leaning out' is undeniable, but it seems to us that there's a tendency to take the 'setting' for granted and to underestimate its mutability.

Ultimately, it's a matter of balance; of adapting settings to sets a little bit less than too much.

Summary

- People take costs as well as benefits into account when deciding whether or not to seek high office.

- People only seek high office if their 'sets' are compatible with the 'setting'.
- Opinion is divided on the extent to which 'settings' can be adapted to 'sets'.
- 'Sets' change with age and circumstances.
- Leaders can change 'settings' by example.
- People who don't seek high office, because they won't adapt their 'sets' to the 'setting', represent an enormous loss.
- The mutability of 'settings' is often underestimated.

chapter 7

The Pipeline Challenge

Imagine a time many years from now, when the 'settings' at the top of organisations have been adapted to accommodate a wider range of 'sets', the gender-balanced board is unremarkable and women occupy roughly half the board seats of the average large company, year in and year out.

What else will have changed?

Cranfield's annual *Female FTSE Report* will have ceased publication for one thing. Women on boards quota laws will have been repealed, or have joined the inert pile of junk legislation that clutters up statute books long after its relevance has been lost. Single issue pressure groups that once campaigned for gender balance on boards will have celebrated victory long ago, and either shut up shop or turned their attention to another issue. Gender parity will be the norm on headhunter shortlists for board appointments.

Business will be perceived by ordinary people as an enterprise led by able and talented people, of both sexes. There will be no more complaints about 'glass ceilings' or 'cliffs'. Women will account for over half business school graduates as they do already for all university graduates.

It seems probable that if women occupy more or less half the board seats of the average company, year in and year out, the same will be true of the average Executive Committee (ExCo). Gender parity will also prevail among executive, as well as non-executive, board members, and within the so-called 'marzipan' management layer just below the board and the ExCo.

There seems no reason to suppose gender splits will be appreciably different at other levels of management hierarchies, apart perhaps from a slight preponderance of men at child-bearing age to reflect the more time-consuming role of women in procreation. It is also likely that, many years from now, when women occupy half the board seats of the average organisation, maternity and paternity leave provision will have converged significantly, and employer-financed childcare provision will be generous and widespread.

By then, rewards and assignments of roles between the sexes should also have become more even-handed. The so-called 'gender pay gap' will have disappeared; the notion that there are so-called 'pink collar' jobs particularly suited to women (HR and PR, for example) will have been dispensed with, and functional routes to the top of the organisation will have become more varied and gender-neutral.

Elisabeth Kelan, Associate Professor (Reader) in the Department of Management at King's College London, distinguishes between, on the one hand, 'outcome' variables (the jobs people end up holding), and on the other, 'formative' variables (the jobs people have before the jobs they end up holding). It is generally accepted today that if young executives are to stand any chance of reaching the board, they must be 'blooded' in key areas or on key assignments, such as crucial projects, overseas postings and external training courses for high-potential employees. These are the key stepping-stones to high office. Insofar as they are reserved for either gender, there is sure to be a preponderance of that favoured gender later on, at the top of the organisation.

If women occupy half the board seats of a company, it's reasonable to assume that earlier on, favoured routes to the top, whatever they were, were open to both sexes, and that roughly half of those who took them were women.

It's also reasonable to assume that if women occupy half the board seats of the average large company, women's 'networking' will have become more sophisticated than it is now, and much more effective. It is unclear how this will come about – will high-potential women develop their own networking system, or will they, by joining the existing male-orientated system, change it? Either way, networking (putting yourself about a bit – see Chapter 5) will cease to be an area in which men have an advantage.

The purpose of this thought experiment is to draw attention to how much remains to be done. Gender parity on boards is not a thing in itself; a target that can be aimed at (and must be hit, if the law demands), independently of the rest of the organisation. If gender parity on boards is to last, it must be an outcome; a consequence of a deeper and more complicated change within the organisation as a whole.

It all boils down to culture. Many years from now, the cultures of the dominant business organisations will be androgynous; a mixture of masculine and feminine. Such cultures will be dominant, because insofar as management styles associated with men and women differ, their integration will be synergistic – their combined output will be greater than either gender could have produced on its own.

Inside these dominant business organisations, the most conspicuous difference from the present will be a much larger number of female role models for men as well as for women. This will be the culture and it will, therefore, be unremarkable.

That's many years from now, but we need to make a start.

New plumbing

When attention focuses on the supply-side of the market for female directors, the term 'pipeline' immediately crops up. It implies an idea of an organisation as a network of tubes of varying diameters conveying human resources, in the form of skilful, talented, able and experienced people, from one part or level of the organisation to another.

When we say there's a 'pipeline problem' with board-ready women we mean that too few women are emerging from the top of the pipe that conveys skilful, talented, able, and experienced people from lower down the organisation up to the board.

There could be various reasons for this insufficiency.

The diameter of the pipe may be too small. This would suggest that there are too few routes to the top of the organisation for women; that the 'pink collar' fallacy is diverting women into departments or functional areas with no direct connection to the high echelons of management.

The pipe's flow rate may be too slow, suggesting too few women are joining the pipe at the bottom. This is the case in the financial services industry. A survey conducted for Bank of America Merrill Lynch and North London Collegiate School found that only one third of women aged 16 to 20 would consider working in what they saw as the 'male-dominated' financial world. In 2013, when girls' schools topped UK GCSE and A level league tables, women accounted for only 19% of applications for graduate jobs in financial services.[1]

There may be leaks in the pipe, suggesting too many able women are leaving to join competitors, or are not returning after maternity leave, or are being deterred by something – the risks they perceive in seeking high office, perhaps, or the pressure, the work load, the impoverishment of their family life that they fear would accompany promotion to high office.

Before anything can be done about a pipeline problem, the pipework must be analysed in detail to establish the pattern of attenuation in the proportion of women at intake, as the pipe's human contents flow upwards. Once the pattern has been revealed the diagnosis can begin.

To return to our thought experiment briefly: if the same number of men and women enter the company and begin to make their way up the pipe leading to the board, an efficient pipe carrying human talent upwards will deliver the same number of men and women from the top of the pipe to the board. If the proportion of women emerging from the top of the pipe is less than 50% then the attenuation of women on the upward journey must have been greater than the attenuation of men. A pipework diagnosis will identify the points at which the attenuation of women was greater than that of men, and examine the reasons for the difference at each point.

Before looking at how The Mentoring Foundation has been addressing the issue, we will look a little more closely at the nature of the so-called 'pipeline problem'.

The executive pipeline

At The Mentoring Foundation's Colloquium at the Bank of England in October 2013, Nigel Wilson, CEO of Legal & General Group, spoke of the need for 'infrastructure that enables talented and committed women to progress their careers'.

He said 'helping women grow, through increasingly senior executive positions is more important and more challenging' than increasing the representation of women among non-executive directors (NEDs). Wilson believes appointing female NEDs is worthwhile in its own right, because it increases diversity, helps to reduce groupthink on boards and swells the still underpopulated ranks of board-level female role models. But in distinguishing between appointing NEDs to boards and promoting women to 'increasingly senior executive positions', he highlighted an important, often overlooked quality of the pipeline problem; it has very little to do with non-executives.

When an organisation's leaders express a wish for a larger pool of board-ready women or a fuller pipeline from which they emerge, the message heard by the organisation's HR department is 'promote more women to senior executive positions'.

There is no internal pipeline for non-executives, because NEDs are never appointed from within. The market for NEDs operates between companies, beyond the reach of the HR department. The only pipeline that the HR department can help to fill with more women is the one conveying executives up to the ExCo, and the board of a particular company.

It is true that female ExCo members are potentially candidates for NED seats on the boards of other companies. They are, so to speak, ex officio members of the inter-company NED pipeline. But HR staff have no direct contact with that pipeline. They can only influence the executive director (ED) pipeline. They may advise an ExCo member that experience as an NED at another company will improve his or her chances of being invited to join his or her own board as an ED, but their ultimate objective is to maximise the quality of their company's executives (including its ExCo members and its EDs).

Many men and women who become NEDs see these appointments as steps towards their appointments as EDs of their own companies.

In his address to the 2013 Colloquium (see above) L&G's CEO, Nigel Wilson, said L&G's focus was 'on growing female directors'. At the time, a third of L&G's ExCo, and half its 16 'future leaders' were women. He had recently commissioned 'a full review of the women in our key grade 4 and 5 transition jobs, potential future leaders'.

A confluence of pipelines

The more diffuse external pipelines that feed NED appointments and shortlists have several tributaries. FTSE 100 constituents, for instance, may look for NEDs among executive directors of FTSE 250 constituents, and to other countries (as have many of France's CAC 40 constituents; see Chapter 3). Companies may also look for their NEDs in non-business areas, such as the professions, government, academia, the media and politics. As we have seen, they may look for their NEDs in the ExCos of companies in their peer groups. The record shows some companies have seen FTSE Programme alumnae as a source of board-ready NEDs.

But when all is said and done, it is those internal executive-only pipelines to which we must look if many years from now the gender-balanced board is to be unremarkable, and women are to occupy more or less half the board seats of the average company, year in, year out.

We can expect a trickle of NEDs to come from outside business, but with the emphasis now on industry-specific experience for company directors, most female board appointments, both NEDs and EDs, will come from those internal executive pipelines that it is the job of HR departments to fill up and strengthen.

This is fortunate, because in the context of the 'big project' the need for more female EDs is, arguably, more pressing than the need for more female NEDs.

The female ED challenge

If the motivation for improving the gender balance on boards is to improve the quality of business 'management', as well as corporate governance (by capturing the synergy of the fusion of the male and female management styles), it seems likely that the appointment of a female ED will contribute more to achieving that goal, than the appointment of a female NED. Whether this is true in a particular case will depend on the individual. But as we suggested in Chapter 1, it seems reasonable to expect female EDs to have more impact on how organisations are managed, as opposed to governed, than female NEDs.

It also seems fair to say that the cultural change required to get to the position, many years from now, when gender-balanced boards are unremarkable, will proceed more quickly at those organisations that have above average complements of female EDs.

This is another area where the headline 'women on boards' numbers are misleading. As far as the 'big project' is concerned it is not the quantity of female directors that matters, it is the quality; the power and influence women exert over the way our organisations and institutions are run.

According to the *Female FTSE Report 2015*, there were 24 female EDs on FTSE 100 boards in March 2015; an increase of 85% since 1999. Compared with the increase of 241% in the number of female NEDs over the same period, this is pedestrian progress. The situation is not quite as bleak as it seems, however. Thanks to a slight reduction in the size of boards and a sharper reduction in the proportion of EDs on boards, the proportion of EDs who were women rose from just over 2% in 1999, to 8.6% in March 2015.

But the picture is certainly bleaker than the headline numbers (an increase in the percentage of women on FTSE 100 boards from barely 6% in 1999 to 23.5% in March 2015) suggest, because these numbers make no distinction between EDs and NEDs.

Let's suppose, for a moment, that an ED exerts twice as much power and influence over the way his or her organisation is run than an NED. Applying the formula 1ED = 2NEDs to the *Female FTSE Report* numbers suggests the power and influence exerted by women on FTSE 100 boards has risen from 5% of all power and influence exerted by FTSE 100 directors in 1999 to 20.6% in March 2015. One can argue about the most appropriate ED to NED ratio. Perhaps it should be 1ED = 3NEDs. This would produce an increase in the power and influence exerted by women on FTSE 100 boards from 4% of all the power and influence exerted by FTSE 100 directors in 1999 to 18% in 2014 (see Table 7.1).

Whatever ratio seems appropriate, some adjustments to the headline numbers are needed to take account of the differences between the power and influence exerted by executive directors on the one hand and by non-executive directors on the other. The headline numbers overestimate the increase in the power and influence of women on the management (as opposed to governance) of FTSE 100 constituents between 1999 and March 2015 for the simple reason that almost all of the increase was accounted for by female NEDs.

For these reasons we believe the focus of attention following Lord Davies's review of progress should shift from female directors to female EDs and female members of ExCos.

TABLE 7.1   The power and influence of women on FTSE 100 boards, 1999–2014

Ratio	1999 (%)	2015 (%)
1ED = 1NED	6.3	23.5 headline
1ED = 2NEDs	4.8	20.6
1ED = 3NEDs	4.1	18.6

Source: Derived from Cranfield's Female FTSE Reports, 1999–2015.

Executive committees

In his 2011 *Women on Boards* Review, Lord Davies said he expected 'all Chief Executives to review the percentage of women they aim to have on their Executive Committees in 2013 and 2015'. Although his original targets were for women directors (ED and NED), Davies appeared to recognise the danger that his focus on women on boards overall might obscure the importance of the ED/NED split on boards and the male/female split on ExCos.

If this was indeed among his concerns, he was right on the button.

Although correlation doesn't necessarily mean causation, it's very likely that Lord Davies's Review and its targets had a substantial impact on the number of women on FTSE 100 boards, and helped boost the proportion of women from 12.5% in 2010, to 23.5% in March 2015. But this was almost entirely attributable to NED appointments. The proportion of EDs who were women rose only modestly over the five-year period, from 5.5% to 8.6%. And, notwithstanding Lord Davies's exhortation, the proportion of women on ExCos seems to have fallen over the same period.

The statistics on ExCo membership are not as reliable or complete as those for boards, but, thanks to the diligence of the Cranfield researchers, there are enough data to indicate that between 2010 and early 2014 the percentage of women on FTSE 100 ExCos fell from 14.2% to 13.7%. Since it is now widely recognised that the emphasis in the gender-balancing project should now be switching from boards to executive directors and executive committees, we believe it would be helpful if companies were obliged to publish the same information for their ExCos as they are for their boards.

This appears to corroborate the old management maxim 'you get what you measure'. The Davies Review set targets for female directors, and their proportion rose sharply. It set no targets for women on ExCos, and their proportion fell slightly.

It's the same in France.

Véronique Préaux-Cobti and Marie-Claude Peyrache don't believe the gender balance on CAC 40 boards would have changed without the Copé–Zimmermann law (see Chapter 3), and cited as evidence the lack of corresponding change in CAC 40 ExCos, which are not subject to the law.

ExCo membership is the first place to look if you want to get some idea of whether the current proportion of women on boards is going to fall, rise or stay the same. The ExCo is the output end of the pipeline of board candidates (see above); and a source of NEDs for other companies, and of EDs for the company it collectively runs.

If fewer women are joining the average ExCo today it's likely that fewer women will be joining the average board as EDs tomorrow.

ExCo membership is the most important of the 'formative' roles, as Elisabeth Kelan calls them (see page 146), that lead to board seats. In other words, serving on an ExCo is a necessary, but not always sufficient, precondition for being appointed to a board as an ED. Some NEDS come from outside the corporate sector: the professions, government, academia, for instance. But someone who has not served on an ExCo is highly unlikely to be appointed an ED.

Although the recent trend in the proportion of women on ExCos is a cause for concern, there is some evidence that the shackles of the 'pink collar' functions, confining women to careers that peak below the board, are loosening. Until 2006, when the Cranfield team began tracking gender balance on FTSE 100 ExCos, female members were from HR, company secretary/general counsel or finance. Since then the provenance of female ExCo members has become more eclectic. In 2014 the origins of the 160 women on FTSE 100 ExCos (down from 176 in 2013) were as shown in Table 7.2.

Excluding C-suite executives who are already on the board, the two most obviously 'formative' classes of job for the outcome of board seats are Human Resources and Divisional Heads. They account for 47.5% of female ExCo members, equivalent to 44 female ExCo members in early 2014 with good chances of being appointed to boards as EDs.

TABLE 7.2 Origins of female ExCo members, 2014

Origins	%
Human Resources	25.0
Divisional heads (VP, MD, Director)	22.5
Corporate Affairs/Communications	10.0
Company Secretaries/General Counsels	10.0
C-suite (CEO, COO, CFO)	8.5
Marketing	7.0
Finance/Risk	6.0
Legal/compliance	6.0
Strategy/Business Development	5.0

Source: Female FTSE Report, 2014.

That's not enough to provide a reason to be hopeful that the ranks of female EDs will increase significantly any time soon.

Building the ladder

A study by KPMG, business psychologists YSC and the 30% Club sheds some light on the nature and scale of the female ED challenge. The results were based on responses to questions from 19 organisations (including 13 FTSE 100 companies and three FTSE 250 companies) and 4,608 individuals.[2]

The average proportion of women four or more levels below the ExCo was 41%. The proportion fell sharply to 29% three levels below the ExCo and then more slowly to 28% two levels below the ExCo, to 23% immediately below the ExCo and 18% on the ExCo. (The latter figure is on the high side for FTSE 100 companies; it compares with under 14% of women on ExCos in Cranfield's 2014 *Female FTSE Report*.)

This indicates that the seeds of the under-representation of women on ExCos and in the ranks of EDs are sown early, with the greatest attrition rate occurring three levels below the ExCo.

But it is hard to disentangle cause and effect. The attrition rate could be partly attributable to the perception, among women, that their chances of promotion to their ExCo or to their main board as executive directors are relatively poor.

Another deterrent is the lack of room for executives at the top.

The reduction in board size from a FTSE 100 average of about 13 in 1999 to fewer than 11 in October 2014, and the sharp increase in the number of NEDs on FTSE 100 boards following the Higgs Report in 2003, have together led to a sharper reduction in the number of EDs on the average FTSE 100 company, from 6.5 in 1999 to fewer than three in 2014.

If companies sincerely want to get more female executives on their boards, and capture the synergies of gender balance in management (as well as governance), they must welcome women and make room for them. More specifically, they should consider two changes in board policies:

- Relax the criteria relating to necessary experience and appropriate functions for an executive director.
- Increase the proportion of executive directors on their boards.

There were good governance reasons for reducing the ED to NED ratio on boards, but perhaps the rebalancing has gone too far. We don't pretend to be experts on board composition, but if gender balance is a virtue on boards as a whole, it seems reasonable to assume it is a virtue among EDs as well as NEDs. There is some evidence for this. The 2013 *Eversheds Board Report*, an international survey of board effectiveness published by the Eversheds law firm, found one distinctive characteristic of the boards of companies with 'strong share price performance' was a relatively high proportion of EDs.

With fewer than three EDs on the average FTSE 100 board, it's hard to achieve and maintain gender balance among EDs. Only four gender combinations are possible: no women, 33% women, 66% women and 100% women.

Governance and management

The sharp reduction in the ED:NED ratio over the past decade or so has reduced the power of boards (an average of 23% women at FTSE 100 companies) relative to that of ExCos (an average of 14% women at FTSE 100 companies). Insofar as the EDs act as representatives of the ExCo, one can say that, while the headline numbers of women on boards have been rising power has been migrating from the board to the ExCo, where women are less well represented.

As we suggested in Chapter 3, this has led to the 'convergence' of the unitary and two-tier board systems. In a modern unitary system the board and the ExCo effectively comprise a two-tier system; the board takes the place of a 'supervisory board', which concentrates on governance, while the ExCo acts as a 'management board', which concentrates on management. It's not as simple as this, of course, but, as a general rule, one can say that the ExCo focuses on doing the right things, while the board focuses on doing things right.

The increases in the number of NEDs in general, and female NEDs in particular, have addressed perceived weaknesses in governance, but have done little to address management weaknesses associated with gender imbalances among managers. This is regrettable, because the business case for gender balance at the top of organisations rests partly on improvements it is expected to lead to in the quality of management.

Ian Coull, former chairman of Galliford Try, believes this is more true of FTSE 250 than FTSE 100 companies: 'I suspect that for many FTSE 250 CEOs focused on performance, the need to have women coming up through the company, and eventually sitting on their boards, is something that needs to be ticked off; a compliance thing. FTSE 100 chairmen and CEOs, on the other hand, know that having more women in leadership roles brings real skills and knowledge and a different way of thinking, that affect the way that company develops.

'For us, there's this issue of governance – what we have to do, to comply, to satisfy our shareholders and keep our reputation at the right level – when what we really need to do is build houses.

'For me, the main benefit of having women in very senior executive roles or around a boardroom is that they bring slightly different ways of thinking. But I also feel that women intuitively are more sensitive. If your product has women at some point in the consumer process, then having that bit of thinking in the mix is important. We sell a house, which is our core business. No man who is married or with a partner is going to make that decision on his own. They will have women who say "the kitchen isn't right or the front door doesn't convey the right impression or the backyard is too small". Having women in senior positions who can contribute as part of the consumer group, is hugely important.

'I think having a board, or ExCo, without representation from your customer base is ridiculous. So if I go back to SEGRO [where Coull was CEO until October 2010], we were the largest industrial real estate group in Europe. A very substantial part of our core market was the Asian community, because small warehouses and industrial units in Slough were, overwhelmingly, used by the Asian and Indian communities. We didn't have anyone from those groups on the board. I realised that that was ridiculous. We brought someone in who was terrific.

'It is the same with women. If you are selling women's fashion, it is madness not to have representatives of the consumer base on the board.'

We asked him how relaxed he was about Galliford Try's female executive pipeline.

'I'm not at all relaxed. We do have a few female project managers now and I suspect there will be more. But I'm not sanguine about the numbers that will come through our business. In office-type roles we have a female HR Director, and we have one or two women in the finance area who will work their way through. But in terms of the core business I am not hopeful. But I'm also not too bothered about it, because it is just the way the industry is.

Women who come into the built environment industry, as architects or engineers, tend to gravitate towards the advisory side. So they join an engineering or architectural practice, rather than come in through the corporate side. I'm not hopeful about getting more women up through the building side, but that is a relatively minor part of the business. Buying land at one end, and selling houses at the other end, are the two critical bits and they're open to both genders. I think that we as a company have opened up, and I think that we will see more female executives near the top of the business in the next five years.'

Filling the pipeline

The pipeline challenge is the same, whether one sees the objective as more female EDs or more women on ExCos. In both cases, the aim is to stimulate the ambition of women at 'sub-marzipan' levels and add upward momentum to their careers.

In his 2011 *Women on Boards* Review Lord Davies acknowledged that a crucial obstacle to the advance of women to the top of companies was a high drop-out rate in the middle of women's careers.

'The reasons for this drop are complex,' Davies said, 'and relate to factors such as lack of access to flexible working arrangements, difficulties in achieving work-life balance, or disillusionment at a lack of career progression.' It is worth thinking about the last factor for a moment. The lack of women at the top of companies is caused partly by women quitting companies because they are fed up with their 'lack of career progression'? The 'pipeline problem' is full of such ironies.

Various suggestions have been proposed over the years for reducing the high drop-out rate. We wanted to see whether the cross-company model we had developed for the FTSE Programme could make a helpful contribution.

Prompted by Legal & General Group whose chairman, John Stewart, is a mentor on, and a supporter of, the FTSE Programme, The Mentoring Foundation launched a Pipeline Pilot Programme in August 2012.

We wanted the Pipeline Pilot Programme to retain the cross-company quality and ethos of the FTSE Programme with its emphasis on building self-confidence, passing on the knowledge and experience of mentors and external networking, all of which are valued highly by the mentors and mentees on the existing Programme.

But who should be the mentors on the pipeline pilot?

We did not think it would be appropriate to ask our mentors on the original Programme, what we now call the Executive Programme, to mentor women at sub-marzipan levels, for three reasons. First, the Executive Programme mentors are busy people. In addition to acting as mentors of senior women on the Executive Programme, many mentor senior executives within their own organisations. Second, chairmen and CEOs are too senior, too remote in position and age from sub-marzipan women to be effective mentors. Third, the mentoring needs of women at a sub-marzipan level are quite different from those of mentees on the Executive Programme. The latter have already made a number of important choices and decided they want to join boards, win promotions or otherwise advance their careers. The former need mentors to help them form and ignite their ambitions as well as to advise them on how to realise those ambitions.

The solution was under our noses. We decided to ask the alumnae of The Mentoring Foundation's Executive Programme to act as mentors on the Pipeline Pilot Programme. They are all strong supporters of the Executive Programme, to which the Pipeline Programme mentees might hope to graduate. Many are active networkers, witness the attendance at the Unilever Mentee Network (see Chapter 5). All are well connected, thanks to their relationships with their Executive Programme mentors and events organised by The Mentoring Foundation. They're all in senior management positions in the marzipan layer or above, and are excellent role models for sub-marzipan women.

Most important of all, women at that crucial middle stage of their careers, when they have to make important life choices, will find it much easier to talk to other women than to men about their motherhood, childcare and work–life balance concerns.

Thankfully but not surprisingly there was no shortage of volunteer mentors among Executive Programme alumnae. Many were eager to give something back; to share their knowledge and understanding, and to pass on to the next generation of senior female executives some of the lessons they had learned from the main Programme.

FTSE Programme participating organisations were enthusiastic. Some had been made aware, by their involvement in the Programme, of the shortage of able women below the marzipan level. They saw in the pilot, and any full-scale programme that might be rolled out if the pilot was a success, an opportunity to demonstrate to their high-potential sub-marzipan women that they value them highly, are keen to keep them and want them to come back after maternity leave. One also saw in the pilot's cross-company arrangement a way to add new vigour to a conservative, insufficiently innovative mid-management culture.

With these fair winds behind us we approached companies and people we thought might be interested in getting involved.

Seven organisations, together contributing 11 mentees, participated in the Pilot Programme:

- BAE Systems
- Bank of England
- HSBC Group
- Legal & General Group
- Lloyds Banking Group
- Royal Bank of Scotland Group
- Tesco

Interested observers inclined to join the Programme if and when it was rolled out included PwC, Rolls-Royce and Royal Dutch Shell.

A steering group was formed, consisting of senior HR executives of participating organisations, a FTSE Programme alumna to represent the pilot mentors and an observer from an organisation disinclined to commit immediately. (It did so later.) It was generally felt to be important, in the pilot stage, for this group to be independent of mentees, because we were experimenting and testing.

The Steering Group acted like a well-functioning board. It kept us all up to date with developments and produced a specification for the pilot, covering the length of the mentoring relationships and other Programme features. Mentoring relationships were to last for 12 months, with a minimum of four face-to-face meetings.

The pilot included an 'action learning' component designed both to inform mentees and to give the mentee group cohesion and networking experience. It consisted of a learning session each quarter, with an agenda and, when appropriate, an invited external speaker. From time to time, The Mentoring Foundation invited a mentor or mentee from the Executive Programme for an 'in conversation' session.

It was left up to the Steering Group to decide whether the results of the pilot justified a full roll-out. They felt it did, and what we now call the Next Generation Women Leaders Programme (NGWL) was formally launched in January 2014.

Before officially joining the NGWL Programme each mentee has a one hour session with The Mentoring Foundation's chief executive, to ensure the mentee understands the process, to give her an opportunity to ask questions and to discuss her career journey and aspirations. Somewhat to our surprise, it emerged during these talks that, perhaps because of the unusual nature of the Pilot Programme (cross-company, cross-industry, female mentors), some mentees had no idea why they had been nominated for the Programme. Did it mean they were regarded as 'high potential' by their organisation, they wondered, or that they were seen to be underperforming and in need of remedial training?

The puzzlement revealed something we believe to be important about talent management in general, and about cross-company mentoring in particular. By nominating a young woman for the NGWL, for example, the nominator is sending a strong but not always self-explanatory signal to the nominee. When the invitation is accepted the nominee not only enters a new relationship with her mentor, but also a new relationship with her organisation. All of those involved with the nominee: her immediate sponsor, her line manager and the HR people who manage talent need to be consulted and involved throughout the process. The Mentoring Foundation does most of the work during an Executive Programme or NGWL assignment, but the mentee's employer also needs to be actively engaged in evaluating and monitoring the results of an assignment and modifying, if necessary, the mentee's position or role in the organisation subsequently.

High-level cross-company mentoring has, and is intended to have, a powerful impact on mentees. It improves self-confidence, increases self-sufficiency, widens horizons and often adds significantly to the mentee's and, indirectly, the organisation's 'network capital' (see Chapter 5). If an organisation is to extract full value from such human enrichment it must adapt appropriately to the person or persons so enriched.

The NGWL Programme exemplifies the 'reaching down' dynamics of the pipeline challenge. To enrich and fill up the pipeline, women who have already risen high and are aiming higher are reaching down to women who are following them, and struggling with the problems and dilemmas they themselves had to solve and resolve.

Summary

- Gender parity on boards will be a consequence of deep change in the organisation.
- The 'pipeline' metaphor is commonly used when discussing the supply of 'board-ready' women.
- The 'pipeline' delivers executives, not non-executives.
- Non-executive directors contribute to governance; executive directors contribute to management.
- Executive directors have more power and exert more influence than non-executive directors.
- The proportion of women on executive committees has fallen.
- Power has been migrating from boards to executive committees.
- Mentoring can help to enrich and fill up the pipeline.

chapter

The Pipeliners

The 'pipeline' metaphor has become commonplace in discussions about the numbers of women who are, or are on track to become, 'board-ready'.

It's a useful metaphor in many ways. Its implications of flows and conduits convey the impression of movement along relatively narrow pathways. The so-called 'pipeline' issue is indeed about the flows of women through organisations. Flow rates are critical. The gauge or bore of the pipe is important. The design of the pipe network is significant too, and the location of the network's exits, entrances and ends are of interest. There are major problems with blockages. All this is true. But the metaphor is too abstract, too mechanical. It obscures as much as it reveals.

When we talk of the pipeline, we're not talking of a real physical pipe. The pipe is virtual. Its existence is inferred from the fact that a group of people of a particular composition reach positions in the organisation where they become candidates for high office.

If the composition of the group is not quite what we want – if it includes too small a proportion of women, for instance – we deduce from this that the routes the group's members have taken to reach positions where they become candidates for high office have proved easier for men to negotiate than for women.

The appropriate response to this deduction is not that of a plumber with a flow-meter and a wrench. It's not a 'hard' mechanical issue to do with fluid dynamics; it's a 'soft' psychological issue to do with perceptions and expectations.

Two case studies

To understand the pipeline issue fully we need to lift the veil and examine what's going on in the minds of people working their way up. We need qualitative as well as quantitative insights. We thought the best place to look for such insights would be inside the pipe. We asked two women rising up it what it was like being a 'pipeliner', these days. Both were mentees on The Mentoring Foundation's Pilot Pipeline Programme (see Chapter 7), since 'rolled out' as the Foundation's Next Generation Women Leaders Programme (NGWL). Their reflections illustrate some of the pressures and uncertainties women experience at this stage of their careers.

Lizzie Rowlands

Senior Manager – Customer Experience, Tesco Stores.

Mentored by Sarah Breeden, Director, International Banks, Bank of England.

When Rowlands was invited to join The Mentoring Foundation's Pilot Pipeline Programme, her reaction was puzzlement: 'My first thought was "why me?" I believed I was well recognised as being a good leader in the job I was doing then, but I wondered "why me, over everyone else?" The person who originally spoke to me about it, and said I would be good, was my boss's boss. I think I was a little shell-shocked. I looked round and thought: "*you* might be more suited to that." But actually, as time went on it became clear it was a kind of recognition that I wanted and needed. It became clear that it was what others in our business wanted for me too.'

She said it felt like a message.

'When I started the Programme, I had just started running Wembley. It's a huge shop – 80,000 square foot, almost 400 colleagues. It's got the largest "world food" offer in the country for us as a business and very ethnically diverse colleague and customer populations, so it is really interesting from that perspective too. It was Brent Park Superstore before it became Wembley Extra, and the 100th store we opened, so it's an iconic store for Tesco. Hugely challenging for someone like me, a country girl from Cornwall; suddenly to be working in such an ethnically diverse store in London; a different world to me, so a huge amount to learn and by far the most difficult year of my career so far.

'Being on the Programme didn't help me much running the day-to-day operation, but it helped a lot in terms of me thinking about what did I really need, in terms of job satisfaction. I think it's the same in many big businesses – when you're in a function it's quite silo'd, so there's a natural path that you would follow in Tesco as an operator, and I was happily working my way along it. That is the honest answer! I would say I was doing better than most in that I had good sponsorship and a good network around the business. I was well thought of for doing it my way and not necessarily just for the results I delivered. But I had never stopped to consider what I actually wanted as opposed to what [would happen] if I just trundled along the train tracks and allowed promotions and job content to come to me. I was almost doing it as a passenger rather than a full contributor to my career path. It never crossed my mind, is the honest answer, that I had a choice in where my career took me.

'Being able to talk to Sarah safely with no political agenda was amazing, because she's not connected to my business. She is a really confident woman, in terms of asking for what she wanted. She had great examples of where she had asked for roles she wanted (I was wondering about where I was going to go). But she also had an outsider's perspective on when I was being a bit "victimey" about the situation I'd found myself in, and when I could be braver. I'd earned the right to be able to say "I think I'd like this instead, actually". So for me it meant, as a result of this different conversation, I had the space and time to think about where I wanted my career to go. For me, it was such a luxury. The journey to see Sarah took

45 minutes, so I had time to really think. I had to know what I wanted to get out of her time and not waste it. I had to know what I wanted out of that conversation. There's something about knowing you're going to have a conversation with someone and you have to take action in the gaps in between. Potentially you might allow time to drift by because you're busy otherwise. It did genuinely feel to me like pauses in time, to have a different conversation solely focused on what I wanted and what was I doing about it: total ownership, that was a big shift for me, and hugely useful in that sense. I have genuinely come out of it feeling like I've stepped off the train I was on, to go and decide what I really wanted to explore.'

'And the organisation managed to accommodate that?' we asked.

'It did. I'm not going to pretend it was easy – the function I was in did not want me to leave so it took some time. The conversation I had been having with Sarah about what I wanted to be doing and how that was going to be of benefit to Tesco if I did, meant that, when I explained that it was proving difficult to make the move but there was a job I thought I'd be useful in, she was able to help with that. I genuinely believe that if I had not joined your Programme, I would probably be working for another company by now, because I would have found myself unsatisfied but not known what to do about it.

'The Pilot Programme gave me the confidence to say "these are my options as I see them, do you see them differently?" And ultimately, I'm now doing a job that I feel I'm really adding value in. I'm challenged and excited about what I am doing. I'm learning loads, and in the longer run, it will make me better as a director for Tesco. I don't think I would have pushed for that though, without the Programme and Sarah's guidance.

'The way I describe it in hindsight to people now is, I could have gone and run a group of stores and I'm sure I would've done a good job. And the team I led would have benefitted from me being there. But I describe the job I have now as working on a project that can make things better for everybody. In my mind, that is a better use of me.

'It's what I wanted as well, in terms of my personal learning. And what I learn, and add to the business, really matters to me in my job.'

Hannah Reynolds

Deputy Secretary, Secretary's Department, Bank of England.

Mentored by Carolyn Bradley, NED Legal & General Group.

'I was really pleased to be selected, and also surprised. I hadn't thought in terms of having an external mentor. My career planning discussions had been entirely internal so being put forward for an external programme wasn't something I'd considered. It was really great to have an external mentor outside the line. And it came at a good time, because it's such a busy job, you don't spend much time thinking about your own development, and where you might want to go next.

'At the time of the Programme, I was the Private Secretary for an Executive Director at the Bank.

'As part of your annual performance assessment review, you write a development plan for the year; things to work on during the year. It might be training, improvement on the job, or more feedback on something. This [the Pipeline Programme] was an addition to things I was already doing.

'I had things around my confidence, which I'd previously worked on and had to cement, particularly speaking up in discussions. Things around thinking about what I might want to do afterwards. That was particularly important, because Private Secretary jobs raise your profile in the organisation. My boss said I had to be careful about where I go next, because you get a chance to springboard from here into what you want to do so don't waste it; make sure you go into something you're really interested in. So some of the things I had on my list were using the position I was in as a Private Secretary to broaden my knowledge of the organisation and then try to make decisions about what I might want to do next on that basis.

'My mentor and I initially met and talked about what we might cover. I told her about the things I had been working on. She got me to work through things with her, particularly my confidence. She also provided me with feedback from a different angle about how I came across to someone new – we spent some time on that. Later we did more specific work: when I was thinking of moving roles, who should I talk to, where I wanted to go. Towards the end of the mentoring, we talked about what I should do when actually moving, like going to meet all the people in the new area or, early on, writing a plan for moving to a new job, because it can be hard to have interim milestones in the early stages. She suggested some reading for me and I had a 30-day plan.

'She said [when moving to new jobs] you get so much reading thrown at you it's sometimes quite hard to achieve things. We also talked about the opportunity you had when you moved to ask questions, and the fact that that window closes after a while. She made me realise that although I enjoyed working for my boss, it was a job that allowed me to shy away from some things I found difficult. I learned a lot, but I was speaking with someone else's authority. And when I moved to another role, I wasn't going to be able to do that.

'We talked quite a lot about how to remain authentic, and not feel as if you are playing a role. I think it's taken me quite a while to find a work "me"; something that feels genuine, and that I feel comfortable with. It's different from my social persona.

'We talked about things like feeling comfortable in meetings. It's all interconnected. Taking up enough space in the meeting, because I tended to "sit small", and not really take part. We talked about how not everything you say in a meeting has to be brilliant. That you can help move a meeting on. It was all things I sort of knew, but hadn't put into practice. Being more aware of how other people do it and then trying those things myself, in my own way.

'A couple of people said they've noticed. I had some nice feedback the other day. Someone I had worked with in internal comms said he'd observed that I'd gone to work on a piece and established myself as a go-to person on it; I'd kind of made it my own. One thing that probably helped is moving roles. That was a chance to reinvent myself. It's kind of drawn a line, and started again, with a slightly different group of people.

'After an Action Learning Group meeting I was speaking to someone and we were saying that these things seem so obvious when you look back, you wonder why it wasn't obvious before. I think it's some time for reflection and a slightly different point of view. I think it's definitely through this Programme that I've acquired a slightly different perspective. I'm also realising that some of the things I stress or worry about are less stressful if I step away from them, rather than making them bigger than they really are.

'My mentor really challenged me, and wasn't afraid to say to me "I don't see why that's such a big issue." Sometimes, I think about doing something, but don't really want to go and talk to that person, or they might get the wrong end of the stick. She didn't really have much truck with my over-analysis of things. She just said "look if you want to go and work in someone's area, go talk to them. You're really over-analysing it. They'll probably be quite pleased that a person who seems relatively good wants to work in their area."

'That was really good, but she never pushed things on to me and it was always done in a very kind way. But it was a good challenge.

'I have to say, the first time we met I was kind of "ooh". I liked her immediately, but I just thought, "wow, she is going to make me think. It's not going to be a little cosy chat."'

We asked Reynolds what she had gained from the Pipeline Programme.

'Two things. First, what we talked about; having self-awareness. The second one, which I talked a lot about with my mentor, was more active management of my career. At the start of my career things happened at various times. When I thought about moving, something came up, and I've kind of just followed my nose a bit; things that I'm interested in. But there's a bit to be done, not only thinking about where I'm going; also when you arrive in the new role, using the chance to ask questions, getting to know the people. Not just arriving, and seeing what happens, but actively managing that, and then thinking about it not in terms of tasks, but more in terms of engagement. Instead of things I want to achieve, like "finish this piece of work", wanting to build an effective team and have a good atmosphere to work in; the bigger things, which enable tasks to be done really well.

'I'm now thinking more strategically both in terms of my career, and where I want it to go, and the role that I'm in now; how I see that, and how I see what my role involves.'

Common factors

It's all too easy to generalise about the pipeline. Each individual in the pipeline is different, and each sees different obstacles and opportunities. But there are some common factors.

For both Rowlands and Reynolds the Programme came at a critical point in their careers when frustration with a current position or with how to move forward began to set in. Their discussions with their mentors encouraged them to take a more active role in managing their careers. It took them outside their organisations and gave them the space and time to reflect, with a trusted external mentor, on their career development. For both, thinking beyond the obvious next step in their current organisation and seeing themselves a little differently enabled them ultimately to renew their commitment to their organisations.

Action Learning Group

As with the Executive Programme the mentoring relationships in the Next Generation Women Leaders (NGWL) Programme are firmly focused on the needs and aspirations of the mentees. Matters discussed are personal and practical, and mainly relate to the mentee's job and career and how she conducts herself in and beyond the workplace.

Discussions during the NGWL's Action Learning Group (ALG) meetings range more widely. From these regular gatherings of NGWL mentees a sense emerges of what kinds of people these 'pipeliners' are, what drives them and how they see the world and their roles in it.

The NGWL's third ALG meeting in London, on 30 October 2014, was a case in point. Following on from discussions at our annual Colloquium earlier that month, we and the mentees discussed the suggestion that the alleged 'self-limiting behaviour' of women is, at least in part, responsible for their failure to advance further. The suggestion is linked to Sheryl Sandberg's 'lean in' prescription,[1] that to climb higher in their organisations women must adapt their behaviour to the organisation.

We at The Mentoring Foundation observed a generational as well as a gender dimension to the debate and that characterising certain kinds of behaviour as 'self-limiting' did not appeal to our pipeliners. Their animated reaction gave us clues about how a younger generation of women of work sees the 'lean in' issue in particular and the future for the world of work in general.

Most of the mentees took issue with the term 'self-limiting' and its implication that the 'behaviours' so characterised by Sandberg in her influential 2013 book were weaknesses. They were of the view that Sandberg failed to acknowledge that her judgement of such 'behaviours' was based on what was considered 'normal' behaviour in many organisations. For the mentees, this judgement could be an example of unconscious bias that was affecting how women perceive themselves and their behaviour.

A detailed discussion followed about such allegedly self-limiting behaviour, including remaining silent in meetings. One mentee gave a very different description of her own behaviour, which was endorsed by the other mentees. She described how, in her case, her silence is due, not to a lack of confidence but to her wish to glean information. 'I already know what I think. What I want to know is what others think.'

The group wondered whether the management literature was making too much of all this. Many believed there were more important issues than Sandberg's 'self-limiting' behaviour that needed to be addressed. One mentee questioned how many of Sandberg's points were really gender-related.

She didn't think there was anything new in Sandberg's list and was at pains to stress the need for more fundamental structural change in the cultures of organisations. 'The world has moved on; 19-year-old tech workers sit in cafés, and bond over a laptop. This is the new working model.'

The group took the view that so-called 'self-limiting' behaviour was symptomatic of unconscious bias more generally. They agreed that organisations need to take a fresh look at their working cultures, identify the skills they need and the behaviour they would like to encourage, and then build an appropriate culture that promotes such behaviour.

Despite largely rejecting the 'lean-in' philosophy, they nonetheless recognised some of the behaviour patterns on Sandberg's list. But they didn't feel defined by them, particularly those about women's perceived lack of self-confidence and how they should address it. The group agreed that there were two dimensions to this issue: how businesses can change and how individuals react and adapt.

The group also suggested we need to look at who is driving culture so that the right behaviour is encouraged. The conventional wisdom is that women should change and improve their skill-sets, to fit into an existing culture.

If anything needed to be changed or reassessed, one of the mentees argued, it was the culture, not the women. By requiring women to adapt, people were less 'genuine' at work and authenticity was an undervalued trait in organisations.

Many commented that the level of diversity in society was changing more quickly than in organisations. The contemporary management literature was too backward-looking, in their view. They said the challenge was how to change, without being purely reactive, and that current thinking about change was within an outdated paradigm. They said this was a generational challenge too. Goals are set, but the ruling hierarchy consisting of men and of like-minded women remained intact, in their view.

The group characterised their generation, generally speaking, as being more socially conscious; more concerned with socio-economic inequality, social issues, and the opportunities (or lack of them) open to those from certain backgrounds. For them, the current focus on women was not just about furthering their own careers; it was also about the social and cultural implications of promoting women and the pursuit of more culturally diverse organisations generally. These aims could not be measured in terms of gender balance alone.

The group came up with seven criteria for bringing about change:

- Understand that the obstacles are intergenerational and socio-economic, as well as gender-related.
- Allow people to be authentic within the organisational context.
- Make an effort to understand why people behave as they do.
- Value EQ (emotional intelligence quotient) as much as IQ.
- Promote honest and open communication.
- Value authenticity.
- Ensure that learning is forward- not backward-looking.

We asked the group to describe the ways in which the conversations of the current generation might differ from the conversations of the previous generation. Their responses revealed that despite their different preoccupations, many of the challenges and dilemmas faced by individuals with career ambitions had essentially remained the same.

One mentee perceived huge social barriers to women's success in the workplace that were not being addressed by the government or business. She spoke of the lack of accessible or affordable childcare, and said this meant that women were faced with a difficult decision: to further their professional careers, and spend all their disposable income on childcare, or to avoid the costs of childcare altogether and become stay-at-home mothers. She observed that men did not have to make the same decision.

Another commented on the dominance of an ostensibly homogenous group of mainly male executives at the top of organisational hierarchies and how their influence on work culture meant that any cultural paradigm shifts had to come from the top. She emphasised the importance of self-awareness in a leader, and asked what behaviour patterns and cultures were being encouraged in our organisations and what were the implications (damaging or otherwise).

Returning to women's perceived behaviours, several of the mentees pointed to ambiguity in the way that confidence and competence were perceived. Sometimes, those who reach the top are those who appear confident, but confidence didn't necessarily mean competence and more introverted behaviour shouldn't be mistaken for a lack of competence.

The mentees believed that organisations often reward 'talking', when they should place more emphasis on 'listening' and more value on people being willing to listen and learn from each other. They questioned the idea that people who can't sell themselves should be valued less than those who can.[2]

When comparing their thoughts with those of our Executive Programme mentors, it seemed to us that our pipeliners might have more in common with the 'homogenous', mostly male group at the top of their organisations than they realise. Or perhaps, just as these women are not defined by the stereotypes used to describe them, so those who are currently running our large organisations are not defined by the stereotypes used to describe them. We know this to be true of the mentors on our Executive Programme. The conversations we facilitate between the mentors on our Executive Programme and the mentees on the Next Generation Women Leaders Programme suggest that a cultural fusion might even now be emerging from the mutual modifications and adaptations of perceived truths that occur when individuals meet and share their different experiences.

An example of this was the reaction of the mentees (expressed at the same Action Learning Group meeting) to their recent meeting with a chairman on the FTSE Executive Programme. They described as 'inspirational' the way he talked about effecting cultural change in his organisation. He had not once mentioned 'female leadership' or attributed perceived 'behaviours' to women. Nor had he spoken about taking risks. Instead, he seemed to be going ahead and making the changes needed. He used honest and open communication in a way that they could relate to and which offered them an attractive role model of leadership.

The mentees also highlighted the question of confidence and competence, and the need not to confuse the two. This point is consistent with research by Cameron Anderson and Gavin Kilduff of UC Berkeley we cited in *Women & the New Business Leadership* (Palgrave Macmillan, 2011).[3]

Anderson and Kilduff divided 68 graduate students into four-person teams and asked each to organise an imaginary charity. The winners would get $400. The work sessions were videotaped. The members of each group were asked to rate each other on their influence on the team, and their competence. Kilduff and Anderson and independent observers did the same. All three sets of judges reached the same conclusions. Those who spoke most were rated highest for desirable qualities, such as 'general intelligence', and 'dependable and self-disciplined.' The people who didn't speak very much scored higher for less desirable traits, such as 'conventional and uncreative'.

Anderson and Kilduff concluded 'more dominant individuals achieved influence in their groups in part because they were seen as more competent by fellow group members'. Maybe they were. To test this, Anderson and Kilduff ran a second study with other volunteers also divided into teams and competing for a $400 prize. The task was to answer maths questions from the Graduate Management Aptitude Test (GMAT), the standard business-school entrance test. All volunteers had taken the GMAT and told the researchers, but not their fellow team members, their scores on the maths section. Once again, those who spoke up more were more likely to be seen as leaders, and more likely to be rated as competent.

But they didn't give the most correct answers, and hadn't achieved the highest GMAT scores.

One conclusion that could be drawn from this is that organisations should heed the views of our NGWL mentees and cease to base their promotion decisions on self-confidence and volubility in meetings. To paraphrase Edmund Burke, it could be that all that is necessary for incompetence to flourish is competent women who say nothing.

The new women

It's hard to know if the views of these pipeliners will remain the same as they approach their goals, but their beliefs suggest that something approaching a new philosophy of business and management is moving up through organisations. It can be characterised by the beliefs that diversity is not all about gender; that the identification of confidence with competence leads to bad promotion decisions; that it is as incumbent on corporate cultures to adapt to women as it is on women to adapt to corporate cultures.

Summary

- The pipeline metaphor is useful, but too mechanical – you need to look inside it at the real people in all their variety.
- Mentoring allows people to focus on their careers, rather than their jobs.
- The timing of a mentoring relationship is crucial.
- Sheryl Sandberg's 'lean-in' thesis is not the whole story.
- There are two issues: how organisations change and how individuals adapt.
- Confidence doesn't necessarily mean competence.

9

HR and the Pipeline

Declarations of intent, statements of belief, policy announcements and other commitments to gender balance on boards come, as they must, from the leaders of companies and other organisations. Many of the most outspoken leaders on the women on boards subject have served, or still serve, as mentors on The Mentoring Foundation's FTSE 100® Cross-Company Mentoring Programme. Their advocacy, and the invaluable contributions they make serving as Programme mentors, have helped to shape the zeitgeist and given the impression that if women want to share the reins of power, in the business world at least, they are pushing at an open door.

Given this evident eagerness for gender-balanced boards at the top of organisations why, the question is begged, has progress been so slow?

Various answers to the question have been proffered: deeply rooted prejudice, male-orientated cultures, hierarchic structures, supine investors, obstructive headhunters, inadequate pipelines. All are alleged to be frustrating in one way or another the clear wish and intent of the leaders of our large organisations.

Another obstruction to progress towards gender-balanced boards and ExCos is the status quo – conventions, traditions and habitual ways of doing things. Attempts to remove such obstructions will usually have unintended and often unwelcome consequences, which have to be managed. That task falls to the HR (human resources) function. The challenge for HR staff is to help fill the pipeline of board-ready women without inflicting too much damage on aspects of the culture that need to be preserved.

It's fortunate, therefore, that it has been estimated that between two-thirds and three-quarters of HR professionals are women. Other things being equal, it is likely that HR professionals will do all they can, within the constraints of their other day-to-day duties, to realise the desire of their organisation's leaders for a fuller pipeline of board-ready and ExCo-ready women.

HR professionals and departments are intimately involved in gender balance. Gender balance at every level of the organisation and the network of pipes conveying talent, skills, ability, and experience from one part, or level of the organisation, to another, are, to a large extent, created and maintained by the HR function. They are the engine-room of gender-balancing. The organisation's leadership decides the general direction, but it's up to HR people to prepare for the journey, plot a course and navigate between the shoals and rocks.

A conspicuous case in point was the announcement by Lloyds Banking Group's CEO António Horta-Osório in January 2014 that the bank was committed to reaching the point, before this decade was out, where women held 40% of the group's top 8,000 jobs.

Challenging times

What was the reaction to Horta-Osório's announcement in the bank's HR department? Some cheers of jubilation for a bold declaration of intent; a weary sigh at the sheer scale of the HR challenge posed by the target; perhaps a muffled 'dream on'? Some may have thought it was a public relations stunt. If so, they were soon disabused.

The clock was ticking – six short years to meet the most ambitious gender-balance target ever set by a publicly listed UK company.

Yet the target wasn't quite as ambitious as it was widely perceived at the time. With 27% already held by women, LBG's top 8,000 jobs were above the gender-balance average in the financial services sector. But there were 13 percentage points to go – that's two more percentage points a year, for six years. Another 1,040 women in top jobs by 2020; that was an average of another 173 each year, for six years. Each year, for six years, an average of 173 top male executives would have to leave, for one reason or another, and be replaced by 173 women.

The goal itself may be useful here, because it will give women who might otherwise have left the impression that their prospects for promotion are relatively good. (But, by the same token, it might also give men who would otherwise have stayed, the impression that their prospects for promotion are relatively poor.) Latest survey results show female employees (or 'colleagues', as Horta-Osório calls them) are more likely than male employees to say they're proud to work for the bank.

Management gurus talk of 'stretch goals' that can't be achieved by incremental improvements; they require extraordinary effort and an entirely different approach. A shift from walking to leaping. 'You can't cross a chasm in two steps,' as they say. Horta-Osório's goal is clearly of the 'stretch' kind. Small incremental steps will not be enough to meet the target.

Horta-Osório acknowledged as much when he talked about the target at The Mentoring Foundation's Colloquium on 2 October 2014: 'Like any good target, it is stretching and ambitious, especially as our aim this year is to achieve 29% representation, up from 27% last year.' But he was confident the target was achievable 'with effort and focus.' He said the time frame provided a window 'to develop a more inclusive organisation', and that LBG was 'looking to develop long term sustainable change, not a quick fix.'

The rationale for this pioneering commitment was the belief of the LBG leadership team that 'we will be better placed to understand our customers' needs and gain the deepest insight if the diversity of our colleagues matches that of our customer base.' Horta-Osório added: 'Most importantly, it's about creating a truly meritocratic organisation' and the positive impact that will have on the bank's 'effectiveness as an organisation …we know too from the extensive research … that organisations with strong female representation at the most senior levels often outperform less diverse competitors. This is, in my view, a compelling case for action.'

But however enthused they may be by the commitment, the HR staff at LBG cannot neglect the day job. Apart from routine administrative tasks required to keep the company's workforce up to strength and engaged, they have a host of other things to do – succession and workforce planning, talent management, leadership assessment and development, operating programmes for 'high-potential' employees, performance management and monitoring, designing and operating the reward and incentive systems, compliance with labour, and health and safety law, and advising executives and board committees on a range of issues.

Somehow or other the CEO's new 'stretch goal' must be accommodated in this busy schedule, and progress towards reaching the target of 40% women in the top 8,000 jobs must be made without compromising the day-to-day efficiency of the HR function.

This won't be easy, and it will be harder still to ensure that the actions and policy changes needed to meet the target are not seen by employees, particularly male employees, as 'unfair' or breaches of the meritocratic principle.

That it is axiomatic, nowadays, that a gender-balancing initiative improves fairness, by subordinating deep-seated cultural obstacles to the advancement of women to the gender balance goal, is in many ways beside the point. It's how these policies and initiatives are seen that matters. If the actions taken to achieve Horta-Osório's target succeed in increasing the retention of women, for instance, at the expense of a deterioration in the retention rate of men, it will be hard to see them as being anything better than a qualified success.

It follows from this that the real challenge for LBG's HR staff is not meeting the 40% target by the 2020 deadline, but changing the culture in such a way that actions taken to achieve the target are perceived by all employees to be fair and reasonable.

Horta-Osório is aware of this danger. He said 'we are taking steps to ensure our systems and processes support our goals in terms of how we recruit and develop talent.' These included monitoring all longlists and shortlists for senior appointments, to ensure 'an appropriate gender mix. But not forgetting that our processes must ultimately remain meritocratic.'

The goal and the reality – insights from Lloyds Banking Group

The Lloyds Banking Group commitment was a major milestone in the progress towards a more equal distribution of executive power between the genders. We were very curious about how it was received within the group. We spoke to LBG's Group Director, Diversity & Inclusion, Fiona Cannon OBE, in January 2015, a year after the 40% target was announced.

'The goal emerged from our strategic aim as an organisation; to be the best bank for customers. Underpinning that was having the best team to support that overall objective. The financial services industry has gone through a difficult time in the economic downturn, and it's probably true to say that the industry had lost the trust of the public because of the financial crisis, and that the reputation of the financial services industry was tarnished. We needed to look at how we were going to achieve our strategic goals in that environment. One thing that came out of all that thinking was "how do we make Britain prosper?" We looked at the issues that our customers were facing in their day-to-day lives and at how we could help them to tackle those issues. Our Helping Britain Prosper Plan is Lloyds Banking Group's response to this.

'The Plan sets out seven key commitments and over 25 independently verified "prosper metrics", which cover the areas where we can make the most difference for our customers across households, businesses and communities. And it also directly supports our business strategy to be the best bank for customers.

'We made the Plan public to demonstrate that we are looking to rebuild the trust of our communities and customers. We felt the only way to do that was to make public statements and allow others to measure us against them. While the plan was being developed, we looked at the things we wanted to be known as. A big issue for us, in terms of being the best bank for customers, is that we can only be the best bank if we understand and meet the needs of all our customers. We're the UK's largest retail bank. We operate in every community, and touch practically every household in the UK. A real sense of responsibility comes with that. Since we operate in every community, our customers are very diverse, so one of the seven key commitments of the Plan is that we will better represent the diversity of our customer base and our communities at all levels of the Group. At the end of January 2014, we became the first UK bank to set public goals for diversity.

'There were three specific diversity goals within the metrics, because the overall goal was to represent the communities we serve. The goal that received the most attention is the one we have set to have women make up 40% of our senior management by 2020, and reaching 29% by the end of 2014. The two other goals are to retain our leading-edge status in terms of disability, as part of the Business Disability Forum benchmarking, and to make sure that our ethnic minority, lesbian, gay, bisexual, transgender and disabled colleagues are as engaged with our work as other groups of colleagues in the organisation. The reason we only set numeric goals for gender was that it's the only one for which we have full data. As data become more complete for the other areas, we will set representation goals for them too.

'I have to say that having been involved with diversity for many years, I wish we had set public goals a long time ago, because it very much focuses the mind. Once it's public you have to act, internally and externally.

'One of the first things that our Group Chief Executive, António Horta-Osório, wanted to do was to demonstrate his personal commitment and leadership. When we launched the Plan internally, he also announced that he would personally mentor three women who had the potential to get to Executive Committee level. The second thing António did was ask the CEO of our Commercial Bank, Andrew Bester, to deliver the Programme: to run it on a day-to-day basis, and to make sure we delivered what we said we were going to.

'The other key thing was to raise awareness, and communicate to all of our colleagues, because such a public focus on diversity and inclusion wasn't something our colleagues had seen before.

'Communication was really important, because we needed to explain to colleagues why we had set these goals, what the implications of setting them were and how we were going to achieve them. This wasn't a one-off piece of work. It went on throughout the year. The initial piece, however, was very much about "why are we doing this?", and trying to ensure colleagues understood. And I have to say there was a reaction, internally, from men and from women: women worrying that they would be seen as the "token woman" if they got the job; men worrying that they weren't going to get jobs because they were going to go to women. They thought this meant fewer future roles for them.

'Andrew Bester spent a lot of time talking to colleagues in focus groups round the organisation. We thought it was important that colleagues should be able to come forward and speak up on what their issues were, how they felt about working in the Group and about what they felt needed to be done. We had a clear view of where we wanted to get to, but we also wanted to involve colleagues in developing the programme so they felt they were a part of it. In those groups we said to the men "this is about everybody; the goal focuses on women, but our overall goal is to be more diverse as an organisation. We're not going to discriminate, and appoint [women] for the sake of it. This is about building a diverse pipeline, and removing barriers and obstacles for anyone developing his, or her career. It may well be, for example, that you don't feel you fit a perceived mould of what it takes to be a "success". This is about creating opportunities and a level playing field for everyone.

We were keen to ensure a clear message; that it was about building a meritocracy, not just focussing on women, and that a meritocracy is good for everyone.

'That's António's big focus – creating a meritocracy. So the listening sessions were really important from a communications perspective in allowing people to participate, and for giving us some pointers in terms of where our colleagues felt we needed to be focussing. And the insights that came out of those groups were the foundation for the work we did subsequently.

'They generated some really important opinions and focus points. We captured everything that was said, so we could look back at the end of the year and ask ourselves how close we were to addressing some of these issues.

'People need to feel reassured that we're not trying to fix individual problems – this is about real cultural change. The first thing Andrew did following on from that work was to set up an Operating Committee, consisting of all the business unit managing directors.

'All of the diversity and inclusion goals are in their balanced scorecards. They have accountability for driving action in their divisions. The Operating Committee meets monthly so it's very much a "hands-on", live, in real-time, Operating Committee. It's the way we do business. We treat the diversity and inclusion agenda like every other business issue and monitor it in real time.

'There's a strong infrastructure in place, and I also go to the Group Executive Committee meetings monthly to report on numbers, actions, insights and where our focus needs to be on a month-to-month basis.

'Another thing we did at the beginning was to focus on numbers and data; not to the point where the numbers drive everything, but to allow us to see immediately where the issues are so we have really detailed monthly information on recruitment, promotions and leavers that we can track. So if there's an issue we're able to see it and break it down both at a group and a divisional level. It is really detailed granular information, and it's made a huge difference because actually what you end up dealing with are the real issues not the sometimes inaccurate perceptions. Hard data help that. It has been really interesting to see what and where the actual problems are. For instance, we've looked at recruitment and worked out that the issue for us is attraction.

'Once women are in the selection process, for example, there don't seem to be many hurdles. The issue is we're not getting as many women through at the beginning. Before we might have speculated as to what the issues were, but actually the data show that it's attraction, and that's where we need to focus our attention. It took time to get really clean data. I've never looked at it in that much detail before. That's part of treating this as a business issue. This is being monitored now as part of our balanced scorecard – we can't get away with not having proper data. I know in the past that diversity and inclusion haven't been treated as being of as much importance as other areas, and weren't seen as business-critical. Now, people really want to know what's going on with the numbers. The data have become more important, not to show we haven't got enough women, but to identify in an objective way where the issues are.

'Another thing António did at the beginning was to insist that all shortlists for promotion to the top two layers of the organisation should include at least one woman. That's been really interesting. Every week, António's office look at what vacancies there are; where we are with the headhunters; what's coming through. The system is that if you want to put up a shortlist without a woman, you must get a waiver from António's office to say that it's OK to continue. It's comply or explain. The interesting thing is how the waiver broadens the conversation. So you say "OK, fine, you tried to get more diversity on the shortlist but show me your workings. What else are you doing for your pipeline further back?" It allows those kinds of conversations to be had. We've had a lot of women coming through that way. So that principle has been cascaded down because it works. It is more difficult, of course, because the population below the top two layers is much bigger.

'It's also been important to spend time with headhunters. We've had the same conversation with all our recruitment agencies for the larger population. They all have targets in terms of what we're expecting them to deliver. We're using our size to influence the supply chain, because that is the only way it can work.

'Another thing we're doing at a senior level is talent mapping. We are looking now at external female talent. We might not have a job right now, but we want to build relationships now, because we know that one of the issues when recruiting women at senior executive level is that they can sometimes take longer [than men] to make the move, often because they have a broader support system in place and don't want to disrupt that ... so it's important we understand.

'It's not a quick fix. The focus on recruitment and promotions has been really important. We did some detailed analysis which showed how many vacancies we would have coming up this year, and who and where our talent is currently. We've placed a real focus on talent - not just in women, but for everyone. How can we ensure we're starting to move that talent upwards in the right way? Some of that was having conversations with women themselves. We spent a lot of time talking to female colleagues to see what's stopping them from moving up. Of course we heard the usual things – confidence; believing the myths about bigger jobs: "I won't be able to do that job because I've got kids", or "I won't be able to do that job, because I have other commitments and I can't do both". We recently ran a programme called "Inspirational People", which identifies inspiring people at all levels of the organisation. We ask them to talk about what they've achieved, how they've done it and about what they've learned.

'It's about dispelling myths. When we were holding those focus groups, we spoke to a woman who was a branch manager. She said "If I look at the next role up, what I see is someone who has to be in the office from 7am in the morning and travels a lot. I can't do that because I've got kids". When we got her to speak to the person in the next role up, he said "I do it that way, because that works for me in my particular circumstances. But you don't have to do it that way ... you could do it a different way." So one of the big things, for us, has been myth-busting about what the next role up means for you, whoever you are. We want to give everybody, women in particular, the confidence to think "I will think about that role. Maybe I can manage it."

'We, as an organisation, are saying that we're open to having discussions with our colleagues about how they might work differently, in a way that works for them and for us. In the "Inspirational People" programme a whole range of people have shown that it's OK to be different, and highlighted the ways in which they have succeeded despite that difference. We found that some very senior people were doing things in very different ways that we never knew about, because they never spoke about it.

'We have job-sharing between very senior executives and senior executives working part-time that only some people knew about. So some really interesting things have come out. It feels like we've opened the door and people are saying "phew, I've been allowed to talk about who I am, and what I do". The energy that has come from that has been phenomenal.

'We have supported our systemic focus on recruitment and promotion processes by ensuring that each member of our Executive Committee makes a specific and visible commitment – they're all either mentoring colleagues or sponsoring diversity strands, and of course they're responsible for their own areas too. The diversity team used to be the people who "did diversity". Now, everyone's doing it.

'All our Executive Committee members have spoken about diversity in their "town hall" meetings or established their own local focus groups. They've really understood the issues in their areas, and are taking action. Communications have been in constant flow throughout the year. We've done some specific things, too. We've developed a "Women in Leadership Programme" about how you move from the level just below senior management into senior management. That has been phenomenally inspirational and successful. All the women have had a sponsor to help move them to the next level, and we've seen real results coming through from that. So development activity is vital as well.

'The other piece is around agile working. Every single focus group talked about this; it didn't matter who they were – male, female, old or young. That leads to the work we're doing in the Agile Future Forum and making sure this organisation is fit for purpose in the 21st century, by understanding and meeting the differing needs of colleagues and the lives they live, and of our customers too. Agile working has been fundamental and has really focussed our attention. We have been looking at lots of other areas, because these things are interrelated. For instance, how are performance management systems applied to those who work differently? If you only work three days a week, how can your performance be compared with that of someone who works five days a week? If you can't work extra hours because you have to look after your children and you're working alongside someone who does extra hours, how do you differentiate?

'And how do we embed this in the organisation? That's another area we're starting to look at; we're looking much more fundamentally at our customer piece as well, doing some research analysis around that whole area. And of course, we're working with our communities through our community focused work – so there's very much a holistic approach to all of this. We are still at the start however, but we have made good progress over this past year driven by António, Andrew and their teams. We've exceeded our first year gender goal and that gives everyone a sense that this is doable.

'But it's hard, because you have to keep at it. That's what public goals make you do; you can't relax. This year, for example, we've just been declared the top private sector employer in the Stonewall Top 100 Employers ranking [for gay-friendly workplaces]; we won awards on gender last year and we're on the Working Families Top Employers for Families list – and that is fantastic, because it shows that the work we have been doing is being recognised. We know that we have more to do to complete the culture change we have started, but we've got a clear focus on the actions we are taking.

'The energy of colleagues and line managers is driving this. Our women's network for example, with 11,000 members, is the largest employee network in the UK – wow! And the number of things they and our other networks are doing is incredible. The support of our colleagues is what is making this work fly.

'What interests me most is what we are unleashing – not only energy but interest and a wish to be different and embrace difference. I don't think there is a line manager in the organisation who doesn't feel really strongly, particularly at the top, and doesn't genuinely believe that this is fundamentally important. They want to do something about it and are delighted that we've got a framework in place that allows them to do it. That has been the game-changer.

'You could have that energy without the public goals, but the goals really make you focus. That's what I like about the goals. The data tell us what we need to do to achieve them. Aligning that with what our colleagues are telling us is what is going to make the difference. This is what drives the plan. The monthly operating committee means that you are dealing with things in real time.

'The great thing about Andrew's Operating Committee and our managing directors is that it's a safe place for people to say "I've had this issue come up, so what do I do?"

'It has created a place where they feel they can ask the questions they maybe wouldn't normally ask. But we didn't get there immediately. That's about building trust that this is real, and that it's OK to say "what does that mean?", "I don't understand" and questioning each other. Someone said recently "women just don't want to apply for these jobs". It was a genuinely held view. Someone asked "have you asked why they don't want them?"' He replied "it's because they've got kids, or whatever". Someone then said: "Hang on a minute, shouldn't you explore that? That sounds like unconscious bias. You're making assumptions on their behalf. Have you asked those women?" There are a few things our managing directors have learned, including "don't take no for an answer". If a woman says no, don't say "OK that's fine". Try and find out why she said no. Don't give up.

'The most illuminating thing for me was before Christmas hearing our Group Executive Committee talk about bisexual colleagues. It was an in-depth discussion about a group we know is less engaged than others and I don't think this would ever have happened before, but here we are having a practical discussion about it, as we would have had about anything else. We had some data that showed there was an issue. They asked "what are the issues? What do we need to do? How do we need to react?" That was a real milestone for me. I know other organisations are focusing on similar issues and in no way am I suggesting that we've got all the answers, but we are the first to set public goals on diversity and that has changed things fundamentally.

'We have been very robust in our responses to the reactions of men and women. It has been important for the organisation to explain that this is about creating a meritocracy and not about special treatment for certain groups, and it's also about ensuring our organisation reflects our customers and a robust response to the gender goal: "Women will not be recruited into more senior positions unless they are good enough. We are a heavily regulated business and we can't appoint people to roles who can't do the job. We wouldn't be allowed to."

'I've spent a lot of time speaking to women about this. You have to prove yourself to get the job and then you will still have to prove you're good enough. But you will only get it in the first place if we think you're good enough and once you are in that position, your job now is to make a success of it. If you don't want it, if you don't want the opportunity, stand aside and let somebody else do it.

'Opportunities come in different shapes and sizes, and the mark of a leader is that you seize your opportunity when you see it. Don't erect barriers in your own mind that stop you. We have been very insistent with women about that. There are plenty of men who have failed and there'll be lots of women who fail too, but that's life.

'Our message from the start has been this is the right thing to do for us, organisationally. This is about being fairer, and creating a more level playing field. We're not doing it because we want to be nice. We're doing this because we want to be the best bank for customers.'

Responding to the zeitgeist – insights from BP and Royal Bank of Scotland Group

Fiona Cannon spoke to us about the power of stretch goals to focus the mind and stimulate action. But although a public goal may be a sufficient stimulus to action, it is not a necessary one. Kirsty Bashforth, Group Head of Organisational Effectiveness at oil giant BP, and Elaine Arden, Group HR Director at Royal Bank of Scotland (RBS), spoke of the power of peer pressure and a gender balance zeitgeist to concentrate minds.

'Lord Davies's report was an amazing behavioural economics exercise,' said Bashforth in January 2015 'because it created peer pressure the like of which no legislation could have achieved. It has changed behaviour and mind-sets profoundly. It could have slapped stuff on; people would have ticked a box. But it kicked everyone, including us, into action. It gave me a license to push harder and set goals. For the first two and a half years you say to yourself "well, good, the goals have created the conversation, but what needs to happen to get there?" It becomes less about "are these goals right?", and more about "it's not just hiring; it's retention, development, engagement; it's all that". In the first two and a half years you find you can make a lot of progress, because people are suddenly saying "why haven't we progressed?" You move forward and women get more confidence and more men come out of the woodwork going "oh I get that, I could do more on this". So you make progress. Then a bit of change or topic fatigue sets in ("are we still on this?") and you get to the stage when you've picked the low hanging fruit; when the stuff that should have happened earlier has happened, and it starts to be the hard yards.

'The people who should've been at that level we've moved up. Now we have to start moving people up more equally than we had been doing before. Perhaps it was bias. We don't know. So we got to the middle of last year, and I was tracking it. I said "are the numbers going up, because you're putting them up? I'm tracking everything you're doing and the number progression seems to have flattened. I'm just not hearing enough focus from certain parts of the company." A number of leaders at the time sat down with their leadership teams, and said "oh yeah, we haven't really done enough". And people found data saying "you may think you're doing enough, but all these promotions had to be filled, all of which had women on the candidate lists, but only a tiny number of women got the jobs". Those data really opened people's eyes in certain parts of the company.

'We definitely made progress last year. That's great because at some point in the year I was thinking "we're going to have a year that is completely flat, compared to the previous year". That's not good. We've started to make progress, but there are two areas where we need to make more progress.

'The first is leading operations, which can be quite a challenge given perceptions, though we're making some key appointments there and they act as a real beacon for others.

'The other is in the areas where we tend to have a much bigger natural talent pool – the staff function areas such as finance and other subjects. That's a place we need to overtly push harder, because we can fall into an unconscious complacency that women will rise through the senior ranks anyway, given the bigger talent pool. We need to really focus here.

'So, we do need to keep stepping back and asking "would I do anything differently?"

'I believe you need three things to make progress – a plan, a vision of what good looks like, and engagement; people who own it and are up for it. You need focused co-ordination so that you can prioritise. I would love to do all three at once, but where we were with diversity and inclusion three or four years ago, if I tried the focussed governance, we'd never have got off the ground. We would've got stuck in a process loop of everybody ticking boxes. So I did the "what does good look like?" and getting the engagement going, but it does mean right now that we've got too many people, doing too much stuff and you're starting to hear people saying "could we coordinate this a bit more?" So that's sort of progress for this year.

'What's happening now is that I've got more and more senior men and women saying "Kirsty, this all feels a bit uncoordinated, we're all doing this a bit part-time, and making great progress, but could you just tighten it up?" I think "yes, great! I would be delighted to tighten it up!" I'd rather have that than people yawn and say "are we still doing this?"

'So I'm using all possible channels; company-wide communications via email, or intranet; whether it's Yammer, social media internally or whether it's trying to provide little beacons of confidence. And then setting those people off. I think of it as a bunch of spinning plates. I will always adopt that approach to change.

'I do think that's the way to move things forward. And when you've got enough plates spinning, you need the right co-ordinator.

'Once you've got that momentum, you have a license to be bolder. For a number of people this topic felt scary; like an additional burden; felt a bit "Oh, do we have to? Here we go again. We've tried this." It didn't feel like front of mind conversation, or a business driver to some people. I would say it's definitely front of mind, as a talent plan. It's increasingly seen as a business driver. You only have to look at Japan; they're trying to engage their women, because they've realised their economy isn't growing. They have two choices; immigration or increase the percentage of women working. It is being seen more now as that kind of macro lever for growth, which is fantastic. It's still exhausting and I think the external context will become challenging, because the oil price has more than halved.

'In such an environment behaviour can revert. People might look for the toughest person around here to manage a crisis. You could end up with some stereotypical views of "Who manages risk well? Who can manage a crisis?" Part of my role at the moment is to keep that front of mind.

'I don't think we or many companies are at a tipping point yet, when you could say we don't have to do anything on gender any more. At BP 27.6% of our working population across the world are women. Sounds a lot, but then you look at the grade distribution. At entry level 38% of our graduates were female last year. When you go right to the top you've got one woman in ten around the management team table.

'We're making that pyramid fatter, rather than a pointy pencil. From looking like the Shard, we're trying to make it look more like a fat pyramid.

'There's more to do and I think topic fatigue, change fatigue in the context of spiralling down oil prices, is going to be tough. When a senior male colleague comes to me and says "how can I help?" I sort of leap all over him. Don't quote me on that – but you know what I mean. I go "OK right! What can you do?" because the more it comes from the establishment, the better.'

We asked her whether she thought the so-called Generation Next posed significantly different challenges.

'I suppose I noticed it both with my elder son George, who is nearly 13 and can't sit down without being on Instagram or whatever, and a 23- year-old-woman I mentor. She's fabulous. There's a bunch of great women coming through, but she's an extreme example. We meet once a quarter. She came in with a list of questions, and ticked them off. She's very specific. She said: "I'm in this situation with my boss. He's asked me this question. How do I respond?" Or "I'm trying to find myself a new role. Exactly which pieces of information should I get, and exactly how should I move forward?"

'After about six of these questions I told her, "I can't give you the answers. Why do you have this list of questions? I thought this was about your development." She said: "This is about my development. I just want to make sure I get it right." It really struck me there is so much information at hand that it's almost weakening the muscle of curiosity. You have to accept that you may not find the answer; that there may be no right answer. You may have to just sort of go a bit with your gut, use your judgment, and call it. And you could almost see her widening eyes going "you want me to come to a view without having all the facts?" She lacked this sense that sometimes, you have to use your gut and your judgment based on experience, as well as data, as you move up an organisation.

'She said "what happens if I get it wrong?". I said "well, sometimes you will". And I look back at my own background and think well, hang on, as I've got older I seem to be much more comfortable using judgment, although at the start of my career I was still a bit "well how will I know if I got it right". But there was far less readily available information to us. You know, when I was growing up, if it wasn't in Pears Cyclopaedia or your Mum or Dad didn't know, you were stuck. Go to the library.

'And if you couldn't find it, you had to make it up and say "this is what I think might happen". So you sort of got used to the world as being a bit of a grey place. You can never say the next generation is better than the current generation; it is just different. It uses different muscles that are far more honed.

'On average (this is hugely stereotypical) people in Generation Next know far more, are far more globally and culturally aware, and their CVs are far more impressive. They've experienced a lot and have more facets to their lives than I have, to be honest. But I worry they may be rabbits stuck in headlights when they are faced with "we're just going to have to talk it through together and come to some consensus or somebody's going to have to take the lead and make a judgement".'

We asked Bashforth whether she felt this was anything to do with the way younger people communicate.

'I'm trying to think of my own communications. I'm not a huge fan of the phone; never have been. I would rather do text, or face to face, or video. I'm not good when I can't see somebody. So one day, in the summer, the email system went down at BP for a whole day, and it was a revelation. A lot more of us got on our video link. Somebody would ping you and ask "do you have two minutes to talk?" So then you open the video. We had far more video conversations when there wasn't an easy way to send messages you can file away for a bit. I think what is happening is we're living our lives faster, and doing more stuff, and trying to manage more things. We're more restless, and therefore maybe we're providing less time for discussion. I don't know if it's the electronic tools that are weakening that muscle for discussion, because in some ways, I find they help it; we can do webcasts now on a global basis, and online calling at the same time, whereas I might have just been broadcasting before. It's more interactive.

'I love change, and I'm curious about change, and moving forward and I'm an optimist; I think it's a great opportunity. Finding the time to reflect, making the time to slow down is the thing that we're not doing as much. But I think the tools are enabling us to be much more interactive.'

Elaine Arden, Group HR Director at Royal Bank of Scotland, has lived through some very interesting times. When we spoke to her in November, 2014, she told us how the "Women on Boards" initiative had been implemented in the bank alongside the unfolding events.

'I feel strongly that it was peer pressure that drove the Women on Boards thing, or rather system pressure. It was almost as if you would be frowned upon, by the establishment, if you didn't address the Davies report. It was more than peer pressure - it was a whole system shift.'

Why the recent shift of emphasis from NEDs to executives?

'It's the zeitgeist. It wasn't so much that dominoes fell. It just became the topic. The "tick the box" focus had obviously fallen on NEDs, but there was an element of the Davies Review that talked about the executive teams and, looking at the NEDs, led chairmen and others to say "so what does that mean down there?" The spotlight has been on one thing and now it's shifting on to another. I think a driver of that was the dialogue about why NEDs. Why that number? Why that percentage? It opened up the "why women?" question.

'At first, the two were quite separate, given everything else that was going on. Sir Philip Hampton was part of the whole thing. He just tackled the board, but with gusto. I would say the area where the conversation mattered most was the Wholesale Bank, and it was not really linked to Davies. It was more to do with the financial crash and the fact that how things had been - the tenure of people, numbers of people, pay structures – couldn't continue. You couldn't do that by chopping away at what existed. To use the words of John Hourican, we had to "ventilate the organisation, create space, and pull through".

'We had to create space and bring in something fresh. The strategy in 2009 shifted to the graduate talent pool. We thought pulling them through would help to achieve the broader goal of ventilating the organisation of those who wouldn't be a part of the future. We would change the organisation with a different breed of people and gender diversity was part of that. We felt gender diversity would be one of the biggest cultural shifts, so we did set targets (only known to very few people). My team had a target to get the gender diversity of graduates up. It had been down in the low 20 per cents of women. Our target was to get that to 50/50, which we just about achieved this year. We're at about 49%. It has been a really hard slog. We knew it would take a few years, and, of course, the pull through would take a few years. So, while Sir Philip was tackling the Board we were "ventilating" the organisation, very much driven by a pretty visionary leader, John Hourican.

'As we got past the crisis phase here, and began to look at talent and bench strength, and reinventing the leadership of the bank, we decided to dispense with the form-filling in the talent and bench review, and just ask a few key questions. One was: "who are your female pipeline, and how are you pulling them through? How do you expect gender diversity in your team to change in the next few years?" I just asked those questions, and said "There's no template; there's no date; come back with how you want to answer that question". Stephen [Hester, CEO until December, 2013] and I would have half a day with business heads once a year, to look at the overall talent bench. It focused the minds on "what does good look like, anyway?"

'We restructured the organisation this year. For us one of the big challenges has been working out how to change an organisation that is downsizing. Because as you downsize, the scope for pull through gets less and less. If the organisation is static you need to hire more women than men for the new roles. But RBS isn't static, its senior cadre is getting smaller, partly because the bank's getting smaller, and partly because we felt we were over-managed and we're stripping out management layers. That is a big part of the change. This restructuring affects the top more than the bottom. So, fewer roles, which means the ratio of women appointments at senior level has to be higher, to make the shift.

'We have recently agreed a target. We have targets for the bank as a whole – to be number one bank for customer service, and customer advocacy by 2020. That sounds a long way off, but it's only five years away. There wasn't a diversity target, but we've recently agreed we want our senior teams to be 30% women by 2020. We've asked ourselves if that is aspirational enough. We feel it is.

'We've worked out the number of appointments that need to be women and it's a big number. It has forced us to say "OK, well if that's our over-all goal, that means you need to do this, so what's your pull through like?" We've actually gone up in terms of the numbers of women, but if you look at our statistics back to 2006 or 2007, you see that it's the middle that never shifts. We're managing to pull through what we call "executive level", but we're not getting the middle ranks. Data make a difference, so we've done the pull through stats for appointments to manager and senior manager – how many appointed women, how many appointed men. That begs questions. What does that mean? Why is that? Why is it one in five? That's getting a different conversation going.

'It's for the very senior people. In February [2015], when we go out with the plan to 2017 and 2020 we'll add in a line on gender diversity. Other organisations have done that. Lloyds, for instance. It seems inevitable to me that you would get a reaction from men. Why would you not?

'The most powerful intervention I've seen in my time here was some years ago, when one of the HR Directors instituted the First Line Manager Programme. It was all about people we promote to managing teams for the first time. They set up this training programme that actually became an accreditation programme, so you had to pass the test, to be a people manager. Then they said (it was a time when a lot of banks were grow-ing) that we have to build a pipeline of people who are ready. So we had a pipeline of people who'd passed the test. We based the nominations process on the test, and it was opened up to self-nomination. Before that, your manager nominated you. We opened that up. It was up to indi-viduals to put themselves forward. We doubled the number of women coming out, graduating, if you like.

'That told us is that if you left it to the managers [those women would not be nominated]. Funnily enough I'd just come back from maternity leave. We were all blown away by it. And then, of course, the bank went bust. We had lots of people ready for people manager jobs, but we had to slash and burn so the opportunities weren't always there for them.'

We asked Arden if she was encouraged by the way things were going now in the organisation.

'Yes, but less about anything specific to do with gender. I'm more encouraged by what the strategy's trying to achieve, the clarity of goals and the connectedness of the organisation to those goals. The first five years after the crash was about "can the businesses stand up? Should we shut them down? Can you make money? How do we manage out the legacy?" You need to remember we were throwing off the equivalent of some countries' GDPs. We were the biggest bank in the world and we had the most loans in the world when the financial crash happened. A very particular financial reengineering had to go on. We're towards the back end of that now. We are shrinking certain things and selling off. We're cleaning up. It's a cleaner business – it needs to be a bank again and we've put out some very clear goals for 2017 and 2020, and they're about the customer. One of the first slides you will see in our strategy deck is that, if you're going to give customers great service and get them to trust you, you need to have great people, who are very engaged with your business and your customers. Then your customers do more business with you and you make more money.

'The chief executive puts that slide up at the front. What we have been doing for the past year is about getting momentum and buy-in. The capital rebuild programme – selling Citizens, biggest IPO ever in US banking; we'll get a billion pounds of cost out. Then there is the system's resilience – we had that awful IT incident – so we had £800 million going into the resilience of our systems. Then reorganising, which my team have led. We're about to set out some quite clear targets for the next few years. So those were the four things for this year. There will be four or five things for next year, the year after, and the year after that, and we are agreeing a people management programme. The CEO [Ross McEwan] talked with 7,000 people leaders on a call last week, about the importance of people leadership and what he expected of them. There will be much more opportunity for future leaders. We'll have a consistency we haven't had before, a simplicity and a focus on what matters. And woven into that will be an aspirational goal for gender.

'The people thing is part of the strategy, and the gender thing is part of the people thing; good people leadership and a common view of what is good and right. I worked in a part of the business that created a good system [First Line Manager Programme]; we got great customer and employee feedback, hit financial targets and had good risk scores. I think we can do that for this bank now, but it will take to 2020 to make the change.'

The birth of a new culture

We felt privileged to be given such fascinating insights into the inner workings of three large organisations, as they adapt to the gender-balance zeitgeist. The reflections of Cannon, Bashforth and Arden suggest Lord Davies's targets and the peer pressures they've generated have created an environment in which corporate cultures have become more malleable.

Targets and goals are being pursued systematically, on many fronts at once, and are being guided and monitored by a detailed analysis of gender balances at every level of the organisation.

The actions taken to meet gender-balance targets have stimulated a period of questioning, introspection and myth-busting that may, in retrospect, be seen as the beginnings of a new stage in the evolution of corporate cultures.

It is possible "topic fatigue" as Bashforth calls it, and pressing external developments, such as the halving of the oil price for BP and the downsizing at RBS, will put a brake on the change process after the Davies target has been met. We don't think so. It seems to us that, deep down, both men and women want the cultural change that has been set in motion and that the increases in the adaptability of cultures will prove permanent.

Summary

- HR is the engine-room of gender-balancing.
- The challenge is to fill the pipeline without unduly damaging the culture.
- Public goals concentrate minds.
- Focusing on the numbers identifies the issues.
- Dispelling myths identifies new opportunities.
- The Davies Review is an exercise in behavioural economics.
- Corporate cultures can become more malleable.

chapter 10

Beyond the Davies Review

In the grand scheme of things 31 December 2015, the date by which Lord Davies wanted FTSE 100 companies to have boards consisting of at least 25% women, is a milestone on a journey, the destination of which remains unspecified.

There are various views about what should happen next and in which direction the gender-balance momentum started by Lord Davies, his Steering Group and many other interested parties, including The Mentoring Foundation, should take us in 2016, and thereafter. The focus of attention and targets should shift to the 'pipeline', for example. The emphasis should switch from boards, to EDs and ExCos. Organisations should look to their settings and 'lean out' more to women.

There is a general belief, however, that no one should suppose the 'job', however it is defined, is done, or even half done.

Some clues about future directions of travel, the numbers, and the debates can be gleaned from a series of interviews with leaders of FTSE 350 companies and other organisations conducted in late 2014 and early 2015.

Six chairmen reflect on the future

Sir Philip Hampton, former Chairman,
Royal Bank of Scotland Group, Chairman, GlaxoSmithKline

Sir Philip, speaking in the last months of his chairmanship of RBS, recalled the discussions on gender diversity after his appointment as chairman in 2009. 'I think we fairly quickly realised that we should have more women on the board. This was two years before the Davies Review, but it was increasingly becoming a talking point. We relatively rapidly got three excellent women on the board. Our board varies between 11 and 12 directors, depending on where we are with recruitment. We got to 25% before Lord Davies identified 25% as a target.

'We're very happy to be at that percentage. We certainly wanted to have women, and we thought one, isolated woman was never quite the same as having two, three, four, five or whatever. Oddly enough we very recently got very close to putting another woman on the board so we're not thinking "we get to 25% and that's the job done", as it were. There certainly isn't a maximum.

'The two decisions I took early on in consultation with others was that the board should be smaller (I said let's get it down from 17 or 18, to 11 or 12), and let's have that very fundamental element of diversity; gender diversity. There are other types of diversity that are important, but gender is probably the most fundamental.

'All the women who have been brought onto the board have been very effective non-executive directors. To be honest, we don't really think about gender differences any more. It sort of becomes normal. The Company Secretary is also a woman, so, actually, sitting round the board table at the moment, it's four out of 12.'

Female directors improve a board, according to Sir Philip, because they 'bring particular skills and change the dynamics of meetings. There is something about a mixed gender meeting that is different from an all-male meeting...I doubt whether all-male groups have got sufficient balance and diversity, and attitudes to life to produce the best judgment and decisions. I would think that you were very peculiar if you had an all–male board. It would seem an unusual gathering. It's very rare at RBS at any level, board or management meeting, to see an all-male group.'

But Sir Philip does not believe the move towards gender balance on boards had anything to do with fashion. 'What's important is that you have effective boards, and part of that is a particular set of skills and experiences that you will want to accumulate. But part of it is also the dynamics, the style, the character of discussion at a board meeting and that isn't just about particular skills and experiences. That's about the blend of contributions or attitudes to life and attitudes to other people, that people round the table bring … if you want a debate about strategy, or judgements about people or – more difficult – judgements about situations, which is reflective and brings in a range of different viewpoints, I find it extraordinary now we would think a single gender group – of men or women – would be the most effective.'

John Stewart, Chairman, Legal & General Group

John Stewart finds his female directors are 'more thoughtful than their male co-directors' and says L&G 'wants at least three women on the board, because … you need at least three women in a committee to get critical mass.

'So ideally, over time, we would like to have three female NEDs on the board and hopefully one female ED, which would make about four out of 12. The whole board would probably vote for that – the ExCo too. But making it happen is quite difficult. If you insist people must be appointed on merit you have to make sure you get the right person, at the right time.'

He warns against rushing things.

'If you address the pipeline over time, the right people will come up. When you try to adjust it suddenly, with relatively short-term targets, you will probably get some push-back. Someone's promotion is someone else's demotion, so men will start to feel that way. We must always run a meritocracy; it has to be the right person. What we need to do is get women really young, build up their confidence and push them through.'

We asked Stewart what he thought of the commitment made by the CEO of Lloyds Banking Group (LBG), António Horta-Osório, to have 40% of LBG's top 8,000 jobs held by women by 2020. Stewart sees a dilemma here: 'forcing it will cause male resentment ... but if you set soft targets, you won't reach critical mass, so you will never get there. You have to strike the right balance ... We're making slow progress, but we really need targets, like António's. Even if he doesn't make it, he will get 30%, so he will change the culture of the whole institution, and good for him.'

Stewart then speculated about the future for the female executive.

'Will we ever get 50:50 [gender parity] among executives? Probably not, because women have the children, and will often take a break. So if we can't hope for 50:50 you have to think maybe of 60:40, at the most. With anything less than two thirds men, one third women, you don't have critical mass, so we really must make the political and business changes to make sure we are at least a third women in say a decade.' Seems like a target; 33% women on ExCos by 2024.

Sir Win Bischoff, Chairman, Financial Reporting Council

Sir Win was chairman of Lloyds Banking Group until April, 2014. He agrees with John Stewart and Sir Philip Hampton that the focus now should be on ExCos.

When we spoke to him in July, 2014, Sir Win was sanguine about the chances of meeting the Davies target. But he thought targeting EDs was 'the wrong measure', and we should look, instead, at executive committees. Getting female ExCo members to 25% 'will take longer', because CEOs can't appoint anyone. There must be a track record of achievement. 'It's a much more complex thing.'

He has asked the 30% Club to consider saying women should account for 30% of ExCo members by 2020.

Sir Win says putting women on shortlists is all well and good, but if they are not getting the jobs, companies must know why and try to help them get the jobs.

As chairman of the FRC, Sir Win wants to make succession planning 'more central' to governance. He welcomes the high number of non-British CEOs and chairmen in the FTSE 100, because 'we want to fish in the widest pool'. He wants investing institutions to take more of an interest in succession planning and diversity, because they have a powerful voice they don't use enough.

He says one of the main advantages of women on boards is that they are more thoughtful about risk, and that groups that include women are better at evaluating risk than male-only groups. 'Of course if it is total risk aversion then it is not good, because you have to take risk in business, but to be thoughtful about risk, I think is a good thing and I think it goes with the female DNA.'

Niall FitzGerald, KBE, Chairman, The Leverhulme Trust

When we interviewed him in July, 2014, we asked FitzGerald, former CEO of Unilever, how he thought things were going.

'In terms of raising awareness that has gone very well - everybody is now conscious of the need to have a more balanced grouping at the top; not balanced for balance's sake, but balance to draw from the total pool of talent that's available. I doubt there's anybody in corporate Britain, anyway, who is unaware of the issue. Doesn't always mean they agree, by the way. But they are aware.

'They are aware that it has become an increasing area of focus for shareholders, regulators and society at large. And it is, therefore, in their self-interest to be aligned, even if they don't entirely agree.

'The spectrum goes from people who passionately believe in it, for very strong business reasons; a group in the middle who feel it is the right thing to do and we should try to do it better; and those who don't really believe in it, but feel public opinion requires them to act as if they do. I think as people get more involved the balance of the spectrum starts to change, and more people move to the positive end of the spectrum. But that is a slow process – it doesn't happen overnight. So awareness, and public shareholder and regulatory pressure are in a much better place than they were some years ago.

'In terms of numbers [of women] on boards, I don't think it is yet where it should be, nor do we have anything like enough in the C-suite', for reasons 'including inadequately prepared candidates and the lack of a pipeline coming through the executive ranks. If you look where male NEDs come from, you see a majority are people who have all been senior executives, CEOs, or whatever. If that source isn't producing decent numbers of women, there will be a shortage of women who are well prepared for board roles.'

'In terms of raw numbers it looks better, but are all of the women who have joined boards as well prepared and well qualified as they need to be? I question that. I suspect, when there's a choice, the external pressure is to choose the woman, which is not always the right thing.'

FitzGerald also thinks more must be done to encourage women to put themselves forward. He still has too many conversations with women who say 'they don't feel ready, or don't think they have the right background. There's a need to build up their aspirations and their self-confidence.

'There's a fourth area. It is very difficult to get inside it, but it is a real issue. On balance, fewer women than men are prepared to make the kind of life sacrifices that are perceived to be needed to pursue that part of their career. I'm not saying it is good or bad. I'm saying it is a fact. That's partly about families, and having a different view on life. It is also fed by a macho perspective of toughness which is largely an illusion.

'An important issue that runs through all of this is that more and more boards want directors with real operating experience, who can deal with real crises; people who can judge the performance of the executive based in part of their own experience of having done it. I am not saying a board should be entirely composed of people like that, but I think if you were talking to any chairman today he/she would say "the area in which I am really short is people with real operating experience". This brings you right back to the fact that the area in which we have made the least progress is getting women through to the executive suite.'

David Cruickshank, Chairman, Deloitte LLP

Deloitte had two female board members when Cruickshank began his first stint as Chairman in 2007. When we spoke to him in August 2014 the UK Board of Partners included four women. If Board Secretary Caryl Longley is included, 5 out of 18 (28%) directors are women.

'As you get into the chairman's role you become more sensitised to the board dynamics, and how important it is to get the environment right. This is one of the main parts of the chairman role; getting the environment right so that debate can happen. You want the best debate and best ideas on the table, to reach the best conclusion. This is something you learn. A good board meeting is when you have some gritty conversation and lots of diversity to reach an outcome everyone's happy with. You learn about what makes for a good board discussion.

'I was very conscious, when we were recruiting our independent NED around the beginning of my second term, of the fit and dynamics.

'I've been very fortunate that we've a lot of diversity and a wide range of skills. It would be hard to form a project committee with no diversity. You wouldn't know you would be able to get the right answers.'

He agreed with Sir Philip Hampton that it was hard to imagine such a group now that wasn't a mix of genders.

'We have set ourselves targets, as a firm, for the number of women partners. We want to have 25% by 2020 and 30% by 2030. The fact of the matter is the professional services firms, generally, have not moved as much in the last few years as big companies. I say to the partners the good news is that we are no worse than anybody else. The bad news is that we're no better and this is very frustrating. So we are giving a big push to try and improve the chance of women coming through. We lose a lot of women around child-bearing years, late 20s, and again in the run up to partner. They think it's too hard to make their partner case. So we have introduced "agility" – working flexibly and having permission in the culture to choose to work flexibly as one of the responses to it. We find the reason we lose women is that they can't work out how to juggle the hours, so they leave to do something easier. Our Head of Talent, Emma Codd, leads our forensic team. They are mostly women. They work flexibly. Most of them have children. Emma and David Sproul [Senior Partner and Chief Executive] lead on the Agility Programme, hoping this will change the culture. But it's an uphill struggle.

'The "agility" programme's firm-wide and people-wide. If I go back even ten years you would never have heard of a man taking paternity leave. Now it's very common. We have set it up so that we can have 10–15% of our people working this way, at any time. So we have set ourselves targets for new partners.

'It will only work over time if the vast majority "buy into" doing the right thing. The agility programme's still relatively new, but people are talking about it.

'Attitudes are changing in the workplace, men are far more attuned to getting the balance right themselves. The vast majority of our major clients are grappling with the same issues, so there is much more understanding.'

Sir David Walker, Chairman, Barclays

We asked Sir David whether he thought the governance weaknesses he identified in his 2009 report, *A Review of Corporate Governance in UK Banks and Other Financial Industry Entities* had been addressed.

'It's a journey,' he replied. 'You don't get to your destination in a short period of time. I would say the recommendations I made and the analysis I presented have been widely embraced. My proposal that every major bank should have a board level risk committee has been fully implemented.

'But that is something discrete. [Companies] say "right! We've now got that!" I have made other recommendations subsequently, about changing the behavioural dynamics of a board, to embrace challenge as a normal way of proceeding; the fact that you and I challenge each other does not mean we are not collegial in a unitary board. It just means I can say: "I think you are wrong. I think we should spend more time on this."

'It's the role of a chairman to facilitate appropriate behavioural dynamics and, for me, good governance will allow you to challenge. It's perfectly reasonable to disagree. You're not a wrecking ball if you question. It is for the chairman to facilitate, encourage and expect challenge. If directors don't meet that expectation and are incapable of challenging, the chairman should say: "well, you know what, if you can't do that then you're not really welcome on my board."

'There's a particular poison here; short term thinking. "I want to do something now!" I think women are less prone to that. It's a rather macho thing "I want to do something now! Let's go, now! This afternoon!" Gang-busters. It's my observation on the board that we have here, that women reflect more.

'I would say that since the crisis boards generally have been more cautious about transactions. A board isn't a place where you take a decision, and say "let's do something!" It is a place where you can think. It's a journey, but I think boards are more thoughtful. The crisis was probably helpful in that it made people realise the things they'd previously taken for granted. For example, access to the money market for banks shouldn't be taken for granted. During the crisis there wasn't a money market. It just dried up.

'It made people think "Hang on a minute. We better be sure some of these parameters that we thought were dependable, are there."'

Sir David is an admirer of *Thinking, Fast and Slow* by the behavioural economist Daniel Kahneman. 'He says instinctive ["system 1" of the Kahneman model] responses, even for people who know a lot about the subject, are often wrong. What I've done here is encourage "thinking slow"; to have a "first reading" debate, a "second reading" debate, and a "third reading" debate. The key is to say before the discussion starts, "we're not going to reach any decision. I want you all to speak freely about all the considerations you think are relevant. In due course we'll have a second reading, and a third reading."

'We have to curb the proclivity to want to "do stuff now". This is not an old man wanting to put stuff off at all. There's some stuff I really need to decide, like, you know, 10 minutes ago.

'One of the chairman's roles is to help boards distinguish between the times they have to think fast and the times they have to think slow. A problem in thinking fast when you ought to think slowly is that deciding to do something now could reduce your options in the medium term.'

We asked Sir David if he felt the movement to more gender-balanced boards should be seen as a part of a more general re-configuration of institutional governance.

'If 50% of the population decline to join boards, or only have 10% or 15% participation on boards, you can't be comfortable that your board represents an array of different views. I'm not sure whether it is part of a more general re-configuration, but we are talking about intelligent, well-educated, and experienced women. Why deny yourself access to a larger talent pool, or think your board is in good shape if you're not taking advantage of what's available?

'One thing that we have to do, certainly in financial services, is manage risk and the way we conduct ourselves. This can create huge risk exposure not only in a bank. There are three lines of defence against this; the business unit (guys on the trading floor lending money to mortgagees, etc.), the compliance department to make sure people are acting in accordance with the regulations and the audit department to make sure everything was done right, on a spot-check basis, after the event.

'The trick is to get most of it done in the business unit, because people can "own" good conduct. People act properly not because the compliance policemen are looking over their shoulders, but because it's natural to act properly. One problem in financial services is that compliance is seen as a bit of a policeman or woman.

'There is friction between business units and the policeman, which might go "I'm trying to make money for the firm. All you're doing is messing it all up, and telling me I can't do it." The other way around is when people in a business unit say "I don't like this moral dilemma. I'll ask compliance. If they say it's OK, I will do it." That's a tick box thing. I want business unit people to say "Is this the right thing to do?", not "Is it legal? Is it allowed? What can I get away with? Will compliance let it through?"

'That's why we've set up, with the Judge Business School in Cambridge, the Barclays and Cambridge Compliance Academy.

'It's not training in a black and white way. It's not "this is how to tick this or that box." What's new in this space is behavioural psychology. One of the ways in which it's finding its legs is in the much wider acceptance now that, in the boardroom, you evaluate the performance on a regular basis with external help.'

Sir David then asked how many additional female directors would be required to get every FTSE 100 board to 30% women. We didn't have the figures to hand at the time, but the Cranfield team were clearly asking themselves a similar question. Their analysis, in the *Female FTSE Report 2015*, suggests that because the high intake of female directors immediately after the Davies Review was not sustained subsequently, on current forecasts, the proportion of women on FTSE 100 boards will rise to 28% by 2020 and then level off. Any calculations to answer Sir David's question are likely to understate the challenge in three ways. As noted in Chapter 3, fractions have to be rounded up, because you can't have part of a woman. The figures are averages, and Sir David asked how many more female directors were needed to get *every* FTSE 100 board to 30% women. The figures take no account of the need to replace a female director who leaves with another female director.

'I think as chairman of the board and as the female candidate, you have to take risks. A woman may be very ambitious, self-assured and all that, but she can't know it's going to work. Chairmen have to take more risks, too. I am a little bit disappointed that we're not going faster to 30%.'

Sir David also had trenchant views on another dimension of what we have called 'the big project'; inter-generational power sharing.

'Everything's totally new, totally different. The older generation is not part of the new technology that is changing everything, at an exponential rate. But technology has two sides. There's facilitating what you do. I can tell you minute by minute where we are in relation to a benchmark, for example. It is quite handy to know that, and getting that technology is just a matter of mechanics. You buy the right box and have an IT person work it out for you. The hard part is knowing how to stay on top of the technology, not in a technical sense, but in its use, and not to be driven by it. You must keep hold of the steering wheel. I don't like the analogy of the self-driving car. It's all right for a car to drive itself to the West Country, for instance, but you must be able to resume control, if you need to.

'That is the generation thing. Bringing experience to bear is part of dealing with the problem. That's quite hard to do unless you've got an older generation.

'We have to be careful about this. Discipline is required on the part of those who bring experience to the table. They have to know what experience is relevant. You must promote openness. I believe good judgement comes from experience. The trouble, in banking, is that experience comes from earlier, bad judgements. Most accidents have already happened.

'It goes back to thinking fast and slow; how to encourage thinking slow. Don't allow technology to seduce you into thinking fast all the time. Just because you can get information instantly, does not mean you have to make decisions instantly.'

Targets and challenges

The views of these distinguished business leaders do not amount to a blueprint for the future. However, some indication of the speed and direction of change from January 2016 onwards, desired by the incumbent elite can be inferred from them.

New milestones

There are no signs among the business leaders we interviewed of an inclination to pause for breath after the passing of Lord Davies's deadline at the end of 2015.

Sir Philip Hampton, speaking of RBS, said: 'we're not thinking "we get to 25% and that's the job done." There certainly isn't a maximum.'

Niall FitzGerald doesn't think the job's done either: 'In terms of numbers on boards, I don't think it is yet where it should be. Nor do we have anything like enough in the C-suite.'

Sir David Walker of Barclays implied that he wanted every FTSE 100 board to consist of at least 30% women.

John Stewart at Legal & General is interested not so much in the numbers as in what he calls 'critical mass': 'With anything less than one third women you don't have critical mass.' He thinks that gender parity among executives is out of reach, but we should try to ensure we're 'at least a third women in, say, a decade.' Taking targets for female executives as implied targets for ExCos, that's tantamount to a target of 33% women on ExCos by 2024.

Sir Win Bischoff has a similar ambition. He wants women to account for 30% of ExCo members by 2020. That compares with the commitment by António Horta-Osório, the CEO of LBG where Sir Win was chairman until April 2014, to have 40% of LBG's most senior 8,000 jobs held by women by 2020. If this target is met, it would be surprising if the composition of the ExCo did not approximately reflect it.

LBG is also committed to ensuring that a quarter of all main board seats are occupied by women.

David Cruickshank, then chairman and now Global Chairman of Deloitte, said the firm had set themselves two targets for the proportion of female partners – 25% by 2020 and 30% by 2030.

Simon Davies, the Firmwide Managing Partner of Linklaters, said the firm's aspiration was that its Executive Committee and International Board would each consist of at least 30% women by 2018 and that all future elections to partnership would comprise at least 30% women (see Chapter 1).

At Unilever, 42% of NEDs and 43.3% of managers are women. The proportion of women at Senior Vice President level has doubled in the past five years and 20% of Unilever's top executives are now women. The pattern is similar geographically and functionally; the 43.3% of managers figure is a good representation of the reality in all Unilever's countries of operation and functions. The company's stated aim is 'to build a gender-balanced organisation'.

New challenges

There is a general view that the emphasis should switch from board members to executives. Most chairmen we talked to felt it was more appropriate to focus on members of ExCos, than executive directors (EDs). This may be partly to do with the fact that CEOs have more influence than chairmen on ED, as opposed to NED appointments. But beliefs about board size, and specifically a distaste for unwieldy boards, are also said to make increasing the proportions of female EDs more challenging.

The boards of FTSE 250 companies are lagging behind those of the FTSE 100 constituents in female representation. However, an odd and perhaps significant anomaly in the *Female FTSE Report 2014* figures (see Chapter 2) is that, at that time FTSE 250 constituents had, on average, a higher percentage of women on their ExCos (18%, in 2014) than FTSE 100 companies (14%, in 2014).

Sir David Walker reminded us that bringing more women on to boards and ExCos is part of a broader programme of reform of governance and management. He spoke eloquently of the importance of behavioural psychology, and the dynamics of leadership groups, such as boards. Sir Philip Hampton, John Stewart, and David Cruickshank mentioned the beneficial effects of the presence of women on the dynamics of meetings of all kinds, including board meetings.

It is also suggested that the presence of women on boards improves the boards' ability to evaluate and manage risk.

A particularly interesting inference from these interviews is that a 'new normal' seems to be emerging in board and other meetings. A decade ago, all-male boards and ExCos were commonplace. Nowadays, they are unusual and thus remarkable. Sir Philip Hampton said that he 'would think that you were very peculiar if you had an all-male board. It would seem an unusual gathering' and 'it is very rare at RBS at any level, board, or management meeting, to see an all-male group.'

This change in what is regarded as 'normal' casts new light on the debate about whether one woman on a board or ExCo is enough. Would she be too isolated, too intimidated or too inclined to 'lean in', to contribute, as a woman, to group discussions and deliberations? This is a transitional issue from which we're already emerging. As gender diversity becomes 'normal' concerns about a single woman on a board or ExCo being 'isolated' will disappear.

Behind the numbers

Targets and goals are outcomes: they don't tell us much about the cultural changes that are required if they are to be met.

We asked Kirsty Bashforth at BP and Elaine Arden at RBS to tell us how they thought the HR function could, or should, develop, and how companies should accommodate the new generations of men and women, with different outlooks and demands who will be approaching boards and ExCos in the next decade or so (see Chapter 9).

Bashforth isn't an HR Director, but she is a senior executive in a field that's part of human resources in the wider sense.

'There is a mix of perception about what HR does and the skills in the HR function' she said. 'One all too common perception is that HR is "pay and rations", and "they don't understand the business case anyway, so why bring them in?" The reality is sometimes we're loading our HR function with too much process; pay, rations and compliance. It's not that HR people can't do more. It's that we're not creating any expectations of a broader role, so you can end up with the perception feeding the reality.

'So where we're trying to go is to ask: "How can HR managers be both change leaders, with change expertise business leaders should call on, and coaches on people issues, built on the foundation of knowing the policies, rules and regulations?" We need to make our processes smoother, better, more systematic, but we also need to build a bit of confidence and judg-ment in the people so that we don't fall back on "the rule says we can't do it", or "I'm worried this person might fall foul ...".

'We're in a slightly challenging position at the moment so we want to break out of that and set wider expectations. But we can't give up the pay, rations, compliance, incidents, grievances things. Too often large com-panies fail to set out what they expect of leaders. They promote people because of their technical expertise, but they don't say "by the way, 70% of your role is leading the people, designing your organisation, improv-ing the effectiveness of the organisation, the values of the organisation, the teamwork, the engagement, the motivation, how you're going to develop the capability for the future – all of that. And maximising value for the company." So, unless the person is naturally good at that he or she becomes the senior technical person and runs the team by the rules and technical capability.

'I would love to see an HR function that really focuses the mind of who-ever is making the promotion decisions on the broader role; they have the IQ to do the job, and the drive to do the job, but do they have the EQ to do the job, because you're managing people? You're no longer using a technical skill, because the team have the technical skill. We want an HR function with a broader role as a coach, change manager and "organisational nurturer", a function that asks "how does the organisation and its people become more effective and build capability for the future?"

'If you look back at the global financial crisis we didn't have that much diversity round the world in terms of background thinking about the banking system. We had people comfortable with a level of risk that could never work. There was a behavioural side to it. People often talk of behaviour, leadership, and coaching as the add-ons, the soft stuff. But the break-down of the soft stuff, its misalignment and mismanagement was the fundamental cause of the financial crisis. That's not an add-on, that's not a soft issue. So for me, we need an HR function to which the business leader can turn and say "something's gone wrong with my results. We need to optimise here. I'm going to speak to my HR direc-tor or partner and ask how I'm doing as a leader. What's the capability of the organisation? How are people coping with change?" That would make the HR function as a career much more attractive, not just for HR people who want to go into it anyway, but people who are leading in the line and may want a stint in an HR function. We send people off into treasury and other functions, but we don't send them off into HR.'

Bashforth agrees with Sir David Walker that behavioural psychology is becoming a new leitmotiv.

'I would say the real expertise and mastery of behavioural economics as a key business driver is in its infancy. There are those who love the topic, who wouldn't label it as a topic, but actually "get it", and there are those who can see projects that help the business, but can't make that leap in their guts or their minds, or if they can in their minds, they can't in their guts to "oh, that's actually a core functional activity." This is particularly true when there are lots of other big topics to be looked at. Even when a company isn't in crisis, there may be five or six things that are so obvious that you have to sort them out.

'It takes a long time for people and organisations to shift, because large organisations have been around a long time, and typically have people who have been in their careers in that organisation or in that industry for decades. The reason they've got to the top is that they have certain traits, approaches and attitudes. It's unrealistic to expect people suddenly to shift, unless you find they've actually been hiding something for 30 years and then sort of become released, which is very rare. So I do understand that it is quite hard.

'There is naïveté and baggage in male and female mind-sets on gender balance and getting more women through pipelines in an organisation. Too many women expect all the men to change, and too many men assume women don't want to take risks. For us to make progress there has to be change in both perceptions, with men and women working together. One gender may go a little bit further or faster than the other, but then the other one has to catch up because as a woman I can't expect a male-dominated work environment to provide me naturally with more opportunities and better conversations, just because someone says it should happen. I have got to play my role in that. I as a woman need to play my part.

'If the working environment is predominantly male, the conversational tone I'm playing into at that moment is male so I could say "I don't have to change who I am, but I have to recognise the dynamics of the situation to be able to influence the situation." I can't as a woman sit here and hope I'll be offered lots of nice things, and hope that people will want to give me a stretching opportunity, without saying what I want it to be. That doesn't mean I'll get it, but if I don't say it, I can't expect telepathy. Quite often in a male environment there will be a more direct communication style. So to be heard, I'm going to have to be a bit more direct. Similarly, if I want to exert influence in a male dominated environment, I may have to get used to having a bit of power; if you want to influence situations, you just have to deal with the fact that you have power; deal with it or else decide not to play' (see page 138).

We asked Elaine Arden whether it was her impression that the new generation of executives, the 'millennials', had different expectations.

'I've just come from our millennials. I'm really torn about it. We worked closely with the London Business School, which is leading a study on the future of work. All the leading companies are in it. They talked about the workforce today being more diverse than it's ever been in terms of its expectations from work. We have the baby boomers, generation X, generation Y and now we have the "connected generation", brought up with phones. My seven-year-old said "Dad, how old were you when you had your first phone?" (because you know he wants a phone). His dad said "30." My son couldn't believe it.

'So we are all asking "what do the millennial generation want?" We have all got flexible working; clearly the technology enablement of work is really critical, and loads of us have done that. In the last few weeks RBS teams have been doing senior manager 360-degree feedback. They're all sitting at home on Sunday night, doing it on iPads, because they don't need to be in the office. We're enabling people to work in different ways. They don't have to have their own desk; they book a desk for when they come in. We've done a lot of the flexible working thing. I was talking to my millennials just now. One question they asked was "how can you motivate such a diverse mass?" I said "I don't know, I've no idea how to motivate you. You tell me." They said "some of us, we want to start work at 12 noon and work on until 10 o'clock at night, but we want to dip in and out", because they're used to multi-tasking. I told them that when I was doing my homework, I used to get told off for having my stereo on, and of course, when I was doing homework I was writing [with a pen]. They are typing their homework, watching TV, texting pals – and on another device, they may be looking up something. They are used to multi-tasking. They want to work for half an hour and then go and talk a bit with their pals.

'We have to think about what that means and how we feel about it.

'Another question is about career paths. They thirst for knowledge and want to dip in to different areas, to get breadth. I said "you also need depth, you need to get a grip on something." They told me they expected to do a few years here, and a few years there. I remember talking to one of my early bosses. He said "I only joined the bank for a couple of years. I didn't know what I wanted to do. Here I am, 35 years later." It was just the same with me; I didn't know what I would be. Some of them will still be here in 30 years. Some won't. So I don't know how much has changed. Workplaces can't ignore the environment, but some things will stay the same.

'The reality is you grow up in your zone. The people you spend the most time with at work are usually in a zone of 10 years, give or take. I overheard someone say "don't worry about feeling old, you never actually feel old as long as you stay with the people in the zone." The new generation will manage it for themselves.

'Another thing I find, when I talk to the millennials is that, not surprisingly their thirst for learning is very high. So was yours. So was mine. It's normal, but you didn't have judgement because you didn't really have experience, so you hadn't built the muscle. How different is that really? The evolution of the human being through the ages - the environment is different, some of the things you do are different, but some fundamental truths remain unchanged.'

There is considerable consensus among the six Chairmen and three HR leaders we interviewed for this chapter, in particular their belief that the job of achieving gender equality and culture change is still a work in progress. It seems to us that business leaders, in their efforts to understand and address the shifting priorities of younger generations of men as well as women, are actively seeking to shape innovative ways of working that will equip their organisations for the future.

Summary

- Everyone recognises that the 'job' is not even half done.
- New, more ambitious goals are replacing Lord Davies's target.
- Behavioural psychology and economics are coming to the fore.
- The problem of the 'isolated' woman is disappearing.
- The HR function should play a broader role.
- A major challenge is accommodating the new generations.
- Numbers are outcome variables. The changes the 'big project' seeks are cultural.

Culture, Culture

The importance of 'culture' (defined in the *Shorter Oxford English Dictionary* as 'Training and refinement of mind, tastes and manners ... the intellectual side of civilisation') has long been recognised in the management discourse.

An organisation's 'culture' is its intangible internal environment – its prevailing ambience ('the smell of the place', as the late Sumantra Ghoshal put it); its conventions, traditions and habitual patterns of behaviour ('the way we do things around here', as the McKinsey & Co. philosophy has it); its attitudes, predilections and propensities; its visions and missions (explicit or implicit); its actual (as opposed to espoused) ethos and values. 'Culture' is an important part of the 'setting' within which an organisation's employees work (see Chapter 6).

Management thinkers have exhorted us to understand the competitive dimensions of organisational cultures and to acknowledge that, in particular circumstances at particular times, one culture could be better than another at creating 'value', however that is defined.

For historical reasons, most organisational cultures bear the mark of their predominantly male creators. The emphasis on and efforts to promote gender balance in the top echelons of our organisations and institutions are still relatively new and have barely begun to change organisational and institutional cultures from male-only to male and female. Having more women on an organisation's board doesn't, on its own, change the culture.

For an individual organisation, the sooner this cultural change is effected the better, because, in common with most of those we have spoken to while writing this book, we believe that, in the endless competitive struggles in which organisations are engaged, male and female cultures will prevail over male-only cultures.

A three-stage cultural change

In considering the cultural aspects of increasing gender diversity it is useful to think in terms of a sequence of cultural changes:

1. Senior people become convinced that gender balance on their boards (or equivalents), and among their senior executives, is advantageous.
2. Organisations begin actively to promote gender diversity through their recruitment, promotion, talent management and succession planning policies.
3. Gender-balanced boards and executive committees (ExCos) and their equivalents, become the norm.

There is nothing neat or tidy about this sequence. The stages will overlap in different parts of the same organisation, and different organisations will move at different speeds through the stages. It seems fair to say, however, that overall the UK's large companies and organisations are in the second stage of cultural change, when organisations actively seek gender diversity through recruitment, promotion, talent management and succession planning. In the UK an additional stimulus has been provided by Lord Davies's target, and has since been sustained by the Davies Steering Group.

During this three-stage cultural transformation, the role of women changes.

In the first stage, women are junior managers and 'associates' (in law firms, for instance) who, in the view of their senior managers who favour gender diversity, are not progressing up the hierarchy far enough or in sufficient numbers. The common assumption at this stage is that the problem lies with women and attention focuses on changing their attitudes and management styles, through, for example, mentoring, networks and education, so that they become more suitable candidates for high office. During this period the organisational culture remains unchanged. All the adaptive pressure is on women. The 'setting' as defined in Chapter 6 is taken for granted.

In the second stage active promotion of gender diversity on boards (driven in part in the UK by the Davies target) reveals more about the causes of the under-representation of women on boards. Efforts to redress the imbalances are encountering obstacles of increasing subtlety. The low-hanging NED fruit are soon picked, and the focus of attention shifts from boards to executive committees, senior executives and the 'pipeline.' Interventions are occurring at all levels, from annual intakes, to boards. Internal targets are being set and tough questions are arising, such as whether, and if so to what extent, women can be favoured in promotion decisions, without breaking equal opportunity laws or compromising the organisation's commitment to the meritocratic principle.

During this stage women become gradually more common at the top of organisations, and their role changes. From aspirants, they become much sought after, 'board-ready' human resources, influential role models and well-connected members of the ruling elite.

As progress slows, the realisation dawns that something may, after all, have to be done about the 'setting'; that what can be gained without changing the culture (through women 'leaning in' as Sheryl Sandberg put it) has been gained, and further progress towards the goal of gender balance will require real cultural change.

In the final stage many years from now, the cultures of most large organisations will have become male and female, gender balance at the top will have become the norm and as far as the proportions of women at the tops of organisations and institutions are concerned, the goals of the 'big project' will have been achieved.

In this final speculative chapter we want to address two questions about culture:

- What cultural changes are needed to get from stage two, which is where we are now, to the final stage three?
- In what ways will the organisational cultures characteristic of stage three differ from the cultures that characterise stages one and two?

Confronting culture

In a successful organisation, there is much to be said for leaving things as they are. Things as they are have led to success and 'if it ain't broke, why fix it?'

But, because the causes of success are many and their interactions are complicated, it is sometimes hard to be sure what it was about 'things as they are' that led to the success. It is possible, the leadership team may acknowledge, that the organisation would have been more successful if things had been different. But since they don't know exactly what led to the success in the first place, or what would have to be different to achieve greater success, 'don't fix it' is the smart play.

No more so than with the culture, much the most complicated of all the organisation's assets. It is known to be important, assumed to be healthy in a successful organisation (witness the success), but thought to be fragile.

But it's also true that companies that fail to adapt to a changing environment will run into trouble.

This tension between the reluctance to change, for fear of adverse unintended consequences, on the one hand, and the need to adapt to environmental changes on the other, means that there comes a time when cultural conservatism ceases to be the smart play. For gender diversity at the top of large organisations, that time is now.

There are some signs that the assumption that 'you tinker with the culture at your peril' is slowly being replaced by the recognition that a culture that, for whatever reason, is deterring able people from seeking high office, is a liability and overdue for reform.

Digital detox – culture change case study

Thierry Breton, French Finance Minister from 2005 to 2007, and CEO of the IT services group Atos, launched a 'zero email initiative' in late 2011. He estimated that only 10% of the 200 or so messages his employees received, on average, each day were useful, 18% were 'spam' and his managers were spending between 5 and 20 hours a week dealing with emails. 'We're producing data on a massive scale that is fast polluting our working environments and … encroaching into our personal lives' he said. 'At Atos we're taking action now to reverse this trend.'

In November 2011, German chemicals group Henkel, maker of Persil washing powder, declared an email 'amnesty' for employees between Christmas and New Year, and said that during those holidays emails should only be sent in emergencies.

In December 2013 German carmaker Volkswagen confirmed that, after complaints that the divisions between its employees' work and home lives were becoming blurred, it had agreed with the works council to stop its BlackBerry servers sending emails to certain employees when they were off-shift. The arrangement does not apply to senior managers.

In the summer of 2014 the *Financial Times* reported that the German car and truck giant Daimler had leap-frogged Volkswagen and was offering German employees the option to have their incoming emails automatically deleted when they were on holiday.[1] The policy was a response to government-funded research into work–life balance carried out by Daimler in 2010 and 2011 with psychologists at the University of Heidelberg.

A deal signed by French employers' federations and French unions in April 2014 requires employees to switch off work phones and avoid looking at work emails outside work hours, and bans companies from insisting their staff check messages when they're not at work. The move can be seen as an attempt to protect the 133 hours a week of non-working time won by French unions in 1998 when they negotiated France's 35-hour working week.

These developments are not directly related to gender diversity of course, but they do help to dispel the idea that cultures and work 'settings' are immutable. They show that some continental European companies not only acknowledge that the pressures of modern email-saturated work are excessive, but also accept that they should, in the interests of efficiency, do something about them.

Until now it has been taken for granted that the pressures of work grow naturally as one climbs up the organisational hierarchy. More pressure after each promotion is what your pay rise is for. It may be regrettable that a successful career crowds out home life, but business is what it is. The conventional wisdom is that in today's increasingly competitive global markets nothing less than pressure to the point of nervous break-down will do.

The conventional wisdom is usually out of date and often downright wrong. The conventional wisdoms about modern work pressures are no exception. Much of modern work pressure is artificial in the sense that it stimulates activity that is unproductive at best, if not counter-productive. It's generated, not by the need for it, but by the ease with which it can be imposed.

Because it's so easy to command another's attention, there's a lot of such 'commanding' going on. Instant communication, the marginal cost of which is close to zero, and the perceived need to respond to it, fill in the gaps that used to separate the tasks of the day and so rob us of the quiet moments needed for reflection.

Instant communication is a boon, and it would be folly to impose a blanket ban on all e-communication. Thierry Breton's initiative at Atos only proscribes internal emails. He favours use of enterprise social networks instead. A June 2014 report on Atos's 'zero email' policy by analysts at IT market research firm Gartner found that the initiative had led to the emergence of more effective ways of working among the company's 76,000 employees.[2] Almost all Atos employees are now registered on the company's blueKiwi social network. The advantage of using a social network platform is that, unlike emails, posts to the social network are broadcast and don't require individual responses.

As Paracelsus said, 'the poison is in the dose'. These developments indicate a growing recognition that 'overdosing' on email can lead to dangerous and counter-productive addiction, and practical steps can and should be taken to reduce it.

They are the beginnings of a more general acceptance that it's not the quantity of work that matters so much as the quality. This is clearly the rationale for the announcement by Sir Richard Branson in September 2014 that staff at Virgin Group's head office could take as much holiday as they liked whenever they liked, as long as their performance at work was not affected. Sir Richard's move was thought to have been inspired by a similar move at video-streaming company Netflix.

The conventional wisdoms about work are being challenged. They are giving way to new wisdoms. Work need not be a 24/7 commitment for executives. The needs of the individual should not be subordinated to the needs of the organisation. Executives who feel they have to sacrifice their home lives to win the next promotion won't realise their full potential. When the pressure of executive work is eased a little, the productivity of executives improves, and more people are encouraged to seek executive positions.

Daimler executives are trained to set good work–life examples and encouraged to set aside time when no meetings would be scheduled. The company told the BBC that the objective was 'to maintain the balance between the work and home life of Daimler employees, so as to safeguard their performance in the long run'.

This is reminiscent of the example Niall FitzGerald established at Unilever, when he told his staff that he would not accept meetings or travel schedules that required him to leave on Sunday or return on Saturday, and would not have breakfast meetings 'because I want to have breakfast with my daughter' (see Chapter 6).

It seems probable that organisations that follow Daimler and begin to dismantle, or disable the artificial pressure generators, will find it much easier to attract and keep good people, particularly women.

Cultures or 'settings' that were once strengths, become weaknesses when they don't adapt to changed circumstances, such as the advent of free, instant communications, or when they become incompatible with the 'sets' of the able and talented people organisations need to remain competitive.

The male and female culture

Healthy cultures are always evolving as they adapt to the demands of a constantly changing environment. At any one time a corporate culture may seem set in stone, but there will always be some areas of innovation and experimentation on the periphery, where changing circumstances expose cultural weaknesses and inadequacies. Healthy cultures encourage experiments and adopt their useful results.

When gathering information on work patterns at Lloyds Banking Group (LBG) following the bank's public commitment to reaching 40% women in its top 8,000 jobs by 2020, Fiona Cannon discovered that changes in work patterns, including job-sharing by senior staff, had been taking place below the threshold of the organisation's awareness (see Chapter 9). The phenomenon is known as 'job crafting', and was first identified by Amy Wrzesniewski and Jane Dutton.[3] Unofficial attempts by individuals to 'craft' their jobs to suit their needs can be powerful agents of cultural change.

Three other cultural change principles emerged from our interviews with Fiona Cannon and Kirsty Bashforth (see Chapter 9). First, the importance of maintaining the meritocratic principle; LBG insisted appointments would continue to be made on merit. Second, gender diversity at LBG was a business project spearheaded by the CEO and run like any other business project. Third, diversity work within LBG and BP is guided by detailed data analysis that tracks changes and identifies the key issues at all levels.

No corporate culture is ever wholly adapted. To paraphrase Stephen Jay Gould, the eloquent evolutionist, '[A culture] is a quirky mass of imperfections, working well enough (often admirably); a jury-rigged set of adaptations, built of curious parts, made available by past histories in different contexts.'[4]

Although management has become generally more 'enlightened' during the past half-century, the cultures right at the top of companies and organisations have changed little since William Whyte bemoaned the subjugation of employees to the needs of organisations.[5] The demands of work in the top echelons remain overwhelming and unrelenting. They 'crowd out' any chance of a reasonable work–life balance and deter people who want a reasonable work-life balance from seeking the top jobs. In other words, the jury-rigged set of adaptations of which corporate cultures and settings consist is no longer working well enough to ensure that all the talent rises to the top.

We believe the solution to this cultural maladaptation is to cease to expect women to do all the adapting to prevailing cultures, and to permit corporate cultures to 'lean out' to women, and so become male and female.

What would such a male and female culture be like?

The short answer is that it's very hard to say. Evolution works in mysterious ways and travels in unpredictable directions. Who would have predicted the dinosaurs would have evolved into birds or that telephones would have evolved into computers?

But we can speculate.

What it's all for?

When the setting at the top of an organisation is modified in ways designed to attract women, it becomes open to further modification by the previously incompatible 'sets' of incoming women. One such modification might be a change in the ways its leaders look at the world and see their roles.

The changes may be subtle. In business, for example, the male-only leadership may have seen the organisation's underlying purpose, or raison d'être, as creating shareholder value. After gender balance has been achieved, the leadership may see the organisation as part of the societies in which it operates with a duty to create social as well as shareholder value.

Most of the time, the practical consequences of the change will be insignificant, because a prudent shareholder value maximiser will take the interests of employees, suppliers, customers, neighbours, and society at large *into* account, even though these non-owning constituencies cannot hold it *to* account. But occasionally, such a change in the leadership's conception of the company and its roles could lead to different decisions.

Whether the change is for the better or worse, time and the market will tell. Some will predict that the loss of focus will lead to a deterioration in economic performance. Others will argue that the conception of the company as a social as well as an economic actor will make it more adaptable, and less likely to be wrong-footed by unexpected social and political developments.

Attitude to risk

We asked Sir Win Bischoff, the chairman of the Financial Reporting Council and ex-chairman of Lloyds Banking Group, why he thought a more gender-balanced board was a better board. He said that it was partly to do with risk.

'People are becoming much more conscious of political risk, in the wider sense; not whether Cameron or Miliband will be elected, but political risk in the way the world is evolving. What is happening in Ukraine and Gaza has an impact on companies and economies.

'One of the main advantages of having diversity on a board is that women are more thoughtful about risk. You might say they are less willing to take risks, and that may be true, but there is more to it than that. They think of the downside, they are very thoughtful about it. Men look at risk in a very different way. They focus too much on the upside; they're less sensitive to risk. There is a lot to be said for having a risk sensitivity. Of course, if it's total risk aversion, that's not good, because you have to take risks in business. But to be thoughtful about risk is a good thing.

'I think it goes with the female DNA. You have to be careful about risk and women are; about their parents, their children and so on. You have to take risks, but they have to be calculated. You must evaluate a risk – grade it, gauge it. Groups that include women are better at that than male-only groups.'

Some might feel Sir Win was straying onto politically risky ground when he suggested a more 'thoughtful' attitude to risk 'goes with the female DNA'. Others might claim it is a gender stereotype. But if it is a stereotype, or an unwarranted generalisation, must Sir Win's view be discounted for that reason? Stereotypes can be very misleading and should be avoided, but there's no escaping the fact that we all use stereotypes, and we all change our perceptions and views, by modifying, and replacing our stereo-types. Whether it is because of their DNA or their cultural conditioning, men and women have different aptitudes and priorities, and assume roles and take positions characteristic of their genders when they work together.

This is the value of diversity, of all kinds.

The tensions between different attitudes, beliefs, and perceptions can often produce compromises that accommodate and give due weight to the different points of view.

Personal agency

Alison Wolf says that women who get to the top adapt completely to the setting and become at one with the male culture.[6] This is not the impression left on us by the women who have been through or are going through The Mentoring Foundation's Executive and NGWL Programmes. Our mentees feel different and stay different – they don't acquire male outlooks.

When we launched the FTSE 100® Cross-Company Mentoring Programme we were a little surprised by a lack of self-confidence in several of the able and already successful women who joined the Programme as mentees.

We expected the problem to ease as the years passed, and all of us working in this field became more effective. It has eased, but it has not gone away. It is as if, deep down, these formidable women still harbour the remnant of a suspicion that they're intruders in a male space. These things, it seems, take time.

Other Programme alumnae already seem comfortable in their elevated roles at the top of their organisations and are starting to assert themselves. In so doing, they're also starting to modify the male-crafted cultures they are operating within. They have begun to ask themselves some very basic questions.

'OK' they're saying. 'I have this great job. I have the elbow room I wanted. I have the power to act that I've been asking for. And I have my seat at the top table. What am I going to do with it?' The question suggests an intention not only to do their jobs, but also *to use their positions to change their environments*. Their answers to the questions are not yet clear even in their own minds, but it seems likely that when they find their answers and begin to act on them, they will re-craft the cultures, and the 'settings' of their organisations.

Clare Francis, Managing Director, Global Corporate Banking, at LBG (see Chapter 4), says that her values and beliefs have not changed as her position has become more elevated and influential. 'I have to try now to think through how I can use these values and beliefs on a larger scale' she told us.

Culture change creeps up on organisations. The progress is so slow you often don't notice it at the time. It's only when looking back that you realise how far you have come. The gender balance numbers don't tell the whole story of cultural change because there is more to an organisation than the gender mix of its board. A change in the gender mix on boards may presage culture change, but it's not culture change itself.

The external environment

Organisational cultures co-evolve with the broader cultures within which the organisations operate. In other words, a male and female culture is likely to emerge more quickly if its superiority over a male culture is recognised by organisations that comprise the environment.

Among the most important institutions in the corporate environment is the Financial Reporting Council (FRC), which issues, and keeps up to date, codes of best practice for companies and institutional investors.

When we interviewed Sir Win Bischoff in July 2014 he had recently replaced Baroness Hogg, another friend of The Mentoring Foundation and its programmes, as chairman of the FRC. We asked him if he shared Lady Hogg's inclination to use the FRC's 'UK Corporate Governance Code' to promote gender diversity on boards.

'I'm at least as interested as she is about this and the Code does specify that diversity and succession planning are very important. Succession planning is something I would want to consider making even more central to a board's governance thinking. There are some companies that do it very well, but it is usually done under great pressure. We will probably place more emphasis on it in future. It involves looking at all the talent. Succession planning in British companies is becoming more global. The number of non-British CEOs and chairmen in the FTSE 100 is quite high. That's to be welcomed. We want to fish in the widest pool. The same applies to diversity. It's going to be more important in succession planning rather than less important.'

During Baroness Hogg's tenure of the FRC chair, the requirement to report on gender diversity targets on a 'comply or explain' basis in annual reports was added to the UK Corporate Governance Code. We asked Sir Win how companies were responding.

'We've noticed that reporting isn't yet well developed. There's no standard template. People are still feeling their way through it. They don't go very far down [the organisation] – it is usually the board, and the ExCo. Some companies are being more open about what they are doing and what they plan to do. Others will follow them.

'The better company secretaries will point out to the Chairman and the CEO that the company actually is doing what it should be doing and should say so. It's quite interesting. We [Sir Win retired as chairman of LBG in April 2014] appointed our Chief Risk Officer [CRO] as a third executive director on the board, and within a few weeks HSBC put their CRO on their board.'

We asked Sir Win whether there were signs shareholders were taking more of an interest in these issues.

'We want shareholders to take an interest in a number of areas; to engage with management on the long-term viability of the company, for example. One of the things they should engage in is succession planning. I believe that shareholders, having seen what can happen when succession planning doesn't go well, will in fact engage with management more on this. What shareholders do not seem to realise, although I keep telling them, is that directors, chairmen and CEOs basically "jump" for two bodies. One is their regulator, you learn to jump to see whether you can meet their requirements; the second is shareholders (see Chapter 2).

'If I receive a letter from a shareholder with as little as 1%, or 2% of the equity who wants to see me (or anyone else), I arrange a meeting relatively quickly. I don't say "look I'm going on holiday, let's make it September". You have to take your investor relations seriously. Shareholders have a very powerful voice. They don't use it enough. We need to encourage them to use it more, because they can get things done. Their senior people, their governance people, as well as the people who make investments, have a lot of day-to-day contact with companies. They need to take ownership of some of this too. Succession planning and diversity are becoming much more important issues for investing institutions.

'Proxy agencies, which act on behalf of companies in areas such as governance and remuneration, have it on their lists to look at.

'The Stewardship Code, developed by Sarah [Baroness Hogg], has not really got going, yet. A lot of investing institutions have signed up to it, because it's the right thing to sign up to, but are they really doing their job? Ownership brings responsibilities. Some of the bigger institutions are very mindful of that, but some smaller institutions signed up, because they felt they had to, rather than doing anything about it.

'Investors should be encouraged to sign up to the Stewardship Code and abide by it. They won't all have the same concerns. Some will have concerns about succession planning and diversity. Others will be more concerned about transparency in the accounts. Still others will have greater concerns about "going concern" issues. Whatever their concerns, they should get engaged, not just be passive. They own chunks of these organisations. In the past they have taken the view that if they don't like what a company's doing, they can sell the shares. That's one way, but it is the worst default. We want people to get engaged and use their *nous*, and their perceptions of what the company's doing. We want investing institutions to engage with the company and talk about these issues.'

Numbers and cultures

We said in Chapter 1 that in the discussions, arguments and debate about how we can get more women onto the boards of UK companies we tend to get too hung up on gender and numbers.

Culture change can't be done by numbers or by ticking a few boxes or setting and striving towards goals, targets or quotas. Nor can it be done by one gender adapting to the other. It has to be a joint project – the crafting, to which both genders contribute, of a new culture in which both genders feel welcome and comfortable.

There is no getting away from the fact, however, that numbers play an important role in most organisations. They are an integral part of the language of organisational performance. It's not surprising that a general desire for more women on boards, or equivalents, is often expressed as a wish to get some variable, such as the number of women on the board, or ExCo, to some specified higher value by some specified date. So, although culture change cannot be done by numbers, it is natural and inevitable that numbers will be used to monitor and guide the process and measure its performance as they have been at Lloyds Banking Group, RBS and BP (see Chapter 9).

It's less desirable, however, to use numbers and targets to direct or constrain the process by concentrating attention on boards, for example, rather than ExCos, intake or middle management. A culture is the creature of everyone in the organisation, not a particular level or stratum. When targets focus attention on one stratum, and distract it from other strata, they may distort, or interfere with movement towards the goal of a male and female culture.

But there is a trade-off here.

Compliance with targets and quotas focuses attention and treatment on the symptoms of gender imbalances, rather than on its cultural causes. But it can also have a catalytic effect that speeds up the process of culture change. If compliance with targets and quotas brings more women to the top of organisations than would otherwise have been the case, this is likely to make the circumstances more favourable for culture change, and add fuel to the culture change process. It may have unintended consequences, such as the 'golden skirts' phenomenon, but by and large, the more women at the top of the organisation, the greater the chances that the male and female culture will emerge sooner, rather than later.

As we saw in Chapter 3, France's Copé–Zimmermann quota law has, in addition to improving the gender balance on boards, identified and made visible a new generation of 'board-ready' women. There is good reason to believe that without the law, a substantial number of able and ambitious French women wouldn't have risen to the top so soon and become role models for younger women. The law has also helped the male-dominated French business elite get used to the idea of women on boards, and appreciate the value they can add.

Sometimes, treating the symptoms can help to treat the causes.

We believe we are also acting as a catalyst in this culture change process. The Mentoring Foundation's two programmes are helping to forge the connections and friendships, and to promote the mutual understanding, from which male and female cultures are starting to emerge. The driving force of culture change is the gradual accretion of new attitudes, a new language and new relationships based on trust and reciprocity.

The rising tide

Whatever view one takes of where we are in the development of male and female cultures in large organisations, it is clear something dramatic has happened since the dawn of the new century. The number of women on the boards of our largest companies has trebled and if (as seems likely) Lord Davies's target is met, by the end of 2015, the *proportion* of women on FTSE 100 boards will have quadrupled in the period since 1999.

The increases in the numbers and proportions of women on executive committees have been less dramatic, and have become a new focus of attention for that reason. It's likely, however, that looking back the first two decades of the 21st century will be seen as a watershed; the time when a rising tide of women flowed up the pipelines and took their places on the ExCos and boards or their equivalents of our largest organisations and institutions.

It is inconceivable that the cultures of these large organisations and the ways they are governed and managed, will be unaffected by this influx of women. New styles of governance and management will emerge and become established.

Capitalism will enter a new phase in its evolution, because of the influx of women, and also because they are members of a new, interconnected generation, which is demanding changes in the traditional patterns and ways of working.

It is incumbent on all of us to try to ensure that this sea change in our society occurs smoothly, with the minimum of disruption and friction. There are always risks and unintended consequences in a process as complex as culture change, but if we do manage to forge male and female cultures in our large organisations the prize is likely to be well worth the effort.

Conclusion

We have endeavoured in this book to summarise the state of play in respect of the gender-balancing component of the 'big project', to put the situation in the UK in an international context, and point to some of the issues we should now be focussing on, including:

- Shifting the focus from boards to executives.
- Recognising that female executives have more influence on management than female non-executives.
- Paying closer, more systematic, attention to the pipeline.
- Acknowledging the need of companies to adapt their 'settings' to the 'sets' of women and the new connected generation.
- Recognising that behind the numbers there are real people with their own interests.
- Acknowledging the importance of behavioural psychology.
- Recognising that sometimes, treating the symptoms of problems can help to treat their causes.
- Facilitating the emergence of 'male and female' organisational cultures.

We want to leave the final words to Lord Davies of Abersoch, whose personal contribution to the gender-balancing component of what we call the 'big project' is very hard to overestimate.

At The Mentoring Foundation's 2014 Colloquium, and again at the launch of the March 2015 *Female FTSE Report*, he said 'Discussions of Venus and Mars are now generational. The new generation Y/Z is omni-channel. CEOs of today's businesses need to get it, or they won't be around in 20 years. For women, the next challenge is the pipeline, and women's representation on top leadership teams. What I've learned in the past four years is that the female pipeline of talent in the UK is unbelievable – absolutely extraordinary. However, it seems to me that in a lot of companies there is a permafrost and for a variety of reasons a lot of women decide that the work–life balance, the culture, the company or whatever isn't right. So, they get out. We've got to change that.'

Appendix
The Mentoring Foundation FTSE 100® Cross-Company Mentoring Executive Programme Mentors (March 2015)

1.	John Abbott	Downstream Director	Royal Dutch Shell Group plc
2.	Marcus Agius	Chairman	PA Consulting Group
3.	Peter Ayliffe	Chairman	Monitise Group plc
4.	John Barton	Chairman	easyJet plc
5.	Andrew Beeson	Chairman	Schroders plc
6.	Mike Biggs	Chairman	Direct Line Insurance Group plc
7.	Sir Win Bischoff	Chairman	Financial Reporting Council
8.	Clement Booth	Former Member of the Board of Management Former Chairman	Allianz SE Allianz UK
9.	Sir Richard Broadbent, KCB	Chairman	Tesco plc
10.	John F Brock	Chairman & Chief Executive Officer	Coca-Cola Enterprises Inc
11.	Monica Burch	Senior Partner	Addleshaw Goddard LLP
12.	Patrick Burgess, MBE	Chairman	Intu Properties plc
13.	Lord Burns, GCB	Chairman	Santander UK plc
14.	Dame Alison Carnwath	Chairman	Land Securities Group plc
15.	Dominic Casserley	CEO	Willis Group Holdings Ltd
16.	David Cruickshank	Chairman	Deloitte LLP
17.	Spencer Dale	Chief Economist	BP plc
18.	Richard Davey	Chairman	Amlin plc

(continued)

APPENDIX   Continued

19.	Simon Davies	Firmwide Managing Partner	Linklaters LLP
20.	Ian Davis	Chairman	Rolls-Royce plc
21.	David Fass	Chief Executive Officer, EMEA	Macquarie Group Ltd
22.	Nicholas Ferguson CBE	Chairman	Sky plc
23.	Niall FitzGerald KBE	Chairman	The Leverhulme Trust
24.	Douglas Flint, CBE	Group Chairman	HSBC Holdings plc
25.	Sir Simon Fraser, KCMG	Permanent Under-Secretary of State	Foreign and Commonwealth Office
26.	Charlie Geffen	Chair of London Corporate	Gibson, Dunn & Crutcher LLP
27.	Sir Peter Gershon CBE, FREng	Chairman	National Grid plc
28.	Sir Philip Hampton	Chairman	Former Chairman, Royal Bank of Scotland Group plc, Chairman GlaxoSmithKline plc
29.	Richard Haythornthwaite	Chairman	Centrica plc
30.	Andrew Higginson	Chairman	Morrisons plc
31.	Anthony Hobson, FCA	Senior Independent Director	James Dyson Ltd
32.	Baroness Hogg	Former Chairman	Financial Reporting Council
33.	Dennis Holt	Chairman	Beazley plc
34.	António Horta-Osório	Group Chief Executive Officer	Lloyds Banking Group plc
35.	Vivian Hunt	Managing Partner	McKinsey & Company
36.	Glyn Jones	Chairman	Aspen Insurance Holdings Limited
37.	David Kappler	Deputy Chairman	Shire plc
38.	Nigel Keen	Chairman	Syncona Partners LLP
39.	Irwin Lee	Vice President & Managing Director UK & Ireland	Procter & Gamble
40.	Wilson Leech	CEO, EMEA	Northern Trust
41.	Sir Nicholas Macpherson KCB, GCB	Permanent Secretary	HM Treasury
42.	Strone Macpherson	Chairman	Close Brothers Group plc
43.	Sir Rob Margetts, CBE, FREng	Chairman	Ordnance Survey

(continued)

APPENDIX **Continued**

44.	Sir Mark Moody-Stuart, KCMG	Chairman	UN Global Compact Foundation
45.	Sir Richard Olver, FREng	Former Chairman	BAE Systems plc
46.	Patrick O'Sullivan	Chairman	Old Mutual plc
47.	Gavin Patterson	Chief Executive Officer	BT Group plc
48.	Sir John Peace	Chairman	Standard Chartered plc
49.	Jan du Plessis	Chairman	Rio Tinto plc
50.	Ian Powell	Chairman and Senior Partner	PwC LLP
51.	Sir Michael Rake	Chairman President	BT Group plc CBI
52.	Sir David Reid	Chairman	Intertek Group plc
53.	Richard Reid	London Chairman	KPMG LLP
54.	Nigel Rich, CBE	Chairman	SEGRO plc
55.	Don Robert	Chairman	Experian plc
56.	Sir Simon Robertson	Deputy Chairman & Senior Independent Non-Executive Director	HSBC plc
57.	Bill Ronald	Chairman	Dialight plc
58.	Lord Stuart Rose	Chairman	Ocado Group plc
59.	Sir John Sawers, KCMG	Chairman and Partner	Macro Advisory Partners
60.	Charles Sinclair	Chairman	Associated British Foods plc
61.	Nicholas Smith	Chairman	Ophir Energy plc
62.	John Stewart	Chairman	Legal & General Group plc
63.	Richard Stillwell	Chairman	St Ives plc
64.	Carl-Henric Svanberg	Chairman	BP plc
65.	Michael Treschow	Chairman	Unilever plc
66.	David Tyler	Chairman	J Sainsbury plc
67.	Graham van't Hoff	Executive Vice President, Global Chemicals	Shell UK Group Ltd
68.	Sir David Walker	Chairman	Barclays plc

Notes

1 The Big Project

1. Sian Griffiths, 'Cracknell tells workaholic dads: spend more time with kids', *Sunday Times*, 14 September 2014).
2. Martin Wolf, 'Failing elites threaten our future', *Financial Times*, 15 January 2014.
3. Alison Wolf, 'Feminists today are too obsessed with their own elite, metropolitan lives', *The Guardian*, 21 January 2015.
4. Jill Rutter, http://www.instituteforgovernment.org.uk/blog/4688/.
5. 'Talent Action Plan: removing the barriers to success', *Cabinet Office*, September 2014.
6. Caroline Binham, 'Law firms try a female leadership', *FT.com*, 10 March 2014.
7. Pui-Guan Man, 'Following an uncertain path', *Legal Week*, 30 May 2014.
8. Science Council, http://www.sciencecouncil.org/content/100-leading-uk-practising-scientists.
9. Vibeka Mair, 'Steady as she goes', *Charity Finance*, 1 July 2014.
10. Jonathan Dean and John Harlow, 'Cut! Celluloid ceiling must go, says Knightley', *Sunday Times*, 29 June 2014.
11. Dr Martha Lauzen, 'The celluloid ceiling: behind-the-scenes employment of women on the top 250 films of 2014', 2015. Center for the Study of Women in Television and Film at San Diego State University.
12. Sheryl Sandberg, *Lean In: Women, Work and the Will to Lead* (Alfred A. Knopf, New York, 2013).
13. Simon Collins, 'Millennials look to tech stars as finance careers leave them cold', *Financial Times*, 8 November 2014.
14. Chris Bryant, 'Auf Wiedersehen, Post – Daimler staff get break from holiday email', *Financial Times*, 14 August 2014.

2   The Story so Far

1. Ruth Sunderland, 'Cable praise for Glencore', *Daily Mail*, 27 June 2014.
2. Elizabeth Coffey, Peninah Thomson and Clare Huffington, *The Changing Culture of Leadership: Women Leaders' Voices*. The Change Partnership, 1999.
3. Roy Adler, *Women in the Executive Suite Correlate to High Profits*, Pepperdine University, 2001.
4. *Groundbreakers: Using the Strength of Women to Rebuild the Economy*. Ernst & Young, 2009.
5. Charlotte Sweeney, 'Women on boards: voluntary code for executive search firms – taking the next step'. Department for Business, Innovation and Skills March 2014.
6. Sharon Allen, 'The death of groupthink'. *Bloomberg Businessweek*, 5 February 2008.
7. 'IMA stewardship code survey', *Governance + Compliance*, July 2014.

3   The Political Environment

1. *Gender Balance on Corporate Boards: Europe Is Cracking the Glass Ceiling*, European Commission, March 2014.
2. 'Yoshida 'picks up baton' for Japan's women executives', *Financial Times*, 5 March 2015.
3. Danielle Paquette, 'Why American women hate board quotas', *Washington Post*, 9 February 2015.
4. Anne Alstott, 'Gender quotas for corporate boards: options for legal design in the United States', Yale Law School, Public Law Research Paper No.489. 21 November 2013.
5. 'Legislating a woman's seat on the board: institutional factors driving gender quotas for boards of directors', *Journal of Business Ethics*, January 2014.

4   Cross-Company Mentoring Works

1. Sylvia Ann Hewlett, Kerrie Peraino, Laura Sherbin and Karen Sumberg, *The Sponsor Effect: Breaking through the Last Glass Ceiling. Harvard Business Review Research Report*, 12 January 2011.

5   Network Capital

1. Adam Grant, *Give and Take: A Revolutionary Approach to Success* (Weidenfeld & Nicolson, 2013).
2. Athena Vongalis-Macrow, 'Assess the value of your networks'. *Harvard Business Review*, 29 June 2012.
3. Trowers and Hamlins, FDU group (2014) Networking Survey Report, http://www.trowers.com/uploads/Blogs/Networking_survey_report_Final.pdf.
4. Frances Rosenbluth, 'Working capital'. *RSA Journal*, autumn 2010.
5. Avivah Wittenberg-Cox, 'Your company doesn't need a women's network'. *Harvard Business Review,* 12 June 2013.

6   When is the Price Too High?

1. About AFF. History and Context. http://www.agilefutureforum.co.uk.

7   The Pipeline Challenge

1. Brian Groom, 'Male culture puts young women off finance careers', *Financial Times*, 2 May 2014.
2. *Cracking the Code.* KPMG LLP, Young Samuel Chambers Ltd and the 30% Club. 2014.

8   The Pipeliners

1. Sheryl Sandberg, *Lean In: Women, Work and the Will to Lead* (Alfred A. Knopf, 2013).
2. Lisa Petrilli, *The Introvert's Guide to Success in Business and Leadership.*
3. Cameron Anderson and Gavin Kilduff, 'Why do dominant personalities attain influence in face-to-face groups? The competence-signalling effects of trait dominance', *Journal of Personality and Social Psychology*, Vol. 96, No. 2 (2009).

10   Beyond the Davies Review

1. Daniel Kahneman, *Thinking, Fast and Slow* (Farrar, Straus and Giroux, 2011).

11 Culture, Culture

1. Chris Bryant, 'Auf wiedersehen, post – Daimler staff get break from holiday email', *Financial Times*, 14 August 2014.
2. Jessica Twentyman, 'Social networks are one answer to information overload at work', *Financial Times*, 24 September 2014.
3. Amy Wrzesniewski and Jane Dutton, 'Crafting a job: revisioning employees as active crafters of their work', *Academy of Management Review*, Vol. 26, No. 2 (2001), pp. 179–201.
4. Stephen Jay Gould, *The Flamingo's Smile* (W. W. Norton, 1985).
5. William Whyte, *The Organization Man* (Simon & Schuster, 1956).
6. Alison Wolf, *The XX Factor: How Working Women Are Creating A New Society* (London: Profile Books, 2013).

Bibliography

Adler, Roy. (2001) *Women in the Executive Suite Correlate to High Profits*, European Project on Equal Pay.

Agile Future Forum. http://www.agilefutureforum.co.uk.

Allen, Sharon. (July 2014) 'The death of groupthink'. *Bloomberg Business Week* 5 February.

Alstott, Anne (2013) 'Gender Quotas for Corporate Boards: Options for Legal Design in the United States', Yale Law School, Public Law Research Paper No. 489, 21 November.

Anderson, Cameron and Kilduff, Gavin (2009) 'Why do dominant personalities attain influence in face-to-face groups? The competence-signalling effects of trait dominance', *Journal of Personality and Social Psychology*, Vol. 96, No. 2.

BBC News (2014) 'Italy's PM-designate Matteo Renzi names new cabinet' 21 February.

Binham, Caroline (2014) 'Law firms try a female leadership', *FT.com*, 10 March.

Blair, Cherie (2014) 'Japan must embrace "womenomics" to modernise economy', *Guardian*, 16 October.

Bryant, Chris (2013) 'Coalition poised to introduce quotas on German boards', *FT.com*, 18 November.

Bryant, Chris (2014) 'Auf wiedersehen, post – Daimler staff get break from holiday email', *Financial Times*, 14 August.

Cabinet Office 'Talent Action Plan: removing the barriers to success', September 2014.

Charlotte Sweeney Associates (2015) http://www.charlottesweeney.com/.

Coffey, Elizabeth and Huffington, Clare and Thomson, Peninah (1999) *The Changing Culture of Leadership: Women Leaders' Voices*. London: The Change Partnership.

Collins, Simon (2014) 'Millennials look to tech stars as finance careers leave them cold', *Financial Times*, 8 November.

Corporate Women Directors International (2013) *CWDI 2013 Report: Women Board Directors in the Fortune Global 200 and Beyond*, http://www.boarddiversity.ca/sites/default/files/2046_001.pdf.

Cracking the Code. KPMG LLP, Young Samuel Chambers Ltd and the 30% Club, 2014.

Davies, Lord Mervyn (2011) *Women on Boards*, http://www.bis.gov.uk/assets/biscore/business-law/docs/w/11-745-women-on-boards.pdf.

Dean, Jonathan and Harlow, John (2014) 'Cut! Celluloid ceiling must go, says Knightley', *Sunday Times*, 29 June.

Department for Business Innovation & Skills (2014) https://www.gov.uk/government/uploads/system/uploads/attachment_data/file/326241/bis-14-950-standard-voluntary-code-of-conduct-for-executive-search-firms.pdf

Desvaux, Georges, Devillard-Hoellinger, Sandrine and Baumgarten, Pascal (2007) *Women Matter: Gender Diversity, a Corporate Performance Driver*, McKinsey & Company, http://www.asx.com.au/documents/media/women_matter_english.pdf.

Equality and Human Rights Commission (2014) *Appointments to Boards and Equality Law*, http://www.equalityhumanrights.com/sites/default/files/publication_pdf/Appointments%20to%20Boards%20and%20Equality%20Law%2022-07-14%20final.pdf.

Ernst & Young *Groundbreakers. Using the Strength of Women to Rebuild the World Economy*, 2009, http://www.vitalvoices.org/sites/default/files/uploads/Groundbreakers.pdf.

European Commission (2011) *Gender Balance on Corporate Boards: Europe is Cracking the Glass Ceiling*, EC Factsheet, http://ec.europa.eu/justice/gender-equality/files/documents/140303_factsheet_wob_en.pdf.

European Commission (2012) *Women in Economic Decision-Making in the EU: Progress Report: A Europe 2020 Initiative*, http://ec.europa.eu/justice/gender-equality/files/women-on-boards_en.pdf.

European Parliament (2014) Policy Department C, *Citizens' Rights and Constitutional Affairs: The Policy on Gender Equality in Italy*, http://www.europarl.europa.eu/RegData/etudes/note/join/2014/493052/IPOL-FEMM_NT(2014)493052_EN.pdf.

Eversheds Board Report (2013) *The Effective Board*, http://www.eversheds.com/global/en/what/publications/board-report2/request-the-report.page?.

Fiat Boards Director, Annual Report (2013) *Boards of Director*, http://2013interactiveannualreport.fiatspa.com/en/report-operations/corporate-governance/boards-director#start.

Fiat Industrial (2013) *Annual Report on Corporate Governance*, http://www.fcagroup.com/en-US/governance/governance_documents/FiatDocuments/2013/Governance_UK.pdf.

Financial Reporting Council (2008) *The Combined Code on Corporate Governance*, June, https://www.frc.org.uk/getattachment/1a875db9-b06e-4453-8f65-358809084331/The-Combined-Code-on-Corporate-Goverance.aspx.

Financial Reporting Council (2010) *The UK Stewardship Code*, July.

Gould, Stephen Jay (1985) *The Flamingo's Smile*. New York: W. W. Norton.

Grant, Adam (2013) *Give and Take. A Revolutionary Approach to Success*. London: Weidenfeld & Nicolson.

Griffiths, Sian (2014) 'Cracknell tells workaholic dads: spend more time with kids', *Sunday Times*, 14 September.

Groom, Brian (2014) 'Young women shun careers in financial sector, study finds, *FT.com*, May 2.

Grussing, Kate and Springbett, Sally (2014) Quarterly *'Movers & Shakers' Survey of Female Executive Appointments*, Sapphire Partners, http://www.sapphirepartners.co.uk/pdf/Ninth%20edition.pdf.

Hewlett, Sylvia Ann, Peraino, Kerrie, Sherbin, Laura and Sumberg, Karen (2011) *The Sponsor Effect: Breaking through the Last Glass Ceiling. Harvard Business Review Research Report*, 12 January.

Higgs, Derek (2003) *Review of The Role and Effectiveness of Non-Executive Directors*, http://www.ecgi.org/codes/documents/higgs.pdf.

Inagaki, Kana (2015) 'Yoshida "picks up baton" for Japan's women executives', *Financial Times*, 5 March.

Investment Management Association (2014) 'Adherence to the FRC's Stewardship Code', http://www.theinvestmentassociation.org/assets/files/surveys/20140501-01_stewardshipcode.pdf.

Kahneman, Daniel (2011) *Thinking, Fast and Slow*. New York: Farrar, Straus, and Giroux.

Kelan, Elisabeth (2009) *Performing Gender at Work*. Basingstoke: Palgrave Macmillan.

Lauzen, Martha (2015) 'The celluloid ceiling: behind-the-scenes employment of women on the top 250 films of 2014', Center for the Study of Women in Television and Film at San Diego State University.

McCarthy, Helen (2004) *Girlfriends in High Places: How Women's Networks are Changing the Workplace*, Demos, http://www.demos.co.uk/files/girlfriendsinhighplaces.pdf?1240939425.

Mair, Vibeka (2014) 'Steady as she goes', *Charity Finance*, 1 July.

Man, Pui-Guan (2014), 'Following an uncertain path', *Legal Week*, 30 May.

Morris, Nigel (2009) Harriet Harman: 'If only it had been Lehman Sisters', *The Independent*, 4 August.

Paquette, Danielle (2015) 'Why American women hate board quotas', *Washington Post*, 9 February.

Petrilli, Lisa (2011) *The Introvert's Guide to Success in Business and Leadership*. C-Level Strategies, Inc.

Rosenbluth, Frances (2010) 'Working capital', *RSA Journal*, autumn.

Rutter, Jill (2012) 'Undoing GOD's work? Will gains women made at the top of Whitehall prove short-lived?' *Institute for Government*, http://www.instituteforgovernment.org.uk/blog/4688/.

Sandberg, Sheryl, (2013) *Lean In: Women, Work and the Will to Lead*. New York: Alfred A. Knopf.

Sanderson, Rachel (2014) 'Matteo Renzi forces sweeping change at state companies' *FT.com,* 14 April.

Sunderland, Ruth (2014) 'Cable praise for Glencore', *Daily Mail*, 27 June.

Sweeney, Charlotte (2014) 'Women on boards: voluntary code for executive search firms –taking the next step', Department for Business, Innovation and Skills, March.

Terjesen, Siri, Aguilera, Ruth V. and Lorenz, Ruth (2014) 'Legislating a woman's seat on the board: institutional factors driving gender quotas for boards of directors', *Journal of Business Ethics*, January, https://business.illinois.edu/aguilera/pdf/terjesen_aguilera_lorenz_2014_jbe.pdf.

Thomson, Peninah and Huffington, Clare (1999) *The Changing Culture of Leadership: Women Leaders' Voices*, Change Partnership.

Thomson, Peninah, Graham, Jacey and Lloyd, Tom (2008) *A Woman's Place is in the Boardroom*. Basingstoke: Palgrave Macmillan.

Thomson, Peninah and Lloyd, Tom (2011) *Women & The New Business Leadership*. Basingstoke: Palgrave Macmillan.

Trowers and Hamlins, FDU Group (2014) *Networking Survey Report*, http://www.trowers.com/uploads/Blogs/Networking_survey_report_Final.pdf

Tutchell, Eva and Edmonds, John (2015) *Man-Made: Why So Few Women Are in Positions of Power,* Gower.

Twentyman, Jessica (2014) 'Social networks are one answer to information overload at work', *Financial Times*, 24 September.

Vinnicombe, Susan, Dolder, Elena, Sealy, Ruth, Pryce, Patricia, Turner, Caroline (2015) *The Female FTSE Board Report, Putting the UK Progress into a Global Perspective,* Cranfield International Centre For Women Leaders.

Vinnicombe, Susan, Dolder, Elena and Turner, Caroline (2014) *The Female FTSE Board Report 2014, Crossing the Finish Line,* Cranfield International Centre For Women Leaders.

Vongalis-Macrow, Athena (2012) 'Assess the value of your networks'. *Harvard Business Review Blogpost*, 29 June.

Walker Review of Corporate Governance in the UK Banking Industry (2009) 'A Review of corporate governance in UK banks and other financial industry entities,' HM Treasury, July.

Watson, Thomas (2007) *Quintessential Quotes*, http://www-03.ibm.com/ibm/history/documents/pdf/quotes.pdf.

Whyte, William (1956) *The Organization Man*. New York: Simon & Schuster.

Wittenberg-Cox, Avivah (2013) 'Your company doesn't need a women's network' *Harvard Business Review Blogpost*, 12 June.

Wolf, Alison (2013), *The XX Factor: How Working Women Are Creating A New Society* (London: Profile Books).

Wolf, Alison (2015) 'Feminists today are too obsessed with their own elite, metropolitan lives', *The Guardian*, 21 January.

Wolf, Martin (2014) 'Failing elites threaten our future', *Financial Times*, 15 January.

Wrzesniewski, Amy and Dutton, Jane (2001) 'Crafting a job: revisioning employees as active crafters of their work', *Academy of Management Review*, Vol. 26 No. 2, pp. 179–201.

Index

Printed and bound by CPI Group (UK) Ltd, Croydon, CR0 4YY